YOURS, JACK

Spiritual Direction from

C. S. Lewis

Edited by
PAUL F. FORD

HarperOne
An Imprint of HarperCollins*Publishers*

HarperOne

HarperCollins books may be purchased for educational, business, or sales promotional use. For information please write: Special Markets Department, HarperCollins Publishers, 10 East 53rd Street, New York, NY 10022.

HarperCollins Web site: http://www.harpercollins.com
HarperCollins®, ®, and HarperOne™ are trademarks of HarperCollins Publishers.

Designed by Joshua Falconer

FIRST EDITION

Library of Congress Cataloging-in-Publication Data is available upon request.

ISBN: 978-0-06-124059-1

08 09 10 11 12 RRD(H) 10 9 8 7 6 5 4 3 2 1

CONTENTS

EDITOR'S NOTE

Unless you were a person friend of C. S. Lewis, or one of his many correspondents, you are probably not aware that he went by "Jack" to his friends, a name he landed on as a child and decided it suited him better than his given one (Clive Staples Lewis). So at the end of most of his letters, you encountered "Yours, Jack." This book is intended to extend that personal relationship to you, the reader.

The purposes of this collection of letters are (1) to draw attention to how, indirectly and directly, C. S. Lewis experienced spiritual direction, wrote about it, and practiced it, and (2) to allow the reader to benefit from having Lewis as a director.

The letters are arranged chronologically because that seemed to be the best way to demonstrate what Lewis was experiencing, reading, and thinking about at the time.

Lewis's spelling, punctuation, grammar, and various ways of dating letters have been regularized to provide the reader an undistracted experience. His capitalization was generally maintained because he used it for emphasis. Translations of foreign-language quotations are provided in brackets. Biblical references and essential bibliographical references are provided in the footnotes when Lewis did not insert them into the actual letters.

Deletions are to be assumed at the beginnings and endings of letters; ellipsis marks indicate deletions within letters. The complimentary close and the signature of letters are retained when they are significantly different from Lewis's regular style.

Readers who desire more complete bibliographical information about books cited and more complete biographical information about people written to or mentioned are invited to consult the three volumes of *The Collected Letters of C. S. Lewis,* so admirably and lovingly edited by Walter Hooper.[1]

---

[1] *The Collected Letters of C. S. Lewis, Volume I: Family Letters, 1905–1931* (London and New York: HarperCollins, 2000), *The Collected Letters of C. S. Lewis, Volume II: Books, Broadcasts, and the War, 1931–1949* (London and New York: Harper-Collins, 2004), and *The Collected Letters of C. S. Lewis, Volume III: Narnia, Cambridge, and Joy, 1950–1963* (London and New York: HarperCollins, 2006).

This collection contains three kinds of letters. There are letters of spiritual *companionship* (letters between equals) to Arthur Greeves (his oldest friend, twenty-eight letters), Warren Lewis (his brother, eleven letters), Leo Baker (three letters), Owen Barfield (four letters), and Bede Griffiths (twenty-eight letters).

There are letters of spiritual *discipleship* (letters to those from whom Lewis sought spiritual advice) to (Saint) Giovanni Calabria (six letters, written in Latin and translated by Martin Moynihan) and Sister Penelope (Lawson, C.S.M.V., eleven letters). Finally, there are letters of spiritual *direction* (letters to those to whom Lewis gave spiritual advice) to Rhona Bodle (fifteen letters), Michael Edwards (two letters), Vera (Mathews) Gebbert (four letters), Genia Goelz (two letters), Mr. Green (three letters), Mrs. D. Jessup (seven letters), Mrs. Johnson (five letters), Mrs. Frank L. Jones (two letters), Laurence Krieg (two letters), Philinda Krieg (two letters), "Mrs. Lockley" (six letters), Edward Lofstrom (two letters), Mary (née Shelley) Neylan (eleven letters), Mary Willis Shelburne (forty letters), Patricia Thomson (two letters), Sheldon Vanauken (twelve letters), Mary Van Deusen (thirty-three letters), and others who received one letter each.

Abbreviations, Nicknames, and Translations

Minto Mrs. Janie King Moore, Lewis's adopted stepmother.

Oremus pro invicem. Latin for "Let us pray for one another." Lewis often used this at the close of letters in Latin or in English.

Vac. The vacation or holidays. At Oxford there are short vacs. between school terms and the long Vac. during the summer. Oxford and Cambridge terms are eight weeks in length. Oxford terms are named Michaelmas (from the Feast of St. Michael, September 29), Hilary (from the Feast of St. Hilary, January 13), and Trinity (from Trinity Sunday, the first Sunday after Pentecost). Cambridge terms are named Michaelmas, Lent, and Easter. The long Vac. lasts from July through September.

W. "Warnie," i.e., Warren Hamilton Lewis, the older brother and only sibling of C. S. Lewis.

ACKNOWLEDGMENTS

Deep gratitude to my first-ever Harper editor, Roy M. Carlisle, and to Patricia Klein, his successor.

Deep gratitude to Michael Maudlin, editorial director, and to Alison Petersen, production editor, at HarperOne.

Deep gratitude to Joshua Falconer, my assistant, and to my spiritual director, Marilyn Peppin.

1916

TO ARTHUR GREEVES, *his oldest friend: On the book that baptized Lewis's imagination—see* Surprised by Joy, *180–181. Anodos is the hero of the book* Phantastes*; Cosmo is the hero of a story Anodos tells in the book.*[1]

7 MARCH 1916

I have had a great literary experience this week. I have discovered yet another author to add to our circle—our very own set: never since I first read 'The well at the world's end' have I enjoyed a book so much—and indeed I think my new 'find' is quite as good as [Thomas] Malory or [William] Morris himself. The book, to get to the point, is George MacDonald's 'Faerie Romance', *Phantastes,* which I picked up by hazard in a rather tired Everyman copy—by the way isn't it funny, they cost 1/1d. now—on our station bookstall last Saturday. Have you read it? I suppose not, as if you had, you could not have helped telling me about it. At any rate, whatever the book you are reading now, you simply *must* get this at once: and it is quite worth getting in a superior Everyman binding too.

Of course it is hopeless for me to try and describe it, but when you have followed the hero Anodos along that little stream to the faery wood, have heard about the terrible ash tree and how the shadow of his gnarled, knotted hand falls upon the book the hero is reading, when you have read about the faery palace . . . and heard the episode of Cosmo, I know that you will quite agree with me. You must not be disappointed at the first chapter which is rather conventional faery tale style, and after it you won't be able to stop until you have finished. There are one or two poems in the tale—as in the Morris tales you know—which, with one or two exceptions are shockingly bad, so don't *try* to appreciate them: it is just a sign, isn't it, of how some geniuses can't work in metrical forms—another example being the Brontës.

---

[1] *Letters I,* 169–170.

TO ARTHUR GREEVES: *On Lewis's religious views as a seventeen-year-old.*[2]

12 OCTOBER 1916

As to the other question about religion, I was sad to read your letter. You ask me my religious views: you know, I think, that I believe in no religion. There is absolutely no proof for any of them, and from a philosophical standpoint Christianity is not even the best. All religions, that is, all mythologies to give them their proper name are merely man's own invention—Christ as much as Loki. Primitive man found himself surrounded by all sorts of terrible things he didn't understand—thunder, pestilence, snakes et cetera: what more natural than to suppose that these were animated by evil spirits trying to torture him. These he kept off by cringing to them, singing songs and making sacrifices et cetera. Gradually from being mere nature-spirits these supposed being[s] were elevated into more elaborate ideas, such as the old gods: and when man became more refined he pretended that these spirits were good as well as powerful.

Thus religion, that is to say mythology grew up. Often, too, great men were regarded as gods after their death—such as Heracles or Odin: thus after the death of a Hebrew philosopher Yeshua (whose name we have corrupted into Jesus) he became regarded as a god, a cult sprang up, which was afterwards connected with the ancient Hebrew Jahweh-worship, and so Christianity came into being—one mythology among many, but the one that we happen to have been brought up in.

Now all this you must have heard before: it is the recognised scientific account of the growth of religions. Superstition of course in every age has held the common people, but in every age the educated and thinking ones have stood outside it, though usually outwardly conceding to it for convenience. I had thought that you were gradually being emancipated from the old beliefs, but if this is not so, I hope we are too sensible to quarrel about abstract ideas. I must only add that one's views on religious subjects don't make any difference in morals, of course. A good member of society must of course try to be honest, chaste, truthful, kindly et

---

[2] *Letters I*, 230–231.

cetera: these are things we owe to our own manhood and dignity and not to any imagined god or gods.

Of course, mind you, I am not laying down as a certainty that there is nothing outside the material world: considering the discoveries that are always being made, this would be foolish. Anything *may* exist: but until we know that it does, we can't make any assumptions. The universe is an absolute mystery: man has made many guesses at it, but the answer is yet to seek. Whenever any new light can be got as to such matters, I will be glad to welcome it. In the meantime I am not going to go back to the bondage of believing in any old (and already decaying) superstition.

TO ARTHUR GREEVES: *On Lewis's favorite short story by George MacDonald.*[3]

15 NOVEMBER 1916

And talking about books I am surprised that you don't say more of the 'Golden Key': to me it was absolute heaven from the moment when Tangle ran into the wood to the glorious end in those mysterious caves. What a lovely idea 'The country from which the shadows fall'!

[3] *Letters I,* 254.

1920

TO LEO BAKER, *an actor, a teacher of acting, and a friend Lewis made in Oxford in 1919, who introduced Lewis to Owen Barfield, a fellow anthroposophist: On Lewis's growing sense of God.*[1]

5 SEPTEMBER 1920

You will be interested to hear that in the course of my philosophy—on the existence of matter—I have had to postulate some sort of God as the least objectionable theory: but of course we know nothing. At any rate we don't know what the real Good is, and consequently I have stopped defying heaven: it can't know less than I, so perhaps things really are alright. This, to you, will be old news but perhaps you will see it in me as a sign of grace. Don't mistake the position: its no cry of 'all's well with the world': it's only a sense that I have no business to object to the universe as long as I have nothing to offer myself—and in that respect we are all bankrupt.

---

[1] *Letters I*, 386.

1921

TO HIS BROTHER, WARREN LEWIS: *On prayer as writing letters to someone who never replies.*[1]

1 JULY 1921

I was delighted to get your letter this morning; for some reason it had been sent first to a non-existent address in Liverpool. I had deliberately written nothing to you since those two you mention: not that I was tired of the job, but because I did not feel disposed to go on posting into the void until I had some assurance that my effusions would reach you. That seemed a process too like prayer for my taste: as I once said to Baker—my mystical friend with the crowded poetry—the trouble about God is that he is like a person who never acknowledges one's letters and so, in time, one comes to the conclusion either that he does not exist or that you have got the address wrong. I admitted that it was of great moment: but what was the use of going on despatching fervent messages—say to Edinburgh—if they all came back through the dead letter office: nay more, if you couldn't even find Edinburgh on the map. His cryptic reply was that it would be almost worth going to Edinburgh to find out. I am glad however that you have ceased to occupy such a divine position, and will do my best to continue: though I hope it won't be for fifteen months.

---

[1] *Letters I*, 555–556.

_1929_

Sometime in the spring (Trinity Sunday was May 22 that year) Lewis came to believe in God, though not yet in Christ:

You must picture me alone in that room in Magdalen, night after night, feeling, whenever my mind lifted even for a second from my work, the steady, unrelenting approach of Him of whom I so earnestly desired not to meet. That which I greatly feared had at last come upon me. In the Trinity Term of 1929 I gave in, and admitted that God was God, and knelt and prayed: perhaps, that night, the most dejected and reluctant convert in all England. I did not then see what is now the most shining and obvious thing; the Divine humility which will accept a convert even on such terms. The Prodigal Son at least walked home on his own feet. But who can duly adore that Love which will open the high gates to a prodigal who is brought in kicking, struggling, resentful, and darting his eyes in every direction for a chance of escape? The words _compelle intrare,_ compel them to come in, have been so abused by wicked men that we shudder at them; but, properly understood, they plumb the depth of the Divine mercy. The hardness of God is kinder than the softness of men, and His compulsion is our liberation. (_Surprised by Joy,_ Chapter 14)

TO ARTHUR GREEVES: _On Lewis's praise for MacDonald's cycle of prayer-poems._[1]

10 OCTOBER 1929

I am slowly reading a book that we have known about, but not known, for many a long day—MacDonald's _Diary of an Old Soul._

---

[1] _Letters I,_ 834.

How I would have scorned it once! I strongly advise you to try it. He seems to know everything and I find my own experience in it constantly: as regards the literary quality, I am coming to like even his clumsiness. There is a delicious home-spun, earthy flavour about it, as in George Herbert. Indeed for me he is better than Herbert.

1930

TO ARTHUR GREEVES: *On the seven deadly sins.*[1]

10 FEBRUARY 1930

When I said that your besetting sin was Indolence and mine Pride I was thinking of the old classification of the seven deadly sins: They are *Gula* (Gluttony), *Luxuria* (Unchastity), *Accidia* (Indolence), *Ira* (Anger), *Superbia* (Pride), *Invidia* (Envy), *Avaritia* (Avarice). *Accidia,* which is sometimes called *Tristitia* (despondence) is the kind of indolence which comes from indifference to the good—the mood in which though it tries to play on us we have no string to respond. *Pride,* on the other hand, is the mother of *all* sins, and the original sin of Lucifer—so you are rather better off than I am. You at your worst are an instrument unstrung: I am an instrument strung but preferring to play itself because it thinks it knows the tune better than the Musician.

TO A. K. HAMILTON JENKIN, *a friend Lewis made in Oxford in 1919, known for his books on Cornwall and loved by Lewis for his ability to enjoy everything: On Lewis's sense of his coming conversion to Christianity.*[2]

21 MARCH 1930

How extremely disappointing! . . . Is there no chance of your ever being able to do as I suggested and coming to spend a couple of nights with me in College in term? . . .

There will be many changes to take stock of. I can hardly imagine you as a married man of several years standing. . . .

On my side there are changes perhaps bigger: you will be surprised to hear that my outlook is now definitely religious. It is not precisely Christianity, though it may turn out that way in the end. I can't express the change better than by saying that whereas

---

[1] *Letters I,* 882.
[2] *Letters I,* 886–887.

once I would have said 'Shall I adopt Christianity', I now wait to see whether it will adopt me: i.e., I now know there is another Party in the affair—that I'm playing poker, not Patience, as I once supposed.

TO ARTHUR GREEVES: *On melancholy and solitude; on masturbation; on temptation; and on reading Brother Lawrence of the Resurrection and the Gospel of Saint John.*[3]

1 JUNE 1930

On the day you left I went our usual walk, through Old Headington, past that little isolated house which you admired, across the brook, and then over two fields to our soaking machine. It was just such another glorious summer day with a kind of mist that made the grass and buttercups look watery. I felt that sort of melancholy (you probably know it) which comes from going through the same scenes through which you walked with a friend a few hours ago, when he has gone. Now that I come to think of it, you must have had this experience much more often than I: so often in your old letters do I find you describing how you went this or that old walk . . . . Mixed with this melancholy, however, (you will not be offended) there was the freshness of solitude which itself, on such occasions, feels like a friend revisited, and what between the two I fell into an extremely receptive state of mind—a sort of impersonal tenderness, which is the reason why I am mentioning this walk, as one of my good ones which was valuable in itself and will, I hope, become even more so in memory.

Just to give you the other side of the picture (I shall not often tell you these things)—I have 'fallen' twice since you left after a long period of quite untroubled peace in that respect. Serves me right, for I was beginning to pat myself on the back and even (idiotically) beginning to fancy that I had really escaped, if not for good, at any rate for an indefinite time. The interesting thing was that on both occasions the temptation arose when I was almost asleep, quite suddenly, and carried me by storm before I really had

---

[3] *Letters I*, 897–899.

my waking mind fully about me. I don't mean to disclaim responsibility on this account: but I feel grateful that the enemy has been driven to resort to *stratagems* (not by me, but by God) whereas he used to walk boldly up to me for a frontal attack in the face of all my guns. I hope I don't delude myself in thinking that this is an improvement. . . .

Lying on the study sofa and hearing these old favourites I had sensations which you can imagine. And at once (here is the advantage of growing older) I knew that the enemy would take advantage of the vague longings and tendernesses to try and make me believe later on that *he* had the fulfilment which I really wanted: so I baulked him by letting the longings go even deeper and turning my mind to the One, the real object of all desire, which (you know my view) is what we are *really* wanting in all wants. . . .

In reading I have of course little to record, and never shall have much in term time. I read in two evenings a little book . . . called *The Practice of the Presence of God* which I picked up and put in the study when I was there last because it seemed to me a promising title. It is by a Seventeenth century monk. It is full of truth but somehow I didn't like it: it seemed to me a little unctuous. That sort of stuff, when it is not splendid beyond words, is terribly repulsive, or can be, can't it? No doubt it depends very largely on one's mood. I had just finished the fourth Gospel in Greek (as I think you know) before you came, and after that most other things are a come down.

TO ARTHUR GREEVES: *On how imagination differs from mere fancy and how holiness differs from mere morality; on Coventry Patmore's* Angel in the House; *on asceticism and marriage; on good humiliation; and on love for one's own father. Lawson and Keir are Oxford dons Lewis's age.*[4]

7 JUNE 1930

I have managed to get a few evenings free this week and have read two new books. The first was Kingsley's *Water Babies*. It was one of the books belonging to my mother which my father had

---

[4] *Letters I*, 901–903.

locked up at her death and I only recovered at the recent clear-ance. It was strange—after the first few pages the most incredibly faint memories began to come about me: she must have read it, or started to read it, to me when I was very small indeed. I had even a curious sense of bringing my mother to life—as if she were reading it through me. The feeling was impressive, but not entirely pleasant. (I don't mean that it was at all unpleasant in the commonplace ghostie sense.) The book itself seems to me not very good. There is some fancy, and I don't object to the preach-ing: but after MacDonald it is tasteless. Put the two side by side and see how imagination differs from mere fancy, and holiness from mere morality. Have you ever read it? As I say it is not *very* good: but well worth reading.

The other was Coventry Patmore's *Angel in the House*. As you know, it is a long poem in a very strict and even monotonous metre, describing a very simple story of love and marriage, inter-spersed with half philosophic, half religious odes on the author's theory of marriage as a mystical image of and approach to divine love. The story parts are deliberately prosaic and hum-drum, and would be very easy to parody . . . though it is surprising how one feels less and less inclined to sneer as you go on. But the bits in between are really often sublime. . . .

He is extremely down on people who take the ascetic view. These will be shut without the fold as 'too good' for God. The whole poem has raised a lot of difficulties in my mind. Even if it were true that marriage is what he says, what help does this give as regards the sexual problem for the innumerable people who can't marry? Surely for them asceticism remains the only path? And if, as he suggests, marriage and romantic love is the real ascent to Spirit, how are we to account for a world in which it is inaccessible to so many, and are we to regard the old saints as sim-ply deluded in thinking it specially denied to them? As a matter of fact he does seem to suggest in one passage that romantic love is *one* ascent, and imagination the other—At all events the book has left me with an extraordinary renewal of my appetite for poetry.

I had an interesting and humiliating experience to-day (Satur-day). I had to go out to tea on Boars' Hill and a man I had been lunching with, Lawson, offered to drive me. I used to know him at [University College] and I lunch with him and Keir once a week for old sake's sake, though Lawson is a most terrible bore. As soon as he got me in the car he decided that we had a good deal of spare time and said he would drive me first to see his old father, recently widowed, whom he has just set up in a little house at the neighbouring village of Holton. On the way I bitterly regretted having been let in for this. Lawson is a tiny little man with puffed out cheeks, a pursed in mouth, and a bristly moustache: very bright staring eyes: and rolls the eyes, jerking his head this way and that, like a ventriloquist's dummy, while he talks, talks, talks, all about himself: or else talks big of university politics, retailing opinions which I know not to be his own and which in any case I despise. I thought 'Now he is going to show me over this house and tell me how he arranged this and why he did that—reams of it.'

When we arrived we found a lovely wild garden with a little red cottage in it. We met an old man speaking with a broad Yorkshire accent and plainly in the technical sense 'not a gentleman'. Point No. I in favour of Lawson—he is not ashamed of his origins: he rose enormously in my eyes. Then Lawson shut up completely and let the old man talk, which he did, describing all he was doing in the garden. He was just like Lawson, only in an old man it was different: and the courage of him setting to work to build up a new life here in his old age was impressive. When we had been round the whole place and into the house, and when I saw so many things out of Lawson's rooms in Merton [College]brought out here, and saw the affection between them, and realised how Lawson had busied himself about the whole—and then remembered how abominably I had treated *my* father—and worst of all how I had dared to despise Lawson, I was, as I said, humiliated. Yet I wouldn't have missed it for anything. It does one good to see the fine side of people we've always seen the worst of. It reminded me very much of the clerk in *Bleak House* (or is it *Great Expectations*) who takes the hero out to see his father and has a cannon on the roof. Do you remember?

TO ARTHUR GREEVES: *On MacDonald's Curdie books; on the dangers of the imagination; and on Mary Webb's* Precious Bane.[5]

15 JUNE 1930

I envy you your shelf of MacDonalds and long to look over them with your guidance. I have read both *The Princess and the Goblin* and *The Princess and Curdie*. In fact I read the former (the other is a sequel to it) for about the third time when I was ill this spring. Read it at once if you have it, it is the better of the two. There is the fine part about the princess discovering her god-mother in the attic spinning.... Another fine thing in *The Pr. and the Goblin* is where Curdie, in a dream, keeps on dreaming that he has waked up and then finding that he is still in bed. This means the same as the passage where Adam says to Lilith 'Unless you unclose your hand you will never die and therefore never wake. *You may think you have died and even that you have risen again*: but both will be a dream.'

This has a terrible meaning, specially for imaginative people. We read of spiritual efforts, and our imagination makes us be-lieve that, because we enjoy the idea of doing them, we have done them. I am appalled to see how much of the change which I thought I had undergone lately was only imaginary. The real work seems still to be done. It is so fatally easy to confuse an aesthetic appreciation of the spiritual life with the life itself—to dream that you have waked, washed, and dressed, and then to find yourself still in bed. . . .

This afternoon I have lounged in the garden and began Mary Webb's *Precious Bane*. I can't remember whether you recom-mended it to me or not. If it goes on as well as it has begun I shall put it very high indeed. In fact I hardly know a book which has given me such a delicious feeling of *country*—homely yet full of eeriness, as in real life.

---

[5] *Letters I*, 905–906.

TO ARTHUR GREEVES: *On Samuel Johnson and Mary Webb.*[6]

22 JUNE 1930

I am delighted to hear that you have taken to Johnson. Yes, isn't it a magnificent style—the very essence of manliness and condensation—I find Johnson very *bracing* when I am in my slack, self pitying mood. The amazing thing is his power of stating platitudes—or what in anyone else would be platitudes—so that we really believe them at last and realise their importance. . . . I personally get more pleasure from the *Rambler* than from anything else of his and at one time I used to read a Rambler every evening as a nightcap. They are so *quieting* in their brave, sensible dignity.

. . . I have finished *Precious Bane* and think I have enjoyed it more than any novel since the Brontës.

TO ARTHUR GREEVES: *On the necessity of charity beginning "at home," through one's own friends and neighbors.*[7]

1 JULY 1930

As to the business about being 'rooted' or 'at home everywhere', I wonder are they really the opposite, or are they the same thing. I mean, don't you enjoy the Alps more precisely because you began by first learning to love in an intimate and homely way our own hills and woods? While the mere globe-trotter, starting not from a home feeling but from guide books and aesthetic chatter, feels *equally* at home everywhere only in the sense that he is really at home nowhere? It is just like the difference between vague general philanthropy (which is all balls) and learning first to love your own friends and neighbours which makes you *more*, not less, able to love the next stranger who comes along. If a man loveth not his brother whom he hath seen—*et cetera.*[8] In other words doesn't one get to the universal (either in people or in inanimate nature) *thro'* the individual—not by going off into a mere generalised mash.

---

[6] *Letters I*, 909.
[7] *Letters I*, 912.
[8] John 4:20.

TO ARTHUR GREEVES: *On the true way to chastity; on Thomas Traherne's* Centuries of Meditations; *on Dante's* Paradiso; *and on diving as preparation for conversion. Prudence Sarn is the heroine of* Precious Bane *and has an experience of God alone in the attic.*[9]

8 JULY 1930

You have I think misunderstood what I said about the return from austerity. I never meant for a moment that I was beginning to doubt whether absolute chastity was the true goal—of that I am certain. What I meant was that I began to think that I was mistaken in aiming at this goal by the means of a stern repression and even a contemptuous distrust of all that emotional and imaginative experience which seems to border on the voluptuous: whether it was well to see in certain romances and certain music nothing but one more wile of the enemy: whether perhaps the right way was not to keep always alive in one's soul a certain tenderness and luxuriousness always reaching out to *that of which* (on my view) sex must be the copy. In other words, whether, while I was right in seeing that a copy must be different from an original, I ought not to have remembered that it must also be *like it*—else how would it be a copy? In the second place, what I feared was *not* lest this mood should be temporary but lest it should turn out to be another wile. What I also ought to have said in my last letter but didn't is that the whole thing has made me feel that I have never given half enough importance to love in the sense of the *affections*. . . .

Almost ever since the Vac. began I have been reading a little every evening in Traherne's *Centuries of Meditations.* . . . I forget whether we have talked of it or not. I think he suffers by making out everything much too easy and really shirking the problem of evil in all its forms: at least, as far as I have got, for it is unfair to say this of a book not yet finished. But apart from this he has extraordinary merits. What do you think of the following;—'The world . . . is the beautiful frontispiece to Eternity'—'You never enjoy the world aright till the sea itself floweth in your veins, till you are clothed with the heavens and crowned with the stars . . . till you can sing and rejoice and delight in God as misers do in

[9] *Letters I,* 913–915.

gold'—'I must lead you out of this into another world to *learn your wants*. For till you find them you will never be happy'—'They (i.e., Souls) were made to love and are dark and vain and comfortless till they do it. Till they love they are idle or misemployed. Till they love they are desolate.' But I could go on quoting from this book forever. . . .

Barfield and I finished the *Paradiso* when I was with him. I think it reaches heights of poetry which you get nowhere else: an ether almost too fine to breathe. It is a pity that I can give you no notion what it is like. Can you imagine Shelley at his most ecstatic combined with Milton at his most solemn and rigid? It sounds impossible I know, but that is what Dante has done. . . .

I also had some lovely bathes with Barfield in a reach of the little river. . . . Picture us lounging naked under the pollards on a flat field: mowers in the next field: and tiny young dragon flies—too small to be frightful yet—darting among the lilies. Here I learned to dive which is a great change in my life and has important (religious) connections. I'll explain that later. They are still very ungraceful dives but I do get in head first.

. . . So glad you approve of *Precious Bane*. Isn't Wizard Beguildy a lovely character: also the scene of Prue Sarn alone in the attic.

TO ARTHUR GREEVES: *On what we get to keep in the life of the world to come.*[10]

29 JULY 1930

It is an interesting and rather grim enquiry—how much of our present selves we could hope to take with us if there were another life. I take it that whatever is *merely* intellectual, *mere* theory, must go, since we probably hold it only by memory habit, which may depend on the matter of the brain. Only what has gone far deeper, what has been incorporated into the unconscious depths, can hope to survive. This often comes over me when I think of religion: and it is a shock to realise that the mere *thinking* it may be nothing, and that only the tiny bit which we really practice is likely to be ours in any sense of which death can not make hay.

---

[10] *Letters I*, 916.

TO ARTHUR GREEVES: *On MacDonald's novels; on worldliness; on hindrances as the raw material of spiritual life; and on the causes of feelings of lack of faith.*[11]

24 DECEMBER 1930

I have of course read very little apart from work. One more MacDonald *Annals of a Quiet Neighbourhood,* which went far to restore my faith in him: badly shaken by an unsuccessful attempt to read the *Seaboard Parish.* Yesterday I picked up ... *Alec Forbes.* ... Do you know it? One reason I enjoyed the *Quiet Neighbourhood* so much was that I read it immediately after Trollope's *Belton Estate:* quite a good book, but all the time one was making excuses for the author on the moral side: saying that this bit of uncharitableness and that bit of unconscious cynicism, and, throughout, the bottomless *worldliness* (not knowing itself for such) belonged to the period. Then you turned to MacDonald, also a Victorian, and after a few pages were ashamed to have spent even an hour in a world so inferior as that of Trollope's.

Have you had glorious fogs—frost-fogs? We have had some of the finest I have ever seen. In fact we have had all sorts of beauty—outside. Inside myself the situation has been quite the reverse. I seem to go steadily downhill and backwards. I am certainly further from self control and charity and light than I was last spring. Now that W. is with us I don't get enough solitude: or so I say to myself in excuse, knowing all the time that what God demands is our solution of the problem set, not of some other problem which we think he ought to have set: and that what we call *hindrances* are really the raw material of spiritual life. As if the fire should call the coal a hindrance! (One can imagine a little young fire, which had been getting on nicely with the sticks and paper, regarding it as a mere cruelty when the big lumps were put on: never dreaming what a huge steady glow, how far surpassing its present crackling infancy, the Tender of the Fire designed when he stoked it.)

I think the trouble with me is *lack of faith.* I have no *rational* ground for going back on the arguments that convinced me of God's existence: but the irrational deadweight of my old sceptical

---

[11] *Letters I,* 944–945.

habits, and the spirit of this age, and the cares of the day, steal away all my lively feeling of the truth, and often when I pray I wonder if I am not posting letters to a non-existent address. Mind you I don't *think* so—the whole of my reasonable mind is convinced: but I often *feel* so. However, there is nothing to do but to peg away. One falls so often that it hardly seems worth while picking oneself up and going through the farce of starting over again as if you could ever hope to walk. Still, this seeming absurdity is the only sensible thing I do, so I must continue it. And all the time, on the other side, the imaginative side, (the fairy angel) I get such glimpses and vanishing memories as often take my breath away: as if they said 'Look what you're losing'—as if they were there just to deprive one of all excuse.

How well I talk about it: how little else I do. I wonder would it be better not to speak to one another of these things at all? Is the talking a substitute for the doing?

1931

TO ARTHUR GREEVES: *On the conversation that led to Lewis's conversion to Christianity; and on the meaning of death. Hugo Dyson, just two years older than Lewis, became his friend in 1930; Maureen was Mrs. Moore's [Minto] daughter, and Tykes, a dog.*[1]

22 SEPTEMBER 1931

Thanks for your letter of the 11th. I couldn't write to you last Sunday because I had a week end guest—a man called Dyson who teaches English at Reading University. I meet him I suppose about four or five times a year and am beginning to regard him as one of my friends of the 2nd class—i.e., not in the same rank as yourself or Barfield, but on a level with Tolkien. . . .

He stayed the night with me in College—I sleeping in in order to be able to talk far into the night as one could hardly do out here [at home]. Tolkien came too, and did not leave till 3 in the morning: and after seeing him out by the little postern on Magdalen bridge Dyson and I found still more to say to one another, strolling up and down the cloister of New Building, so that we did not get to bed till 4. It was really a memorable talk. We began (in Addison's walk just after dinner) on metaphor and myth—interrupted by a rush of wind which came so suddenly on the still, warm evening and sent so many leaves pattering down that we thought it was raining. We all held our breath, the other two appreciating the ecstasy of such a thing almost as you would. We continued (in my room) on Christianity: a good long satisfying talk in which I learned a lot: then discussed the difference between love and friendship—than finally drifted back to poetry and books.

On Sunday he came out here for lunch and Maureen and Minto and I (and Tykes) all motored him to Reading—a very delightful drive with some lovely villages, and the autumn colours are here now.

---

[1] *Letters I*, 916.

I am so glad you have really enjoyed a Morris again. I had the same feeling about it as you, in a way, with this proviso—that I don't think Morris was conscious of the meaning either here or in any of his works, except *Love Is Enough* where the flame actually breaks through the smoke so to speak. I feel more and more that Morris has taught me things he did not understand himself. These hauntingly beautiful lands which somehow never satisfy,—this passion to escape from death plus the certainty that life owes all its charm to mortality—these push you on to the real thing because they fill you with desire and yet prove absolutely clearly that in Morris's world that desire cannot be satisfied.

The MacDonald conception of death[2]—or, to speak more correctly, St. Paul's[3]—is really the answer to Morris: but I don't think I should have understood it without going through Morris. He is an unwilling witness to the truth. He shows you just *how far* you can go without knowing God, and that is far enough to force you (though not poor Morris himself) to go further. If ever you feel inclined to relapse into the mundane point of view—to feel that your book and pipe and chair are enough for happiness—it only needs a page or two of Morris to sting you wide awake into uncontrollable longing and to make you feel that everything is worthless except the hope of finding one of his countries. But if you read any of his romances through you will find the country dull before the end. All he has done is to rouse the desire: but so strongly that you must find the real satisfaction. And then you realise that *death* is at the root of the whole matter, and why he chose the subject of the Earthly Paradise, and how the true solution is one he never saw.

On Monday, 28 September, Warnie took Jack to Whipsnade Zoo in the sidecar of his motorbike, and it was during this outing that Jack took the final step in his conversion:

I know very well when, but hardly how, the final step was taken. I was driven to Whipsnade one sunny morning. When

---

[2] In Lewis's *George MacDonald: An Anthology* (London: Bles, 1946), see Extracts 69–70, 146, 280, 293, and 363.

[3] E.g., Romans 5:12–21; 6:5–23; I Corinthians 15:12–58.

we set out I did not believe that Jesus Christ is the Son of God, and when we reached the zoo I did. Yet I had not exactly spent the journey in thought. Nor in great emotion. 'Emotional' is perhaps the last word we can apply to some of the most important events. It was more like when a man, after long sleep, still lying motionless in bed, becomes aware that he is now awake. (*Surprised by Joy*, Chapter 15)

TO ARTHUR GREEVES: *Thanking him for sending all the letters Lewis wrote to him, so that Warren could type them into what became the Lewis papers, a family history; explaining that he, Lewis, would keep from Warren any letters about their adolescent sexual trespasses, including Lewis's invented fornication with a Belgian evacuee early in World War I; making his first reflections on the meaning of his life up to this time; and announcing his conversion to Christianity.*[4]

I OCTOBER 1931

Very many thanks for the letter and enclosure that arrived this morning. Now, as to their return. I confess that I had not supposed you often read them, and had in view merely an *ultimate* return when W. had finished his editing, that is, in about 4 years' time. If however you want them at once, they are of course your property and will be returned by registered post whenever you wish. I shall follow absolutely your directions. In the meantime you can feel quite confident about their safe keeping. I have spent this morning on them and established a pretty good order for all except about eight. (How maddening my habit of not dating them now becomes! And how ridiculous the arguments by which I defended it!)

All the ones that deal with what we used to call 'It' I am suppressing and will return to you in a day or two. I am surprised to find what a very large percentage of the whole they are. I am now inclined to agree with you in *not* regretting that we confided in each other even on this subject, because it has done no harm in the long run—and how could young adolescents really be friends without it? At the same time, the letters give away some of your secrets as well as mine: and I do not wish to recall things of that

---

[4] *Letters I*, 916.

sort to W's mind, so that in every way they had better be kept out of the final collection. I am also sending back some others in which my replies to you imply that you have said foolish things— you will see what I mean when I return them. Finally, I am suppressing (i.e., sending back at once and keeping from W.—that is what the word 'suppressing' means throughout) all letters that refer to my pretended assignation with the Belgian. I am not at all sure that if Jeremy Taylor were at my elbow he would not tell me that my repentance for that folly was incomplete if I did not submit to the 'mortification' of having them typed and laid open to posterity. I hope, however, this is not really necessary in the case of a sin so old and (I hope) so fully abandoned.

Thanks for all you say about the letters in general. You see mine with too friendly eyes. To me, as I re-read them, the most striking thing is their egotism: sometimes in the form of priggery, intellectual and even social: often in the form of downright affectation (I seem to be posturing and showing off in every letter): and always in the form of complete absorption in ourselves. I have you to thank that it was at least 'ourselves' and not wholly 'myself'. I can now honestly say that I envy you the much more artless letters you were writing me in those days: they all had at least the grace of humility and of affection. How ironical that the very things which I was proud of in my letters then should make the reading of them a humiliation to me now!

Don't suppose from this that I have not enjoyed the other aspect of them—the glorious memories they call up. I think I have got over *wishing* for the past back again. I look at it this way. The delights of those days were given to lure us into the world of the Spirit, as sexual rapture is there to lead to offspring and family life. They were nuptial ardours. To ask that they should return, or should remain is like wishing to prolong the honeymoon at an age when a man should rather be interested in the careers of his growing sons. They have done their work, those days and led on to better things. All the 'homeliness' (which was your chief lesson to me) was the introduction to the Christian virtue of charity or love. I sometimes manage now to get into a state in which I think of all my enemies and can honestly say that I find something lovable (even if it is only an oddity) in them all: and your conception of 'homeliness' is largely the route by which I have reached this. On the other hand, all the 'strangeness' (which was my lesson to you) has turned out to be only the first step in far deeper mysteries.

How deep I am just now beginning to see: for I have just passed on from believing in God to definitely believing in Christ—in Christianity. I will try to explain this another time. My long night talk with Dyson and Tolkien had a good deal to do with it. . . .

Did it strike you in reading those letters how completely *both* of us were wrong in most of our controversies, or rather in the great standing controversy about 'sentiment' which was the root of most of our quarrels? If anyone had said 'There is good feeling and bad: you can't have too much of the first, and you can't have too little of the second' it would have blown the gaff on the whole argument. But we blundered along—my indiscriminate hardness only provoking you into a more profound self pity (which is the root of all bad sentiment) and that bad sentiment in return making me harder and more willing to hurt.

P.S. I have just finished *The Epistle to the Romans,* the first Pauline epistle I have ever seriously read through. It contains many difficult and some horrible things, but the essential idea of Death (the MacDonald idea) is there alright. What I meant about the Earthly Paradise was simply that the whole story turns on a number of people setting out to look for a country where you don't die.

TO ARTHUR GREEVES: *On the intellectual turning point of his conversion—myth become fact (see* God in the Dock *for the essay "Myth Become Fact").*[5]

18 OCTOBER 1931

What has been holding me back (at any rate for the last year or so) has not been so much a difficulty in believing as a difficulty in knowing what the doctrine *meant:* you can't believe a thing while you are ignorant *what* the thing is. My puzzle was the whole doctrine of Redemption: in what sense the life and death of Christ 'saved' or 'opened salvation to' the world. I could see

---

[5] *Letters I,* 976–977.

how miraculous salvation might be necessary: one could see from ordinary experience how sin (e.g. the case of a drunkard) could get a man to such a point that he was bound to reach Hell (i.e., complete degradation and misery) in this life unless something quite beyond mere natural help or effort stepped in. And I could well imagine a whole world being in the same state and similarly in need of miracle. What I couldn't see was how the life and death of Someone Else (whoever he was) 2000 years ago could help us here and now—except in so far as his *example* helped us. And the example business, though true and important, is not Christianity: right in the centre of Christianity, in the Gospels and St. Paul, you keep on getting something quite different and very mysterious expressed in those phrases I have so often ridiculed ('propitiation'—'sacrifice'—'the blood of the Lamb')—expressions which I could only interpret in senses that seemed to me either silly or shocking.

Now what Dyson and Tolkien showed me was this: that if I met the idea of sacrifice in a Pagan story I didn't mind it at all: again, that if I met the idea of a god sacrificing himself to himself..., I liked it very much and was mysteriously moved by it: again, that the idea of the dying and reviving god (Balder, Adonis, Bacchus) similarly moved me provided I met it anywhere *except* in the Gospels. The reason was that in Pagan stories I was prepared to feel the myth as profound and suggestive of meanings beyond my grasp even though I could not say in cold prose 'what it meant'.

Now the story of Christ is simply a true myth: a myth working on us in the same way as the others, but with this tremendous difference that *it really happened:* and one must be content to accept it in the same way, remembering that it is God's myth where the others are men's myths: i.e., the Pagan stories are God expressing Himself through the minds of poets, using such images as He found there, while Christianity is God expressing Himself through what we call 'real things'. Therefore it is *true,* not in the sense of being a 'description' of God (that no finite mind could take in) but in the sense of being the way in which God chooses to (or can) appear to our faculties. The 'doctrines' we get *out of* the true myth are of course *less* true: they are translations into our *concepts* and *ideas* of that which God has already expressed in a language more adequate, namely the actual incarnation, crucifixion, and resurrection. Does this amount to a belief in Christianity? At any rate I am now certain (a) That this Christian story is to be approached, in a sense, as I approach the other myths. (b) That it is the most important and full of meaning. I am also *nearly* certain that it really happened.

TO ARTHUR GREEVES: *On why Christianity doesn't appeal the way Paganism does; and on the spiritual danger of looking for an encore (see* Letters to Malcolm: Chiefly on Prayer, *27 and 90).*[6]

8 NOVEMBER 1931

I, like you, am worried by the fact that the *spontaneous* appeal of the Christian story is so much less to me than that of Paganism. Both the things you suggest (unfavourable associations from early upbringing and the corruption of one's nature) probably are causes: but I have a sort of feeling that *the* cause must be elsewhere, and I have not yet discovered it. I think the thrill of the Pagan stories and of romance may be due to the fact that they are mere beginnings—the first, faint whisper of the wind from beyond the world—while Christianity is the thing itself: and no thing, when you have really started on it, can have for you then and there just the same thrill as the first hint. For example, the experience of being married and bringing up a family, cannot have the old bittersweet of first falling in love. But it is futile (and, I think, wicked) to go on trying to get the old thrill again: you must go forward and not backward. Any *real* advance will in its turn be ushered in by a new thrill, different from the old: doomed in its turn to disappear and to become in its turn a temptation to retrogression. Delight is a bell that rings as you set your foot on the first step of a new flight of stairs leading upwards. Once you have started climbing you will notice only the hard work: it is when you have reached the landing and catch sight of the new stair that you may expect the bell again. This is only an idea, and may be all rot: but it seems to fit in pretty well with the general law (thrills also must die to live) of autumn and spring, sleep and waking, death and resurrection, and 'Whosoever loseth his life,

---

[6] *Letters II*, 12–13.

shall save it.'[7] On the other hand, it may be simply part of our probation—one needs the sweetness to *start* one on the spiritual life but, once started, one must learn to obey God for his own sake, not for the pleasure.

TO ARTHUR GREEVES: *On the theories of the atonement (see* Mere Christianity, *Book II, Chapter 4); and on the defects of Puritanism and of ritualism.*[8]

6 DECEMBER 1931

As to [your cousin] Lucius about the atonement not being in the Gospels, I think he is very probably right. But then nearly everyone seems to think that the Gospels are much later than the Epistles, written for people who had already accepted the *doctrines* and naturally wanted the *story*. I certainly don't think it is historical to regard the Gospels as the *original* and the rest of the New Testament as later elaboration or accretion—though I constantly find myself doing so. But really I feel more and more of a child in the whole matter.

I begin to see how much Puritanism counts in your make up—that both the revulsion from it and the attraction back to it are strong elements. I hardly feel either myself and perhaps am apt to forget in talking to you how different your experience and therefore your feeling is. All I feel that I can say with absolute certainty is this: that if you ever feel that the *whole spirit and system* in which you were brought up was, after all, right and good, then you may be quite sure that that feeling is a mistake (though of course it might, at a given moment—say, of temptation, be present as the alternative to some far bigger mistake).

My reasons for this are 1. That the system denied pleasures to others as well as to the votaries themselves: whatever the merits of self-denial, this is unpardonable interference. 2. It inconsistently kept some worldly pleasures, and always selected the worst ones—gluttony, avarice, et cetera. 3. It was ignorant. It could give no 'reason for the faith that was in it'.[9] Your relations have been

---

[7] Luke 11:24.
[8] *Letters II*, 12–13.
[9] 1 Peter 3:15.

found very ill grounded in the Bible itself and as ignorant as savages of the historical and theological reading needed to make the Bible more than a superstition. 4. 'By their fruits ye shall know them.'[10] Have they the marks of peace, love, wisdom and humility on their faces or in their conversation? Really, you need not bother about that kind of Puritanism. It is simply the form which the memory of Christianity takes just before it finally dies away altogether, in a commercial community: Just as extreme emotional ritualism is the form it takes on just before it dies in a fashionable community.

---

[10]Matthew 7:20.

1932

About Lucius' argument that the evangelists would have put the doctrine of the atonement into the Gospel if they had had the slightest excuse, and, since they didn't, therefore Our Lord didn't teach it: surely, since we know from the Epistles that the Apostles (who had actually known him) *did* teach this doctrine in his name *immediately* after his death, it is clear that he *did* teach it: or else, that they allowed themselves a very free hand. But if people shortly after his death were so very free in interpreting his doctrine, why should people who wrote much later (when such free would be more excusable from lapse of memory in an honest writer, and more likely to escape detection in a dishonest one) become so very much more accurate? The accounts of a thing don't usually get more and more accurate as time goes on. Anyway, if you take the sacrificial idea out of Christianity you deprive both Judaism and Paganism of all significance. Can one believe that there was just *nothing* in that persistent *motif* of blood, death, and resurrection, which runs like a black and scarlet cord through all the greater myths—thro' Balder and Dionysus and Adonis and the Graal too? Surely the history of the human mind hangs together better if you suppose that all this was the first shadowy approach of something whose reality came with Christ—even if we can't at present fully understand that something.

---

[1] *Letters II*, 35.

TO ARTHUR GREEVES: *On love of one's students; on a source of parental disappointment and family tension; and on receiving every good thing as a gift. Tom was Greeves's brother and first employer in Greeves's adolescence; Bookham was the village in which Lewis was tutored as an adolescent.*[2]

27 MARCH 1932

Talking of the past, I had a really delightful experience some weeks ago. An old pupil of mine, one [Arthur] Wood, came to spend a night with me. When I was his tutor he had been a curiously naïf, almost neurotic youth, who was always in love and other troubles, and so childish that he once asked me (as if I were his father!) whether one fell in love less often as one grew older, because he hoped so. Altogether an appealing, but somewhat ridiculous young man. When he went down he was compelled against his will to go into his father's business: and for a year [or] so I got letters from him, and accounts of him from common friends, which seemed to show that he was settling down into a permanent state of self-pity.

You can imagine how pleased I was to find that he had got over this: but above all—that is why I am telling the story—to find that his whole support is romantic reading in those precious evening hours 'after business' which you remember so well. He quoted bits of Middle English poems which he had read with me for the exam. They were mere drudgery to him at the time, but now, in memory, they delight him. He has just re-read the whole of Malory with more delight than ever, and has bought, but not yet begun, *The High History of the Holy Graal*. He also writes a bit—in those same precious evenings, and Saturday afternoons.

In fact as I sat talking to him, hearing his not very articulate, but unmistakable, attempts to express his pleasure, I really felt as if I were meeting *our* former selves. He is just in the stage that we were in when you worked with Tom and I was at Bookham. Of course there was an element of vanity on my side—one liked to feel that one had been the means of starting him on things that now are standing him in such good stead. There was also a less contemptible, and, so to speak, professional, pleasure in thus seeing a proof that the English School here does really do some good. But in the main the pleasure was a spiritual one—a kind of love. It is difficult, without being sentimental, to say how extraordinarily *beautiful*—ravishing—I found the sight of some one just at that point which you and I remember so well. I suppose it is this pleasure which fathers always are hoping to get, and very seldom do get, from their sons.

Do you think a good deal of parental cruelty results from the disappointment of this hope? I mean, it takes a man of some tolerance to resign himself to the fact that his sons are not going to follow the paths that he followed and not going to give him this pleasure. What it all comes to, anyway, is that this pleasure, like everything else worth having, must not be reckoned on, or demanded as a right. If I had thought of it for a moment in the old days when I was teaching Wood, this pleasant evening would probably never have happened.

1933

TO MARY SHELLEY, *a former student and the first of Lewis's "direct-ees," who had just received barely passing grades and the lowest possible degree (fourth class). This letter begins a lifelong friendship.*[1]

21 JULY 1933

Dear Miss Shelley,

If you are not, at the moment, too sick of me and all my kind to read further, it may be worth saying that you must not run away with the idea that you are a Fourth Class mind. What really ruined you was an NS ["not satisfactory"] and a Δ on language, which would of course have spoiled even very good work else-where. In the Lit. your highest mark was ß+ (XIXth century).

Why your literature papers were not better I do not under-stand. I blame myself for not having exhorted more essays from you—but I doubt if that was the whole cause. You were very *short* and *general*. But I am quite clear in my own mind that you have not done yourself justice and that your real quality is far beyond the work you did in Schools [the final examinations].

This is cold comfort to you with the world to face!—but at least it is said quite sincerely and not merely for the sake of con-soling you.

Try to forgive me both as an examiner and as a tutor. If there should at any time be any way in which I can be of use to you, let me know at once. Till then, good-bye and good luck.

---

[1] *Letters II,* 113.

TO ARTHUR GREEVES: *On the sheer goodness of God and the existence of evil; on the nature of temptation and sin; and on obedience.*[2]

12 SEPTEMBER 1933

It was a delightful surprise to get your long and interesting letter: certainly the longest and one of the most interesting letters I have ever had from you.

I have been thinking all morning over your question about God and evil which is very far from being 'elementary' to me—or for that matter, I suppose, to the angels. If I understand you rightly you are not *primarily* concerned with the sort of logical problem as to how the All-Good can produce evil, or produce a world in which there is evil, but with a more personal, practical, and intimate problem as to how far God can sympathise with our evil will as well as with our good—or, to draw it milder, *whether* he does.

I should begin, I think, by objecting to an expression you use: 'God must have a potentiality of His opposite—evil.' For this I would substitute the idea which someone had in the Middle Ages who defined God as '*That which has no opposite*' i.e., we live in a world of clashes, good and evil, true and false, pleasant and painful, body and spirit, time and eternity *et cetera*, but God is not simply (so to speak) *one* of the two clashes but the ultimate thing beyond them all—just as in our constitution the King is neither the Prime Minister nor the Leader of the Opposition, but the thing behind them which alone enables these to be a lawful government and an opposition—or just as space is neither bigness or smallness but that in which the distinctions of big and small arise. This then is my first point. That Evil is not something outside and '*over against*' God, but *in some way* included under Him.

My second point seems to be in direct contradiction to this first one, and is (in scriptural language) as follows: that God 'is the Father of Lights and in Him is *no darkness at all*'.[3] *In some way* there is no evil whatever in God. He is pure Light. All the *heat* that in us is lust or anger in Him is cool light—eternal morning, eternal freshness, eternal springtime: never disturbed, never strained. Go

---

[2] *Letters II*, 121–125.
[3] John 1:5.

out on any perfect morning in early summer before the world is awake and see, not the thing itself, but the material symbol of it.

Well, these are our two starting points. *In one way* (our old phrase!) God includes evil, in another way he does not. What are we to do next? My beginning of the 'next' will be to deny another remark of yours—where you say 'no good without evil'. This on my view is absolutely untrue: but the opposite 'no evil without good' is absolutely true. I will try to explain what I mean by an analogy.

Supposing you are taking a dog on a lead through a turnstile or past a post. You know what happens (apart from his usual ceremonies in passing a post!). He tries to go the wrong side and gets his lead looped round the post. *You* see that he can't do it, and therefore pull him back. You pull him *back* because you want to enable him to go *forward*. He wants exactly the same thing—namely to go *forward*: for that very reason he resists your pull *back,* or, if he is an obedient dog, yields to it reluctantly as a matter of duty which seems to him to be quite in opposition to his own will: though *in fact* it is only by yielding to you that he will ever succeed in getting where he wants.

Now if the dog were a theologian he would regard his own will as a *sin* to which he was tempted, and therefore an *evil:* and he might go on to ask whether you understand and 'contained' his evil. If he did you could only reply 'My dear dog, if by your will you mean what you really want to do, viz. to get forward along the road, I not only understand this desire but *share* it. Forward is exactly where I want you to go. If by your will, on the other hand, you mean your will to pull against the collar and try to force yourself forward in a direction which is no use—why I *understand* it of course: but just because I understand it (and the whole situation, which you *don't* understand) I cannot possibly share it. In fact the more I sympathise with your *real* wish—that is, the wish to get on—the less can I sympathise (in the sense of 'share' or 'agree with') your resistance to the collar: for I see that this is actually rendering the attainment of your real wish impossible.'

I don't know if you will agree at once that this is a parallel to the situation between God and man: but I will work it out on the assumption that you do. Let us go back to the original question—whether and, if so in what sense God contains, say, my evil will—or 'understands' it. The answer is God not only understands but *shares* the desire which is at the root of all my evil—the desire for complete and ecstatic happiness. He made me for no other purpose than to enjoy it. But He knows, and I do not, how it can be really and permanently attained. He knows that most of *my* personal attempts to reach it are actually putting it further and further out of my reach. With these therefore He cannot sympathise or 'agree': His sympathy with my *real* will makes that impossible. (He may *pity* my misdirected struggles, but that is another matter.) The practical results seem to be two.

1. I may always feel looking back on any past sin that in the very heart of my evil passion there was something that God approves and wants me to feel not less but more. Take a sin of Lust. The overwhelming thirst for *rapture* was good and even divine: it has not got to be unsaid (so to speak) and recanted. But it will never be quenched as I tried to quench it. If I refrain—if I submit to the collar and come round the right side of the lamp-post— God will be guiding me as quickly as He can to where I shall get what I really wanted all the time. It will not be very like what I now think I want: but it will be more like it than some suppose. In any case it will be the real thing, not a consolation prize or substitute. If I had it I should not need to fight against sensuality as something impure: rather I should spontaneously turn away from it as something dull, cold, abstract, and artificial. This, I think, is how the doctrine applies to past sins.

2. On the other hand, when we are thinking of a sin in the future, i.e., when we are tempted, we must remember that *just because* God wants for us what we really want and knows the only way to get it, therefore He must, in a sense, be quite ruthless towards sin. He is not like a human authority who can be begged off or caught in an indulgent mood. The more He loves you the more determined He must be to pull you back from your way which leads nowhere into His way which leads where you want to go. Hence MacDonald's words 'The *all-punishing, all-pardoning* Father'. You may go the wrong way again, and again He may forgive you: as the dog's master may extricate the dog after he has tied the whole lead round the lamp-post. But there is no hope *in the end* of getting where you want to go except by going God's way. And what does '*in the end*' mean? This is a terrible question.

If endless time will really help us to go the right way, I believe we shall be given endless time. But perhaps God knows that time makes no difference. Perhaps He knows that if you can't learn the way in 60 or 70 years on this planet (a place probably constructed by Divine skill for the very purpose of teaching you) then you will never learn it anywhere. There may be nothing left for Him but to destroy you (the kindest thing): *if He can.*

I think one may be quite rid of the old haunting suspicion—which raises its head in every temptation—that there is something else than God—some other country . . . into which He forbids us to trespass—some kind of delight which He 'doesn't appreciate' or just chooses to forbid, but which would be real delight if only we were allowed to get it. The thing *just isn't there.* Whatever we desire is either what God is trying to give us as quickly as He can, or else a false picture of what He is trying to give us—a false picture which would not attract us for a moment if we saw the real thing. Therefore God does really in a sense contain evil—i.e., contains what is the real motive power behind all our evil desires. He knows what we want, even in our vilest acts: He is longing to give it to us. He is not looking on from the outside at some new 'taste' or 'separate desire of our own'. Only because he has laid up *real* goods for us to desire are we able to go wrong by snatching at them in greedy, misdirected ways. The truth is that evil is not a real *thing* at all, like God. It is simply good *spoiled.* That is why I say there can be good without evil, but no evil without good. You know what the biologists mean by a parasite—an animal that lives on another animal. Evil is a *parasite.* It is there only because good is there for it to spoil and confuse.

Thus you may well feel that God understands our temptations—understands them a great deal more than we do. But don't forget MacDonald again—'*Only God understands evil and hates it.*' Only the dog's master knows how useless it is to try to get on with the lead knotted round the lamp-post. This is why we must be prepared to find God implacably and immovably forbidding what may seem to us very small and trivial things. But He knows whether they are really small and trivial. How small some of the things that doctors forbid would seem to an ignoramus.

When I suggested that you had changed, I didn't mean that you had changed towards me. I meant that I thought the centre of your interests might have shifted more than mine. This leads on to what you say about being a mere mirror for other people on which each friend can cast his reflection in turn. That certainly is what you might become, just as a hardened bigot shouting every one down till he had no friends left is what I am in danger of becoming. In other words sympathy is your strong point, as stability is mine—if I have a strong point at all, which is doubtful: or weakness is your danger, as Pride is mine. (You have no idea how much of my time I spend just hating people whom I disagree with—though I know them only from their books—and inventing conversations in which I score off them.) In other words, we all have our own burdens, and must do the best we can. I do not know which is the worse, nor do we need to: if each of us could imitate the other.

1934

TO BEDE GRIFFITHS: *On the eternal fate of the virtuous unbeliever; on Lewis's resolution never to discuss differences between Christian denominations; on the devotional value of reading difficult theological books; and on two of the essential problems of prayer—on prayer as illusion and on God's role in every prayer.*[1]

4 APRIL 1934

The question of 'generality' in prayer is not so simple. The doctrine held by your own Church about the position of the virtuous heretic or pagan . . . is, you will find, far from crude. Is it not held that many who have lived and died outside the visible Church are finally saved, because Divine Grace has guided them to concentrate solely on the true elements in their own religions? And if so, must one not admit that it was the mysterious will of God that these persons should be saved in that peculiar way? I use this argument to point out that even such a comparatively general prayer as that for a man's conversion, may yet be too particular.

And while I am on the subject, I had better say once and for all that I do not intend to discuss with you in future, if I can help it, any of the questions at issue between our respective churches. It would have the same unreality as those absurd conversations in which we are invited to speak frankly to a woman about some indelicate matter—which means that she can say what she likes and we can't. I could not, now that you are a monk, use that freedom in attacking your position which you undoubtedly would use in attacking mine. I do not think there is any thing distressing for either of us in agreeing to be silent on this matter: I have had a Catholic among my most intimate friends for many years [Tolkien] and a great deal of our conversation has been religious. When all is said (and truly said) about the divisions of Christendom, there remains, by God's mercy, an enormous common ground. It is abstaining from one tree in the whole garden.

---

[1] *Letters II*, 121–125.

I should rather like to attend your Greek class, for it is a perpetual puzzle to me how New Testament Greek got the reputation of being easy. St. Luke I find particularly difficult. As regards matter—leaving the question of language—you will be glad to hear that I am at last beginning to get some small understanding of St. Paul: hitherto an author quite opaque to me. I am speaking now, of course, of the general drift of whole epistles: short passages, treated devotionally, are of course another matter. And yet the distinction is not, for me, quite a happy one. Devotion is best raised when we intend something else. At least that is my experience. Sit down to meditate devotionally on a single verse, and nothing happens. Hammer your way through a continued argument, just as you would in a profane writer, and the heart will sometimes sing unbidden. . . .

P. S. This has some relevance both to the questions of Prayer and Idealism. I wrote it over a year ago.

They tell me, Lord, that when I seem
To be in speech with You,
Since You make no replies, it's all a dream
—One talker aping two.

And so it is, but not as they
Falsely believe. For I
Seek in myself the things I meant to say,
And lo!, the wells are dry.

Then, seeing me empty, You forsake
The listener's part, and through
My dumb limps breathe and into utterance wake
The thoughts I never knew.

Therefore You neither need reply
Nor can: for while we seem
Two talking, Thou art one forever; and I
No dreamer, but Thy dream.

1935

TO OWEN BARFIELD, *who had given Lewis a copy of one of his favorite books by George MacDonald: On proper self-love.*[1]

9 DECEMBER 1935

The Diary of an Old Soul is magnificent. . . .

Incidentally, since I have begun to pray, I find my extreme view of personality changing. My own empirical self is becoming more important and this is exactly the opposite of self love. You don't teach a seed how to die into treehood by throwing it into the fire: and it has to become a good seed before it's worth burying.

TO ARTHUR GREEVES, *who had just ended an unhealthy friendship with a boy: On doing the right thing; and on the blessing of friendship.*[2]

29 DECEMBER 1935

As regards your news—sympathy and congratulations. Sympathy on the wrench of parting and the gap it will leave: congratulations on having done the right thing and made a sacrifice. The chief consolation at such times, I think, is that the result, however unpleasant, must be a kind of relief after the period of saying 'Shall I really have to—no I won't—and yet perhaps I'd better.' There is always some peace in having submitted to the right. Don't spoil it by worrying about the *results,* if you can help it. It is not your business to succeed (no one can be sure of that) but to do right: when you have done so, the rest lies with God. . . .

I don't think you exaggerate at all in your account of how it feels. After all—though our novels now ignore it—friendship is the greatest of worldly goods. Certainly to me it is the chief happiness of life. If I had to give a piece of advice to a young

---

[1] *Letters II,* 121–125.
[2] *Letters II,* 174.

man about a place to live, I think I should say, 'sacrifice almost everything to live where you can be near your friends.' I know I am very fortunate in that respect, and you much less so. But even for me, it would make a great difference if you (and one or two others) lived in Oxford.

1936

TO BEDE GRIFFITHS: *On unreliable fashions in philosophy and the reliability of the Word; on how it is easier to pray for others than for oneself; on obedience as the whole business of life; and on the obedience of nature as the beauty of nature.*[1]

8 JANUARY 1936

It must be nice to know some Aristotle, and it is a relief to hear that kind of philosophy praised by you who have a right to judge: for in the Oxford world 'Neo-Scholasticism' has become such a fashion among ignorant undergrads. that I am sick of the sound of it. . . .

By the way, I hope that the great religious revival now going on will not get itself too mixed up with Scholasticism, for I am sure that the revival of the latter, however salutary, must be as temporary as any other movement in philosophy. Of things on the natural level, now one, now another, is the ally or the enemy of Faith. The scientists have got us in such a muddle that at present rationalism is on our side, and enthusiasm is an enemy: the opposite was true in the 19th century and will be true again. I mean, we have no abiding city even in philosophy: all passes, except the Word. . . .

Thank you for your prayers: you know mine too, little worth as they are. Have you found, or is it peculiar to me, that it is much easier to pray for *others* than for oneself. Doubtless because every return to one's own situation involves action: or to speak more plainly, obedience. That appears to me more and more the whole business of life, the only road to love and peace—the cross and the crown in one. Did you ever notice a beautiful touch in the *Faerie Queene*

> 'a groom them laid *at rest in easie bedd,*
> His name was meek Obedience.'

---

[1] *Letters II,* 176–178.

What indeed can we imagine Heaven to be but unimpeded obedience. I think this is one of the causes of our love of inanimate nature, that in it we see things which unswervingly carry out the will of their Creator, and are therefore wholly beautiful: and though their *kind* of obedience is infinitely lower than ours, yet the degree is so much more perfect that a Christian can see the reason that the Romantics had in feeling a certain holiness in the wood and water. The Pantheistic conclusions they sometimes drew are false: but their feeling was just and we can safely allow it in ourselves now that we know the real reason.

TO ARTHUR GREEVES, *whose dog Tommy had just died, leaving his other dog John bereft of companionship: On the comfort of pets (Mr. Papworth was Lewis's dog); on the significance of Charles Williams's novel; and on humility as a corrective of the sin of abuse of the intellect.*[2]

26 FEBRUARY 1936

I see to my consternation that it is over a month since your letter came. It certainly deserved an earlier answer but you must forgive me.

I was very sorry indeed to hear about 'Tommy'. I am particularly sorry for John. You know I crossed with the pair of them last time I left home: and I should like to say as impressively as I can—and you to take note—that I was very much impressed by seeing them together and by the fire, almost the spiritual atmosphere of their whole world of mountain climbing. It gave me a new and most favourable sidelight on John: and I am afraid it is most unlikely that he will find any one to take Tommy's place. I am very sorry for him. Try to be as nice to him as you can—but I have no doubt you are doing that already.

For yourself I expect days are pretty dim at present. Do you hear good news of the boy? As I said before, I am sure you have done the right thing, and I'm afraid that is all the comfort I can offer.

I quite understand what you say about the comfort derived from all a dog's 'little affairs', and enjoyed reading that passage as much as any in your letter. They are a *busy* folk. And talking

---

[2] *Letters II,* 179–181.

of dogs, poor old Mr Papworth has been gathered to his fathers. He had been ailing for some time and finally got a bad ulcer on his chin. He was given a strong sleeping draught. When I went to bed he was asleep in his basket and breathing as gently as a child: in the morning he was dead. Minto has been very badly upset—almost as if for a human being. I don't feel it as badly as that myself and would discourage the feeling (I think) if I had it. But it is a parting, and one sometimes remembers his old happy days, especially his puppyhood, with an ache.

I have just read what I think a really great book, *The Place of the Lion* by Charles Williams. It is based on the Platonic theory of the other world in which the archetypes of all earthly qualities exist: and in the novel, owing to a bit of machinery which doesn't matter, these archetypes start sucking our world back. The lion of strength appears in the world and the strength starts going out of houses and things into him. The archetypal butterfly (enormous) appears and all the butterflies of the world fly back into him. But man contains and ought to be able to rule all these forces: and there is one man in the book who does, and the story ends with him as a second Adam 'naming the beasts' and establishing dominion over them.

It is not only a most exciting fantasy, but a deeply religious and (unobtrusively) a profoundly learned book. The reading of it has been a good preparation for Lent as far as I am concerned: for it shows me (through the heroine) the special sin of abuse of intellect to which all my profession are liable, more clearly than I ever saw it before. I have learned more than I ever knew yet about humility. In fact it has been a big experience. Do get it, and don't mind if you don't understand everything the first time. It deserves reading over and over again. It isn't often now-a-days you get a *Christian* fantasy.

TO CHARLES WILLIAMS: *On the impact on Lewis of Williams's novel. This is the letter that begins their friendship. Damaris Tighe is the heroine of the novel, the young philosopher who undergoes a conversion.[3]*

11 MARCH 1936

I never know about writing to an author. If you are older than I, I don't want to seem impertinent: if you are younger, I don't want to seem patronizing. But I feel I must risk it.

A book sometimes crosses one's path which is so like the sound of one's native language in a strange country that it feels almost uncivil not to wave some kind of flag in answer. I have just read your *Place of the Lion* and it is to me one of the major literary events of my life—comparable to my first discovery of George MacDonald, G.K. Chesterton, or Wm. Morris. There are layers and layers—first the pleasure that any good fantasy gives me: then, what is rarely (though not so very rarely) combined with this, the pleasure of a real philosophical and theological stimulus: thirdly, characters: fourthly, what I neither expected nor desired, substantial edification.

I mean the latter with perfect seriousness. I know Damaris very well: in fact I was in course of becoming Damaris (but you have pulled me up). . . . Not only is your diagnosis good: but the very way in which you force one to look at the matter is itself the beginning of a cure. Honestly, I didn't think there was anyone now alive in England who could do it.

Coghill of Exeter put me on to the book: I have put on Tolkien (the Professor of Anglo Saxon and a papist) and my brother. So there are three dons and one soldier all buzzing with excited admiration. We have a sort of informal club called the Inklings: the qualifications (as they have informally evolved) are a tendency to write, and Christianity. Can you come down some day next term (preferably not Sat. or Sunday), spend the night as my guest in College, eat with us at a chop house, and talk with us till the small hours. Meantime, a thousand thanks.

---

[3] *Letters II*, 183–184.

1938

29 APRIL 1938

I have been in considerable trouble over the present danger of war. Twice in one life—and then to find how little I have grown in fortitude despite my conversion. It has done me a lot of good by making me realise how much of my happiness secretly depended on the tacit assumption of at least tolerable conditions for the body: and I see more clearly, I think, the necessity (if one may so put it) which God is under of allowing us to be afflicted—so few of us will *really* rest all on Him if He leaves us any other support.

About our differences: I feel that whenever two members of different communions succeed in sharing the spiritual life so far as they can now share it, and are thus forced to regard each other as Christians, they are really helping on reunion by producing the conditions without which official reunion would be quite barren. I feel sure that this is the layman's chief contribution to the task, and some of us here are being enabled to perform it. You, who are a priest and a theologian, are a different story: and on the purely natural and temperamental level there is, and always has been, a sort of tension between us two which prevents our doing much mutual good. We shall both be nicer, please God, in a better place. Meanwhile you have my daily prayer and good wishes.

---

[1] *Letters II*, 224–226.

1939

TO BEDE GRIFFITHS: *On ecumenical differences; on the poet Coventry Patmore and the age at which to read certain books; on worries about the coming war; on the meaning of temporal evils; on the central importance of Gethsemane in Lewis's own meditations; and on the necessity of every generation learning from its own experience. The Territorials are the part-time soldiers Britain had mobilized for protecting the homeland.*[1]

8 MAY 1939

It was nice to hear from you again. I think I said before that I have no contribution to make about reunion. It was never more needed. A united Christendom should be the answer to the new Paganism. But how reconciliation of the Churches, as opposed to conversions of individuals from a church to another, is to come about, I confess I cannot see. I am inclined to think that the immediate task is vigorous co-operation on the basis of what even now is common—combined, of course, with full admission of the differences. An *experienced* unity on some things might then prove the prelude to a confessional unity on all things. Nothing would give such strong support to the Papal claims as the spectacle of a Pope actually functioning as head of Christendom. But it is not, I feel sure, my vocation to discuss reunion....

I thought we had talked of Patmore. I think him really great within his own limited sphere. To be sure he pushes the parallel between Divine and human love as far as it can sanely or decently go, and perhaps at times a little further. One can imagine his work being most pernicious to a devout person who read it at the wrong age. But a superb poet. Do you remember the comparison of the naturally virtuous person who receives grace at conversion to a man walking along and suddenly hearing a band playing, and then 'His step unchanged, he steps in time.' Or on the poignancy of Spring, 'With it the blackbird breaks the young day's heart.' Or the lightening during a storm at sea which reveals 'The deep/

---

[1] *Letters II*, 256–258.

Standing about in strong heaps.' That is sheer genius. And the *tightness* (if you know what I mean) of all his work. . . .

No, I haven't joined the Territorials. I am too old. It would be hypocrisy to say that I regret this. My memories of the last war haunted my dreams for years. Military service, to be plain, includes the threat of *every* temporal evil: pain and death which is what we fear from sickness: isolation from those we love which is what we fear from exile: toil under arbitrary masters, injustice and humiliation, which is what we fear from slavery: hunger, thirst, cold and exposure which is what we fear from poverty. I'm not a pacifist. If its got to be, its got to be. But the flesh is weak and selfish and I think death would be much better than to live through another war.

Thank God, He has not allowed my *faith* to be greatly tempted by the present horrors. I do not doubt that whatever misery He permits will be for our ultimate good unless, by rebellious will, we convert it to evil. But I get no further than Gethsemane: and am daily thankful that that scene, of all others in Our Lord's life, did not go unrecorded. But what state of affairs in this world can we view with satisfaction? If we are unhappy, then we are unhappy. If we are happy, then we remember that the crown is not promised without the cross and tremble. In fact, one comes to realise, what one always admitted theoretically, that there is nothing here that will do us good: the sooner we are safely out of this world the better. But 'would it were evening, Hal, and all well.' I have even, I'm afraid, caught myself wishing that I had never been born, which is sinful. Also, meaningless if you try to think it out.

The process of living seems to consist in coming to realise truths so ancient and simple that, if stated, they sound like barren platitudes. They cannot sound otherwise to those who have not had the relevant experience: that is why there is no real teaching of such truths possible and every generation starts from scratch.

TO SISTER PENELOPE, *an Anglican nun, in the letter that begins their spiritual friendship: On humility; and on the books of George MacDonald and of Charles Williams.*[2]

---

[2] *Letters II,* 256–258.

9 AUGUST 1939

Thank you very much . . . for your kind letter. The letter raises for me rather an acute problem—do I become more proud in trying to resist or in frankly revelling in, the pleasure it gives me? One hopes there will come a day when one can enjoy nice things said about one's self just in the same innocent way as one enjoys nice things about anyone else—perfect humility will need no modesty. In the meantime, it is not so. . . .

I think your task of finding suitable fiction for the convalescents must be interesting. Do you know George MacDonald's fantasies for grown-ups (his tales for children you probably know already). *Phantastes* and *Lilith* I found endlessly attractive, and full of what I felt to be holiness before I really knew that it was. One of his novels, *Sir Gibbie* (Everyman), though often, like all his novels, amateurish, is worth reading. And do you know the works of Charles Williams? Rather wild, but full of love and excelling in the creation of convincing *good* characters. (The reason these are rare in fiction is that to imagine a man worse than yourself you've only got to stop doing something, while to imagine one better you've got to do something). . . .

Though I'm forty years old as a man I'm only about twelve as a Christian, so it would be a maternal act if you found time sometimes to mention me in your prayers.

TO OWEN BARFIELD: *On the meaning of Jesus' temptations in the wilderness and in the garden of Gethsemane; on fear; on death; and on the meaning of his death on the cross.*[3]

AUGUST 1939

As regards our argument about Gethsemane, I quite see that it sounds odd to attribute to perfect man a fear which imperfect men have often overcome. But one must beware of interpreting 'perfect man' in a sense which would nullify the temptation in the wilderness: a scene on which, at first, one would be tempted to comment (a) As regards the stone and bread 'Imperfect men have voluntarily starved' (b) As regards Satan's demand for

---

[3] *Letters II, 266–269.*

worship 'Most men have never sunk so low as to feel this temptation at all.'

If we are to accept the Gospels however, we must interpret Christ's perfection in a sense which admits of his feeling *both* the commonest and most animal temptations (hunger and the fear of death) and those temptations which usually occur only to the worst of men (devil worship for the sake of power). I am assuming that the stones and bread represent hunger: but if you prefer to regard it as primarily a temptation to *thaumaturgy* [miracle-working] ('If thou be the Son of God, command these stones') then it falls into my second class.

The consideration of this second class at once raises the question 'Are there no temptations proper to the very best and the very worst, which the middle sort of men do not feel?': or, again, 'Do not common temptations attack most fiercely the best and the worst?' I should answer Yes, and say that fear of death was one of these. . . .

. . . Death for Him also is the final defeat, but this time of *real* Free (I am taking it for granted that the spiritual essence of death is 'the opposite of Freedom': hence the most mortal images are rigidity, suffocation *et cetera*).

No doubt, He also knows the answer—that voluntary death . . . makes unfree itself the assertion of freedom. But voluntary submission does not mean that there is nothing to submit to.

What is it to an ordinary man to die, if once he can set his teeth to bear the merely animal fear? To give in—he has been doing that nine times out of ten all his life. To see the lower in him conquer the higher, his animal body turning into lower animals and these finally into the mineral—he has been letting this happen since he was born. To relinquish control—easy for him as slipping on a well worn shoe.

But in Gethsemane it is essential Free that is asked to be bound, unwearied control to throw up the sponge. Life itself to die. Ordinary men have not been so much in love with life as is usually supposed: small as their share of it is they have found it too much to bear without reducing a large portion of it as nearly to non-life as they can: we love drugs, sleep, irresponsibility, amusement, are more than half in love with easeful death—if only we could be sure it wouldn't hurt! Only He who really lived a human life (and I presume that only one did) can fully taste the horror of death.

TO SISTER PENELOPE, *who had given Lewis her book,* Leaves from the Trees, *in which "Consider the Dog: A Study in Right Relationship" is the first chapter: On what he has learned from animals about our relationship to God; and on the possibility of animals in heaven, and even their greeting us with tails wagging as we arrive.*[4]

24 AUGUST 1939

Thank you very much for your most interesting letter and for *Leaves.* . . .

Your book raises a whole host of points that interest me. I have often thought of the parallel between the dog-man and the man-God relation and agree with all you say. I have found it helpful, too, in trying to understand Grace—which I suppose comes in on top of our humanity as the many quasi-human qualities which the dog learns from living with us come in on top of his caninity. . . . I very earnestly hope that you are right on p. 76 about tails wagging as well as trumpets sounding: *not* (as the anti-sentimental do vainly talk!) through sentiment, but because animal suffering raises quite terrifying problems about divine justice. Yet it is difficult to me to accept your suggestion, partly because the whole Christian tradition is so silent on the subject (or is that my ignorance?) and partly—well, what about all the wasps?—remembering, as you well remind us elsewhere, that the living members of any species are such a small minority. Perhaps the real answer is beyond human understanding: we know so little about Time and Individuality.

---

[4] *Letters II,* 264–265.

TO HIS BROTHER, *who had been called back to active duty in the army and to whom Lewis wrote long, newsy letters weekly throughout the war: On the reading of* Introduction to the Devout Life *by St. Francis de Sales.*[5]

3 DECEMBER 1939

And talking of books, I have been looking rapidly through St. François de Sales this week end to find a passage I wanted to quote, and have derived much 'social pleasure' from your pencillings: as I have experienced before, to read a book marked by you in your absence is almost the nearest thing to a conversation. When I read that hares turn white in winter because they eat nothing but snow (used as an argument for frequent communion) and see your mark it is almost as if one of us was pointing the passage out to the other here in the study.

TO HIS BROTHER: *On the center of the Christian experience at the heart of the best of western literature; and on Samuel Johnson.*[6]

18 DECEMBER 1939

Yes, I know well what you mean by the materialistic gains of being a Christian. It more often presents itself to me the other way round—how on earth did we manage to enjoy all these books so much as we did in the days when we had really no conception of what was at the centre of them? Sir, he who embraces the Christian revelation rejoins the main tide of human existence! And I quite agree about Johnson. If one had not experienced it, it would be hard to understand how a dead man out of a book can be almost a member of one's family circle—still harder to realise, even now, that you and I have a chance of someday really meeting him.

---

[5] *Letters II,* 301.
[6] *Letters II,* 304–305. On the center of the Christian experience at the heart of the best of western literature, see "On the Reading of Old Books," *God in the Dark,* (Grand Rapids: Eerdmans, 1970), 200–207.

1940

TO HIS BROTHER, *at the end of a long description of a delight-filled winter walk: On thanksgiving as the necessary completion of a pleasure.*[1]

9 JANUARY 1940

It seems almost brutal to describe a January walk taken without you in a letter *to* you, but I suppose 'concealment is in vain'. . . .

. . . I dined at the Harwoods that night and came away—on Tuesday morning—as you said in your last letter 'thanking the Giver' which, by the way, is the *completion* of a pleasure. One of the things about being an unbeliever is that the steam or 'spirit' (in the chemical sense) given off by experiences has nowhere to go to.

TO BEDE GRIFFITHS: *On Lewis's morning practice of rejoicing.*[2]

17 JANUARY 1940

I agree with you very strongly about the necessity of trying as hard as we can to obey the apostolic 'Rejoice always':[3] and I think we sin by needless neglect of this as often as by anything else. The attempt to obey it is at present one of my three morning resolutions each day. I had not realised its importance till recently.

TO HIS BROTHER: *On patience with the talkative elderly as Lewis's way of making up for the way he treated his father. F.K. is the eighty-year-old Anglican priest Edward Foord-Kelcey, and "old Taylor" is their Headington Quarry neighbor William Taylor.*[4]

3 FEBRUARY 1940

That afternoon I had the coldest dawdle round the estate with old Taylor that I have yet had. In spite of the bitter wind we had

---

[1] *Letters II*, 322.
[2] *Letters II*, 327.
[3] Philippians 4:4.
[4] *Letters II*, 340.

to stop to examine every track and speculate what kind of animal it was—but indeed I am rather ashamed that a man of over 70 should have so much more gust for natural philosophy and so much less shrinking from the wind than I. (Between ourselves, too, I have a sort of faint hope that what I can put in with such as F.K. and old Taylor may be accepted as a kind of penance for my many sins against [our father]: the blackest chapter in my life.)

TO HIS BROTHER: *On the pivotal spiritual event of Charles Williams's lecture on chastity in the poem by Milton.*[5]

11 FEBRUARY 1940

On Monday Charles Williams lectured nominally on *Comus* but really on Chastity. Simply as criticism it was superb—because here was a man who really started from the same point of view as Milton and really cared with every fibre of his being about 'the sage and serious doctrine of virginity' which it would never occur to the ordinary modern critic to take seriously. But it was more important still as a sermon. It was a beautiful sight to see a whole room full of modern young men and women sitting in that absolute silence which can *not* be faked, very puzzled, but spellbound: perhaps with something of the same feeling which a lecture on *un*chastity might have evoked in their grandparents—the forbidden subject broached at last. He forced them to lap it up and I think many, by the end, liked the taste more than they expected to. It was 'borne in upon me' that that beautiful carved room had probably not witnessed anything so important since some of the great medieval or Reformation lectures. I have at last, if only for once, seen a university doing what it was founded to do: teaching Wisdom. And what a wonderful power there is in the direct appeal which disregards the temporary climate of opinion—I wonder is it the case that the man who has the audacity to get up in any corrupt society and squarely preach justice or valour or the like *always* wins? After all, the Nazis largely got into power by simply talking the old straight stuff about heroism in a country full of cynics and buggers.

---

[5] *Letters II,* 345–346.

TO HIS BROTHER: *On the human inability to scatter one's sympathies globally; and on the changing theological and evangelical climate. Sir Roger de Coverley is a fictional character described in various issues of the oldest British periodical still in print,* The Spectator. *Mr. Arabin is a clergyman in Trollope's Barchester novels.*[6]

18 FEBRUARY 1940

Barfield has been up to spend an evening with me. . . .

He is very much depressed having a greater faculty than you or I for feeling the miseries of the world in general—which led to a good deal of argument, how far, as a man and a Christian, one *ought* to be vividly and continuously aware of, say, what it's like on the [front] line at this moment.

I took the line that the present rapidity of communication *et cetera* imposed a burden on sympathy for which sympathy was never made: that the natural thing was to be distressed about what was happening to the poor Jones's in *your own village* and that the modern situation, in which journalism brings the Chinese, Russians, Finns, Poles and Turks to your notice each morning really *could not* be met in the same way. Of course I know the more obvious reply, that you can't do them any good by being miserable, but that is hardly the point, for in the case of the Jones's next door we should think ill of the man who felt nothing whether his feeling did them good or not. I am afraid the truth is in this, as in nearly everything else I think about at present, that the world, as it is now becoming and has partly become, is simply *too much for* people of the old square-rigged type like you and me. I don't understand its economics, or its politics, or any dam' thing about it.

Even its theology—for that is a most distressing discovery I have been making these last two terms as I have been getting to know more and more of the Christian element in Oxford. Did you fondly believe—I did—that where you got among Christians, there, at least, you would escape (as behind a wall from a keen wind) from the horrible ferocity and grimness of modern thought? Not a bit of it. I blundered into it all, imagining that I was the upholder of the old, stern doctrines against modern quasi-

---

[6] *Letters II*, 350–352.

Christian slush: only to find that *my* 'sternness' was *their* 'slush'. They've all been reading a dreadful man called Karl Barth, who seems the right opposite number to Karl Marx. 'Under judgement' is their great expression. They all talk like Covenanters or Old Testament prophets. They don't think human reason or human conscience of any value at all: they maintain, as stoutly as Calvin, that there's no reason why God's dealings should appear just (let alone, merciful) to us: and they maintain the doctrine that *all* our righteousness is filthy rags[7] with a fierceness and sincerity which is like a blow in the face.

Sometimes the results are refreshing: as when Canon Raven (whom you and Dyson and I sat under at Ely) is sharply told in a review in *Theology* that 'it is high time persons of this sort learned that the enjoyment of a chair of theology at Cambridge does not carry with it a right to criticise the Word of God'—that's the kind of rap on the knuckles which has not been delivered for a hundred years!

But the total effect is withering. Of two things I am now persuaded. (1) That a real red-hot Christian revival, with iron dogma, stern discipline, and ruthless asceticism, is very much more possible than I had supposed. (2) That if it comes, people like us will not find it nearly so agreeable as we had expected. 'Why have they desired the Day of the Lord? It is darkness not light.'[8] I have no doubt the young gentlemen are substantially right: this is the goods. We ought to have expected that if the real thing came it would make one sit up (you remember Chesterton 'Never invoke gods unless you really want them to appear. It annoys them very much').

But, in a private letter, one may, for a moment, bewail happier days—the old world when Politics meant Tariff Reform, and war, war with Zulus, and even religion meant (beautiful word) Piety. 'The *decent* church that crowns the neighbouring hill'—Sir Roger at Church—'Mr Arabin sent the farmers home to their baked mutton very well satisfied'.

---

[7] Isaiah 64:6.
[8] Amos 5:18.

TO HIS BROTHER: *On Lewis's chief problem with the attitude one ought to bring to petitionary prayer—the contrast between "Thy will be done" and "believing that we shall receive" (Matthew 21:22).*[9]

3 MARCH 1940

By the bye, 'tell me' as your poor father used to say: how does one in practice (I don't say, intellectually)—in the actual practice of prayer—combine the attitude 'Thy will be done' with obedience to the exhortation that we should ask 'believing that we shall receive'? It seems to me almost impossible. One can choose the first: but surely in the very act of doing so one *ipso facto* abandons all confidence that one's prayer is likely to have any causal efficacy in bringing about the event prayed for? I have never seen the question discussed anywhere nor got an answer from anyone whom I asked.

TO HIS BROTHER: *On reading* The Revelations of Divine Love *by Julian of Norwich; and on Lewis's deepest conviction that "all shall be well."*[10]

21 MARCH 1940

I have been reading this week the 'Revelations' of Mother Julian of Norwich (14th century); not always so profitable as I had expected, but well worth reading. This is a curious vision 'Also He showed me a little thing, the bigness of a hazel-nut, in my hand. I thought, What may this be? And it was answered, it is all that is made. I marvelled how it might last, for methought it might suddenly have fallen to naught for littleness.' Now that is a good turn given to the monkish (or indeed Christian) view of the whole created universe: for to say that it is bad, as some are inclined to do, is blasphemous and Manichean—but to say that it is *small* (with the very odd dream twist 'so small it might fall to bits'), that seems just right. Very odd too is her doctrine of 'the Grand Deed'. Christ tells her again and again 'All shall be well, and all shall be well, and all manner of thing shall be well.' She asks how it can be well, since some are damned. He replied that

---

[9] *Letters II*, 361–362.
[10] *Letters II*, 369–370.

all that is true, but the secret grand deed will make even that 'very well'. 'With you this is impossible, but not with Me.'

My mood changes about this. Sometimes it seems mere drivel—to invent a necessarily inconceivable grand deed which makes everything quite different while leaving it exactly the same. But then at other times it has the unanswerable, illogical convincingness of things heard in a dream and appeals to what is one of my deepest convictions, viz. that reality always escapes prediction by taking a line which was simply not in your thought at all. Imagine oneself as a flat earther questioning whether the Earth was endless or not. If you were told 'It is finite but never comes to an end', one would seem to be up against nonsense. Yet the escape (by being a sphere) is so easy—once you know it. At any rate, this book excites me.

TO MARY NEYLAN, *who had married in 1934 and about whose first daughter, Sarah, two years old, she seems to have consulted Lewis: On obedience; on psychoanalysis as a science and as a philosophy; on living with and/or treating a psychological illness; and on the character and attractiveness of Jesus, with recommendations of many books and authors (some recommendations made again and again throughout Lewis's writings).*[11]

26 MARCH 1940

(1) About obedience. Nearly everyone will find himself in the course of his life in positions where he ought to command and in positions where he ought to obey. Which he ought to be doing in any given situation, or whether he ought to be doing either, of course will always admit of dispute, but that doesn't invalidate the principle—any more than the general rule 'I oughtn't to overeat' is invalidated by the difficulty of saying whether one bun here and now constitutes over-eating. Still less is it invalidated by the fact that some people are too fond of ruling and others too fond of obeying: sooner or later each of them may be a duty for everyone.

Now each of them requires a certain training or habituation if it is to be done well: and indeed the habit of command, or of obedience, may often be more necessary than the most enlightened view as to the ultimate moral grounds for doing either; and certainly,

---

[11] *Letters II*, 371–376.

where there is no training, the enlightened views will either be ineffective, or effective at the cost of great nervous tension. You can't begin training a child to command until it has reason and age enough to command someone or something without absurdity. You can at once begin training it to obey: that is, teaching it the act of obedience *as such*—without prejudice to the views it will later hold as to who should obey whom, or when, or how much. Just as you try to train it in *courage,* without in the least prejudging the question as to which changes in adult life ought to be faced and which ought to be declined.

Of course I personally think (a) That there is in existence a Being so intrinsically authoritative that obedience is the essential business of a human being in a way in which command (though unfortunately humans must sometimes assume it) is not. (b) That humility is in itself good. But you would *not* have to agree with these two purely theological views if you agreed that children ought to learn obedience as such, since it is perfectly obvious that every human being is going to have to spend a great deal of his life in obeying parents, schoolmasters, employers, magistrates *et cetera.* Nor of course am I making any *political* statement. The question whether *persons to be obeyed* should be democratically elected or otherwise (I personally am a democrat) leaves where it was the truth that in any human society there will have to be a lot of obeying.

(2) Psychoanalysis. In talking to me you must beware, because I am conscious of a partly pathological hostility to what is fashionable, of which I think I could give the causes if it were necessary. I may therefore have been betrayed into statements (or, at least, what is perhaps more insidious, a *tone*) on this subject which I am not prepared to defend. No doubt, like every young science, it is full of errors, but so long as it remains a science and doesn't set up to be a philosophy I have no quarrel with it—i.e., as long as people judge whatever it reveals by the best human logic and scheme of values they've got and don't try to derive logic and values from it. In practice, no doubt, as you say, the patient is always influenced by the analyst's own values.

Further, in so far as it attempts to *heal,* i.e., to make *better,* every treatment involves a value judgement. This could be avoided if the analyst said 'Tell me what kind of chap you want to be and I'll see how near that I can make you': but of course he really has his own idea of what goodness and happiness consist in and works to that. And his idea is derived not from his science (it couldn't be) but from his age, sex, class, culture, religion and heredity, and is just as much in need of criticism as the patient's. In fact if you suspect *your* values come from the nursemaid, you may console yourself by reflecting that so do *his*! For no amount of knowledge about how states of mind are produced could of itself teach you which states to prefer: for that, he must be falling back on whatever general philosophy of life he has.

In reality, of course, neither his values nor yours are invalidated by the fact that they have a history in which nursemaids play a part—any more than reason collapses when you realise that you learned most of it from your elders.

Another way in which *any* therapeutic art may have bad philosophical results is this. It must, for the sake of method, take perfection as the Norm and treat every departure from it as disease: hence there is always a danger that those who practise it may come to treat a perfectly ideal perfection as 'normal' in the popular sense and consequently waste their lives in crying for the moon.

When Dr. Sprenger says Sarah is 'nervous' he probably is right *in the sense that* she is not, and never will be, perfectly wise, good, and happy. God-a-mercy! Fancy equating 'happiness' and 'normality'! Worm's meat, neighbour: Adam's sons, Eve's daughters: 'life will not bear refining on'—'think not the doom of man reversed for thee'.

I see no reason why a Christian should not be an analyst. Psychoanalysis after all merely defines what was always admitted, that the moral choices of the human soul operate inside a complex nonmoral situation. Even Hamlet knew that 'the devil' was 'very potent' with men of the melancholy complexion—i.e., men with certain complexes, which really gives the whole thing in a nutshell.

The Christian view would be that every psychological situation, just like every degree of wealth or poverty, talent or stupidity *et cetera,* had its own peculiar temptations and peculiar advantages, that the worst could always be turned to a good use and the best could always be abused to one's spiritual ruin. In fact 'all fortune is good' as Boethius said.

This doesn't mean that it would be wrong to try to cure a complex any more than a stiff leg: but it does mean that if you can't, then, so far from the game being up, life with a complex, or with a stiff leg, is precisely the game you have been set. To the person whom you imagine who says 'I'm a neurotic and can't afford to be analysed and so can't do anything about it', I suppose a Christian would give just the same advice as to a person who needed a holiday and couldn't get it—advice you doubtless heard long ago from that obviously excellent nursemaid. Even a Stoic would not listen to the plea you imagine. We must play the parts we find ourselves given. The despair at not being able to be analysed is really a revolt against the conditions of existence. Once make the medical Norm our ideal of the 'normal' and we shall never lack an excuse for throwing up the sponge. But these are all illegitimate abuses of analysis. The real thing has obviously done you nearly pure good—you've learned from it some of the most valuable lessons, and they needn't be un-learned.

(3) *Christianity.* My own experience in reading the Gospels was at one stage even more depressing than yours. Everyone told me that I should find there a figure whom I couldn't help loving. Well, I could! They told me I would find moral perfection—but one sees so very little of Him in ordinary situations that I couldn't make much of that either. Indeed some of His behaviour seemed to me open to criticism, e.g. accepting an invitation to dine with a Pharisee and then loading him with torrents of abuse.

Now the truth is, I think, that the sweetly-attractive-human-Jesus is a product of 19th century scepticism, produced by people who were ceasing to believe in His divinity but wanted to keep as much of Christianity as they could. It is not what an unbeliever coming to the records with an open mind will (at first) find there. The first thing you really find is that we are simply not *invited,* so to speak, to pass any moral judgement on Him, however favourable: it is only too clear *He* is going to do whatever judging there is: it is we who are *being* judged, sometimes tenderly, sometimes with stunning severity, but always *de haut en bas* [from the top down]. (Have you noticed that you can hardly free your imagination to picture Him as shorter than yourself?) The first real work of the Gospels on a fresh reader is, and ought to be, to raise very acutely the question, 'Who—or What—is This?' For there is a good deal in the character which, *unless* He really is what He says He is—is not lovable nor even tolerable. If He *is,* then of course it's another matter: nor will it then be surprising if much remains puzzling to the end. For if there is anything in Christianity we are now approaching something which will never be fully comprehensible.

On this whole aspect of the subject I should go on (since you've read his *Orthodoxy*) to Chesterton's *The Everlasting Man*. You might also find Mauriac's *Vie de Jésus* useful. . . . By the way, if childish associations are too intrusive in reading the New Testament, it's a good idea to try it in some other language, or in Moffatt's modern translation.

As for theology proper: a good many misunderstandings are cleared away by Edwyn Bevan's *Symbolism and Belief*. A book of composite authorship and of varying merits, but on the whole good is *Essays Catholic and Critical* ed. E. G. Selwyn S.P.C.K. Gore's *The Philosophy of the Good Life* (Everyman) is rather wordy but taught me a lot. If you can stand serious faults of style (and if you can get them, they are long out of print) Geo. MacDonald's 3 vols. of *Unspoken Sermons* go to the very heart of the matter. I think you would also find it most illuminating to re-read now many things you once read in 'Eng. Lit' without knowing their real importance—Herbert, Traherne, *Religio Medici*.

As for a person 'with whom to discuss', choice is more ticklish. L. W. Grensted is very interested in Psychoanalysis and wrote a book on its relations to Christianity: would that be an advantage or the reverse? O. C. Quick is a man whom I know and like. Milford, the present rector of St. Mary's, some like and some don't. Let me know what, or what sort, you want and I'll see what can be done.

I like very much what you say about 'not having it both ways' and something that can't be 'indefinitely avoided'. If it was really psychoanalysis that taught you that, more power to its elbow: but I suspect it is your own. Propaganda, my books? Tut! Only the two that almost profess to be (*Regress* and *Silent Planet*).

TO HIS BROTHER: *On Mrs. Neylan's impeding conversion (the two "Papists" are Bede Griffiths and George Sayer); and on Denis de Rougemont's book,* Love in the Western World.[12]

---

[12] *Letters II*, 378–379.

29 MARCH 1940

This week I received a letter from my former pupil Mrs. Neylan . . . who is trembling on the verge of Christianity—admits that the issue 'can no longer be avoided'—and asks what to read and (more difficult still) who to see. I felt almost overwhelmed by the responsibility of my reply, and naturally the more because the two other people whose conversion had something to do with me became Papists!

After writing at great length I fortunately re-read her letter and discovered that, owing to her omission of inverted commas, I had wholly misunderstood one of her points (will anyone teach women to punctuate) so I had to do nearly the whole job over again. The letter's gone now. I suppose if God intends to have Mrs. Neylan it won't make much difference what I've written!— yet that is a dangerous argument which would lead to its not mattering what you did in any circumstances.

The other thing I've been busy on this week is a book called *L'Amour el l'Occident* by one Denis de Rougemont, apparently a French Protestant, which I have to review. It contains a thoroughly bad historical thesis about medieval love, and an absolutely first class *moral* thesis about the utter incompatibility of *l'amour passion* with Christian marriage, happiness, or even enjoyable physical sexuality. He's a corker of a man, though with some bogus elements in him: I've written to him to-day. If, as I suspect, he is now a *poilu* [soldier], my letter may give a moment's happiness.

TO BEDE GRIFFITHS, *who had just been ordained and who had sent Lewis the traditional prayer-card/bookmark which had the figure of the priest-king Melchizedek of Genesis 14: On healthy and unhealthy attitudes to art, literature, sensual love, any created thing, and the world; on the meaning of the word* spiritual, *on thinking about and praying for one's enemies; and on the providence of books.*[13]

---

[13] *Letters II,* 390–392. On the danger in the premature reading of Lady Julian's book (or any book, for that matter), see the letter below to Mary Neylan, 26 April 1941, *Letters II,* 480–481: "The important thing for each of us about any book is not whether it is wicked in itself but whether it can be safely read by *me* at this particular moment." Lewis often recommended reading this book.

16 APRIL 1940

Congratulations (if that is the right word) on becoming a Priest, and thanks for the pleasing woodcut. Yes: Melchisedech is a figure who might have been intended (nay, was intended, since God provides not for an abstraction called Man but for individual souls) for people who were being led to the truth by the peculiar route that you and I know.

I do most thoroughly agree with what you say about Art and Literature. To my mind they are only healthy when they are either (a) Definitely the handmaids of religious, or at least moral, truth—or (b) Admittedly aiming at nothing but innocent recreation or entertainment. Dante's alright, and *Pickwick* is alright. But the great *serious irreligious* art—art for art's sake—is all balderdash; and, incidentally, never exists when art is really flourishing. In fact one can say of Art as an author [De Rougemont] I recently read says of Love (sensual love, I mean) 'It ceases to be a devil when it ceases to be a god'. Isn't that well put? So many things—nay, every real *thing*—is good if only it will be humble and ordinate.

One thing we want to do is to kill the word 'spiritual' in the sense in which it is used by writers like [Matthew] Arnold and [Benedetto] Croce. Last term I had to make the following remark to a room full of Christian undergraduates 'A man who is eating or lying with his wife or preparing to go to sleep, in humility, thankfulness, and temperance, is, by Christian standards, in an infinitely *higher* state than one who is listening to Bach or reading Plato in a state of pride'—obvious to you, but I could see it was quite a new light to them.

I don't know what to think about the present state of the world. The sins on the side of the democracies are very great. I suppose they differ from those on the other side by being less deliberately blasphemous, fulfilling less the condition of a *perfectly* mortal sin. Anyway, the question 'Who is in the right' (in a given quarrel) is quite distinct from the question 'Who is righteous?'—for the worse of two disputants may always be in the right on one particular issue. It is therefore *not* self righteous to claim that we are in the right now. But I am chary of doing what my emotions prompt me to do every hour; i.e., identifying the enemy with the forces of evil. Surely one of the things we learn from history is that God never allows a human conflict to become unambiguously one between simple good and simple evil?

The practical problem about charity (in our prayers) is very hard work, isn't it? When you pray for Hitler and Stalin, how do you actually teach yourself to make the prayer real? The two things that help me are (a) A continual grasp of the idea that one is only joining one's feeble little voice to the perpetual intercession of Christ, who died for those very men (b) A recollection, as firm as one can make it, of all one's own cruelty which might have blossomed, under different conditions, into something terrible. You and I are not, at bottom, so different from these ghastly creatures.

I have been reading Lady Julian of Norwich. What do you make of her? A dangerous book, clearly, and I'm glad I didn't read it much earlier. (Have you noticed how God so often sends us books at just the right time?) One thing in her pleased me immensely. *Contemptus mundi* [hatred of the world] is dangerous and may lead to Manicheeism. Love of the creature is also dangerous. How the good of each is won, and the danger rejected, in her vision of 'all that is made' as a little thing like a hazel nut 'so small I thought it could hardly endure'. Not bad, you see: just very, very small. . . .

A woman, an ex-pupil of mine called Mary Neylan, seems in her last letter to be hovering on the brink of conversion to Christianity—a proper subject for your prayers.

TO MARY NEYLAN, *who has raised objections to becoming a Christian because of what she perceives as its outdated teachings about women and men, especially in marriage and in the Church's wedding service: On "being in love" and on feelings in general; on the real differences between men and women; on the purposes of sex; on male headship only in marriage and not elsewhere; and on the meaning of the wedding service.*[14]

18 APRIL 1940

(1) On the marriage service [in the Book of Common Prayer]. The three 'reasons' for marrying, in modern English are (a) To have children. (b) Because you are very unlikely to succeed in

---

[14] *Letters II*, 392–397.

leading a life of total sexual abstinence, and marriage is the only innocent outlet, (c) To be in a partnership. What is there to object to in the order in which they are put?

The modern tradition is that the proper reason for marrying is the state described as 'being in love'. Now I have nothing to say against 'being in love': but the idea that this is or ought to be the exclusive reason or that it can ever be by itself an *adequate* basis seems to me simply moonshine.

In the first place, many ages, many cultures, and many individuals don't experience it—and Christianity is for all men, not simply for modern Western Europeans. Secondly, it often unites most unsuitable people. Thirdly, is it not usually transitory? Doesn't the modern emphasis on 'love' lead people either into divorce or into misery, because when that emotion dies down they conclude that their marriage is a 'failure', though in fact they have just reached the point at which *real* marriage begins. Fourthly, it would be undesirable, even if it were possible, for people to be 'in love' all their lives. What a world it would be if most of the people we met were perpetually in this trance!

The Prayer Book therefore begins with something universal and solid—the biological aspect. No one is going to deny that the *biological* end of the sexual functions is offspring. And this is, on any sane view, of more importance than the *feelings* of the parents. Your descendants may be alive a million years hence and may number tens of thousands. In this regard marriages are the fountains of *History*. Surely to put the mere emotional aspects first would be sheer sentimentalism. Then the second reason. Forgive me: but it is simply no good trying to explain this to a woman. The *emotional* temptations may be worse for women than for men: but the pressure of mere *appetite* on the male, they simply don't understand. In this second reason, the Prayer Book is saying 'If you can't be chaste (and most of you can't) the alternative is marriage.' This may be brutal sense, but, to a man, it is *sense,* and that's that. The third reason gives the thing that matters far more than 'being in love' and will last and increase, between good people, long after 'love' in the popular sense is only as a memory of childhood—the partnership, the loyalty to 'the firm', the composite creature. (Remember it is not a *cynic* but a devoted husband and inconsolable widower, Dr. Johnson, who said that a man who has been happy with one woman could have been equally happy with any one of 'tens of thousands' of other women. I.e., the original attraction will turn out in the end to have been almost accidental: it is what is built up on that, or any other, basis which may have brought the people together that matters.)

Now the second reason involves the whole Christian view of sex. It is all contained in Christ's saying that two shall be 'one flesh'.[15] He says nothing about two 'who married for love': the mere fact of marriage *at all*—however it came about—sets up the 'one flesh'. There is a terrible comment on this in I *Cor* VI 16 'he that is joined to a harlot is one flesh'.[16] You see? Apparently, if Christianity is true, the mere fact of sexual intercourse sets up between human beings a relation which has, so to speak, transcendental repercussions—some *eternal* relation is established whether they like it or not.

This sounds very odd. But is it? After all, if there *is* an eternal world and if our world is its manifestation, then you would expect bits of it to 'stick through' into ours. We are like children pulling the levers of a vast machine of which *most* is concealed. We see a few little wheels that buzz round on *this* side when we start it up—but what glorious or frightful processes we are initiating *in there,* we don't know. That's why it is so important to do what we're told (cf.—what does the Holy Communion imply about the real significance of *eating*?).

From this all the rest flows. (1) The seriousness of sexual sin and the importance of marriage as 'a remedy against sin' (I don't mean, of course, that sins of that sort will not, like others, be forgiven if they are repented, nor that the 'eternal relations' which they have set up will not be redeemed. We believe that God will use all repented evil as fuel for fresh good in the end.) (2) The *permanence* of marriage which means that the intention of fidelity matters more than 'being in love'. (3) The *Headship* of the Man.

I'm sorry about this—and I feel that my defence of it would be more convincing if I were a woman. You see, of course, that if marriage is a permanent relation, intended to produce a kind of new organism ('the one flesh') there must be a Head. It's only

---

[15] Matthew 19:5.
[16] 1 Corinthians 6:16.

so long as you make it a temporary arrangement dependent on 'being in love' and changeable by frequent divorce, that it can be strictly democratic—for, on that view, when they really differ, they part. But if they are not to part, if the thing is like a nation not a club, like an organism not a heap of stones, then, in the long run, one party or other must have the casting vote.

That being so, do you really want the Head to be the woman? In a particular instance, no doubt you may. But do you really want a matriarchal world? Do you really like women in authority? When you seek authority yourself, do you naturally seek it in a woman?

Your phrase about the 'slave-wife' is mere rhetoric, because it assumes servile subordination to be the only kind of subordination. Aristotle could have taught you better. 'The householder governs his slaves despotically. He governs his wife and children as being both free—but he governs the children as a constitutional monarch, and the wife politically' (i.e., as a democratic magistrate governs a democratic citizen).

My own feeling is that the Headship of the husband is necessary to protect the outer world against the family. The female has a strong instinct to fight for its cubs. What do nine women out of ten care about justice to the outer world when the health, or career, or happiness of their own children is at stake? That is why I want a 'foreign policy' of the family, so to speak, to be determined by the man: I expect more mercy from him!

Yet this fierce maternal instinct must be preserved, otherwise the enormous sacrifices involved in motherhood would never be borne. The Christian scheme, therefore, does not suppress it but protects us defenceless bachelors from its worst ravages! This, however, is only my own idea.

The Headship doctrine is that of Christianity. I take it to be chiefly about man *as* man and woman *as* woman, and therefore about husbands and wives, since it is only in marriage that they meet *as* epitomes of their sex. Notice that in I Cor XI just after the bit about the man being the Head, St. Paul goes on to add the baffling reservation (verse 11) that the sexes 'in the Lord' don't have any separate existence. I have no idea what this means: but I take it it must imply that the existence of a man or woman is not exhausted by the fact of being male or female, but that they exist in many other modes. I mean, you may be a citizen, a musician, a teacher *et cetera* as well as a woman, and you needn't transfer to all these personalities everything that is said about you as wife *quâ* wife.

I think that is the answer to your view that the Headship doctrine would prevent women going in for education. St. Paul is not a *system* maker, you know. As a Jew, he must, for instance, have believed that a man ought to honour and obey his Mother: but he doesn't stop and put that in when talking about the man being Head in marriage.

As for Martha and Mary, either Christ and St. Paul are inconsistent here, or they are not. If they're not, then, whether you can see how or not, St. Paul's doctrine can't have the sense you give it. If they *are* inconsistent, then the authority of Christ of course completely over-rides that of St. Paul. In either event, you needn't bother.

I very strongly agree that it's no use trying to create a 'feeling'. But what feeling do you want to have? Isn't your problem one of thought, not feeling? The question is 'Is Christianity true—or even, is there some truth mixed up in it?' The thing in reading MacDonald is not to try to have the feelings he has, but to notice whether the whole thing does or does not agree with such *perceptions* (I mean, about good and evil *et cetera*) as you already have—and, where it doesn't, whether it or you are right.

. . . Thank you for taking my mind off the war for an hour or so!

P.S. I don't think the Marriage Service is ascetic, and I think your real objection to it may be that it's not *prudish* enough! The service is *not* a place for celebrating the flesh, but for making a solemn *agreement* in the presence of God and of society—an agreement which involves a good many other things besides the flesh.

Distinguish the Church from the bedroom and don't be silly! Would you really think it suitable for erotic excitement to be expressed by the young couple while visiting the family solicitor, while asking their parents' blessing, while bidding good-bye to the old home? If not, then why when asking God's blessing? Do you think a grace before meals should be so written as actually to make the mouth water? If we began holidays with a religious service, would you take your bathing suit to Church, and practice a few gold strokes in the choir?

'Sober and godly matrons' [a phrase from the marriage service] may be a stickler, if you haven't read the English School: but *you* ought to know that all the associations you are putting into it are modern and accidental. It *means* 'Married women (matrons) who are religious (godly) and have something better and happier to think about than jazz and lipstick (sober).' But you must know that as well as I do!

TO HIS BROTHER: *On forgiving and loving one's enemies (Lewis's nemeses among his colleagues at Magdalen College were William Mackenzie, a political scientist, John Austin, a Leftist philosopher, and Redvers Opie, the obese bursar); and on his and his brother's guilt over the way they treated their father.*[17]

4 MAY 1940

Your other question about loving our enemies has been very much in my mind lately, and it must be faced, every time we say the Lord's Prayer. No exemption seems to be allowed—of Johnson's *Rambler* 185 (for Xmas Eve 1751) which ends thus: 'Of him that hopes to be forgiven, it is indispensably required that he forgive. On this great duty eternity is suspended: and to him that refuses to practise it, the throne of mercy is inaccessible, and the Saviour of the world has been born in vain.' It sounds impossible. I pray every night for the people I am most tempted to hate or despise (the present list is Stalin, Hitler, Mussolini, Mackenzie, Austin and Opie)* and in the effort to make this real I have had to do a good deal of thinking.

(1) There were three words in Gk. which covered most kinds of love (Eros = sexual love, Storge = family affection, Philia = friendship) but the New Testament word for 'love' or 'charity' is Agape, which has hardly any use in classical Gk—i.e., it is a new word for a new thing. It is obvious that it cannot mean 'an involuntary sentiment'. We all *say* that God is wise, and habitually argue as if He were a fool! How could He be commanding the involuntary? Agape is best seen, I think, in the words 'love your

---

[17] *Letters II*, 408–411.

neighbour as yourself',[18] i.e., by an act of will, aim at your neighbour's good in the same way as you aim at your own.

Now you don't 'love' yourself because of your own 'lovable qualities'. You may, in moments of vanity, attribute lovable qualities to yourself, but that is not the *cause* of your self-love but one of the *results* of it. At other moments, when you dislike yourself, you still wish for your own happiness. This attitude to one's own self is dictated by nature: towards other selves it has to be acquired.

I take it, it has nothing in the world to do with trying to pretend that the enemy is 'not so bad after all' or that his sins 'don't matter', or that he is really lovable. Not a bit. It's the old business about 'loving the sinner and hating the sin' which becomes alive to me when I realise that this is what I do to myself all the time. In fact I provisionally define Agape as 'steadily remembering that inside the Gestapo-man there is a thing which says I and Me just as you do, which has just the same grounds (neither more nor less) as your "Me" for being distinguished from all its sins however numerous, which, like you, was made by God for eternal happiness—remembering, and always acting for the real interests of that thing as far as you can.'

(2) If one takes seriously your suggestion that they are literally possessed, really it only makes this point of view easier? Suppose your eyes were opened and you could see the Gestapo man visibly fiend-ridden—a twisted and stunted human form, covered with blood and filth, with a sort of cross between a mandrill and a giant centipede *fastened* onto it? Surely you, and the human remains, become almost allies against the horror which is tormenting you both, him directly and you through him?

(3) Of course there is a further stage. We are not asked to love the damned. When the fiend's victim has wholly ceased to be human, when his will is no longer merely dominated by but unrecoverably identified with his rider, charity is no longer commanded. But we are not allowed to assume that this has taken place in any man still alive, and obviously we don't know enough. But I think the *possibility* is a positive help to charity. These 'swine', as you rightly call them, are to be regarded as people in whom the human self

---

[18] Matthew 22:39.

78 • YOURS, JACK

(made for happiness, like you) is still alive, and steadily moving towards that final identification with its fiend—but still capable (we must assume) of being rescued. From this point of view I do not find it impossible to desire, and pray, that that rescue may occur. (Remember, you are not asked to wish that, *remaining what they now are,* they should be happy: far from it.)

(4) Of course the parable of the servant who wouldn't forgive his fellow servant[19] comes in. You and I take a high line about Nazi cruelties. You and I, of all people. Think it over.

(5) We are told that God desires the salvation of all men.[20] One is to picture Christ perpetually interceding for these swine; when we pray for them we are merely joining our infantile prayer to His. One can put it almost comically 'I don't fancy that man myself, Sir, but of course, if you make a point of it . . .' Of course His intercession for them is not because of any value they have; but so is His intercession for us. My own tendency to give a free rein to hatred and to regard it as virtuous or natural is much cooled by noticing that hatred comes as often from wind-up as from anything else.

*N.B. I don't mean that I'm tempted to hate them equally, of course!

TO OWEN BARFIELD, *whose mother had just died: On Mrs. Barfield's possible "luck" in escaping the war by her death and on fear of war and death; on the great comfort in the writings of Julian of Norwich; on dealing with tribulations one at a time; and on the meaning of their friendship.*[21]

2 JUNE 1940

Mrs. Moore told me yesterday about your loss of your mother. I cannot imagine myself, in similar circumstances, not feeling very strongly *felix opportunitate mortis,* but I daresay, when it comes to the point, that is very far from being the predominant emotion. . . .

I am very sorry you should have this particular desolation added to the general one in which we all are. It is like the first

---

[19] Matthew 18:23–35.
[20] I Timothy 2:3–4.
[21] *Letters II,* 418–419.

act of *Prometheus [Unbound]:* 'Peace is in the grave, the grave hides all things beautiful and good.' [Shelley] was near, however, to his release when he said that, and I accept the omen—that you and I and our friends will soon be past the worst, if not in one way, then in the other. For I am very thankful to say that while my digestion often plays tricks I am ashamed of, I retain my faith, as I have no doubt you do yours.

'All shall be well, and all shall be well, and all manner of thing shall be well'—This is from Lady Julian of Norwich whom I have been reading lately and who seems, in the Fifteenth century, to have rivalled Thomas Aquinas' reconciliation of Aristotle and Christianity by nearly reconciling Christianity with Kant. The real difficulty is, isn't it, to adapt one's steady beliefs about tribulation to this *particular* tribulation; for the particular, when it arrives, always *seems* so peculiarly intolerable. I find it helpful to keep it very particular—to stop thinking about the ruin of the world *et cetera,* for no one is going to experience *that,* and to see it as each individual's personal sufferings, which never can be more than those of one man, or more than one man, if he were very unlucky, might have suffered in peacetime. Do you get sudden lucid intervals? islands of profound peace? I do: and though they don't last, I think one brings something away from them.

I wish we could meet more, but I can hardly reckon on any one evening at present. . . . All is well still—except one's stomach. And oddly enough, I notice that since things got really bad, everyone I meet is less dismayed. MacDonald observes somewhere that 'the approach of any fate is usually also the preparation for it'. I begin to hope he is right. Even at this present moment I don't feel nearly so bad as I should have done if anyone had prophesied it to me eighteen months ago.

1941

TO MARY NEYLAN, *who had told Lewis she was going to resume the practice of her faith after years of alienation and theological struggle: On acting
on the light one has; on the unreliability of religious emotion; on confession of
sins to a spiritual director; and on daily spiritual and Bible reading.*[1]

4 JANUARY 1941

Congratulations . . . on your own decision. I don't think this
decision comes either too late or too soon. One can't go on thinking it over for ever; and one can begin to try to be a disciple before one is a professed theologian. In fact they tell us, don't they,
that in these matters to act on the light one has is almost the only
way to more light. Don't be worried about feeling that, or about
feeling at all. As to what to do, I suppose the normal next step,
after self-examination repentance and restitution, is to make your
Communion; and then to continue as well as you can, praying
as well as you can . . . and fulfilling your daily duties as well as
you can. And remember always that religious *emotion* is only a
servant. . . . This, I say, would be the obvious course. If you want
anything more e.g. Confession and Absolution which our church
enjoins on no-one but leaves free to all—let me know and I'll find
you a *directeur.* If you choose this way, remember it's not the psy-
choanalyst over again: the confessor is the representative of Our
Lord and declares His forgiveness—his advice or 'understanding'
though of real, is of secondary importance.

For daily reading I suggest (in small doses) Thomas à Kempis'
'Imitation of Christ' and the 'Theologia Germanica' . . . and of
course the Psalms and New Testament. Don't worry if your heart
won't respond: do the best you can. You are certainly under the
guidance of the Holy Ghost, or you wouldn't have come where
you now are: and the love that matters is His for you—yours for
Him may at present exist only in the form of obedience. He will
see to the rest.

---

[1] *Letters III,* 1539–1540.

This has been great news for me I need hardly say. You have all my prayers (not that mine are worth much).

TO MARY NEYLAN: *On the need to give and receive encouragement; and on not relying on feelings but rejoicing when good feelings come.*[2]

29 JANUARY 1941

Thanks very much for your kind letter. My own progress is so very slow (indeed sometimes I seem to be going backwards) that the encouragement of having in any degree helped someone else is just what I wanted.

Of course the idea of not relying on emotion carries no implication of not rejoicing in it when it comes. You may remember Donne's *Litanie* 'That our affections kill us not—nor die'. One of the minor rewards of conversion is to be able to see at last the real point of all the old literature which we are brought up to read with the point left out!

TO MARY NEYLAN: *On the meaning of the emotional crisis and spiritual awakening her difficulties with her now three-year-old daughter occasioned; on the essential goodness of the need for approval; on the right and wrong times to read a book; and on the advisability of confessing one's sins to a fellow layperson. The moral of the Aesop fable about the dog in the manger is "People frequently begrudge something to others that they themselves cannot enjoy. Even though it does them no good, they won't let others have it." (Aesop's Fables, trans. Laura Gibbs [Oxford: Oxford University Press-World Classics, 2002], number 163.)*[3]

26 APRIL 1941

(1) I think I understand what you say about Sarah. Since the total experience (which we have inadequately labelled 'maternal jealousy') led you to Him, I agree that some element in it came from Him. It wouldn't follow that the Jealousy considered in the abstract, was good. Cf. a *resentment* as a rebuke which is the beginning of a process that leads to real contrition. The resentment in itself is bad, but only the bad concomitant (at that stage perhaps

---

[2] *Letters II,* 467–468.
[3] *Letters II,* 480–481.

inevitable) of a good thing, self-knowledge. In your experience, I take it, the good thing was the painful realisation of how far you had abdicated your maternal position—a complex privation, of joys missed and duties neglected. The bad element was the 'dog in the manger' indignation at seeing that someone else had picked up what you had dropped. Conjugal jealousy would similarly contain good and bad elements, I suppose.

(2) On being 'patted on the head'... I have just made some new discoveries. Something like a 'pat on the head' is promised ('Well done, thou good and faithful servant').[4] Link that up with 'entering the Kingdom as a child'[5]—then reflect that being praised by those we ought to please, as far from being the vainest, is the humblest and most creaturely of *all* pleasures. It is our Pride (as usual) that has excluded from our idea of Heaven the old picture of the divine accolade.

(3) ... The important thing for each of us about any book is not whether it is wicked in itself but whether it can be safely read by *me* at this particular moment.

(4) You may say you want to confess your sins to God only. The trouble is that in fact you have confessed a good many of them to me! On the medical level, the amateur practitioner gets *prosecuted* for treating a patient if he is unsuccessful and found out. On the spiritual level, I don't know. I feel pretty sure, however, that if I now give you any wrong advice and the matter comes before any objective spiritual tribunal hereafter, both parties would be asked 'Were there no priest in your country?' And quite frankly I am not sure that it is *fitting* for a man who is not protected and supported by the special status of a priest or a doctor to be told too many of his neighbour's secrets—unless, of course, there is some desperate need. It's not a question of being bored at all—more a desire to walk in well established ways which have the approval of Christendom as a whole. I leave the decision to you. But one of the things on which a confessor could give you advice would be precisely the proper use to be made of a lay adviser, and the limitations of that use—specially when the lay adviser has no *natural locus standi* ["recognised position,

---

[4] Matthew 25:21.
[5] Mark 10:15.

acknowledged right or claim"] as a father, brother or even an old family friend might have.

TO MARY NEYLAN: *More on the advisability of confessing one's sins to a fellow layperson and on choosing a priest confessor; in praise of her husband's patience with her religious changes, a remarkably rare gift in an intimate relationship.*[6]

30 APRIL 1941

I see from your letter that you have really acted with great circumspection and made every effort to seek advice in more professional quarters! I hope that my last letter, written in ignorance of this, did not sound dictatorial. You may put out of your head any idea of 'not having a claim' on any help I can give. Every human being, still more every Christian, has an absolute claim on me for any service I can render them without neglecting other duties.

When I spoke of some one with more *locus standi* I didn't mean someone 'on whom you had a claim' in the least. I only meant that certain things were most properly discussed *either* where a professional status makes them impersonal *or* where some natural, objective relation between the speakers renders the personal confidence what our forefathers called 'convenient'. Conversations about *principles* (as opposed to particular facts) are another matter. But I think we both agree on the point.

Now, as to a confessor. The two alternatives that occur to me are (a) Milford, (b) A Cowley Father, preferably my own confessor, Father Adams.

The points *for* Milford are that he is a modern intellectual brought up like yourself, a married man conversant with domestic problems, besides being accustomed to hear confessions. The point *against* him is that he seems (from what we saw of him last term) to hold the traditional faith with rather too many concessions to the modern scientific outlook.

The point *against* Fr Adams is that he is much too close to Rome. I had to tell him that I couldn't follow him in certain directions, and since then he has not pressed me. He would also, in my opinion, be inferior to Milford as an intellectual guide. On

[6] *Letters II,* 481–483.

the other hand (a) He certainly understands the human soul for practical purposes very well indeed. (b) If I have ever met a *holy* man, he is one.

I write this without knowing whether he can take on more penitents than he has at present, for he is very old (an advantage in my opinion) and has had an illness. He knows some psychoanalysis.

I should be free at 12 on Tuesday if you cared to call in and give me your views.

If it is not impertinent to say so, I think your husband must have behaved like an angel. I have had the experience myself of remaining an unbeliever when some of my most intimate friends began to believe, and I've experienced the same situation the other way round when I began to change myself. It is an extraordinarily disagreeable one to the unbelieving party and if he is not good may provoke resentment. I'm afraid for a few years I just took the line of being as nasty as I could and saying everything that could hurt. God forgive me.

TO MARY NEYLAN: *With praise for her gracious acceptance of his diagnosis of jealousy in her relationship with her daughter; and a request for prayer.*[7]

9 MAY 1941

I have a reply from Fr Adams. He would like you to write to him as soon as you please and suggest a time for going to see him. The first interview will not be the Confession itself but to settle preliminaries. The address is The Rev. Fr. Adams, ssje, The Mission House, Marston St., Oxford.

I'm sure you're doing right and that God is leading you and bringing you in pretty fast too. I shall never forget your reply 'It looks like it' when I suggested jealousy as one of the troubles—I never hope to see the human ship take a big wave in better style!

Continue to pray for *me*. I need it all: and may say in general that if I were to tell you as much about myself as you have told me (which I shan't!) the record would be much blacker than your own.

---

[7] *Letters II*, 483–484.

TO ARTHUR HAZARD DAKIN, *who was writing a biography of Paul Elmer More: On the qualities Lewis sought (and found) in an ideal spiritual director.*[8]

3 AUGUST 1941

I have sent under a separate cover copies of the three letters I had from Paul E. More. Please forgive me the delay. I have been so busy for many months now that I hardly know whether I am on my head or my heels. Now for such recollections as I can furnish.

I once told Paul Elmer More that while it would be an exaggeration to call him my spiritual father, I might call him my spiritual uncle. By this I meant, in the first place, that one had in his presence that sense of comfort and security and well-being which a child has in the presence of grown up relatives whom it likes. I began to feel it almost at once. It was something I am not sure we would gather from his books—a real homeliness, almost an affectionateness, the very reverse of that rarefied quality which some people may associate with American 'Humanism'.

In the second place, I meant that quality which a good uncle often has of giving, without the slightest offence, advice and even correction which the child would resent if it came from the father. In our very first conversation he corrected a false Greek accent, and the misuse of a scientific term, which I had perpetrated in print, in a way which ought to be common among old men but is actually rather rare. On the other hand it was so done that even the vainest young author could not have objected to it: on the other, there was no nonsense about all being in the same boat, or 'you don't mind my mentioning it' or anything of that kind. It was quite definitely and undisguisedly the ripe speaking to the unripe—authority without egoism.

At this distance of time I cannot remember much of our conversation. He found that I agreed with him about the futility of much academic 'research', and this led him to tell with great humour, and also great tenderness, the story of a young woman he knew who had refused to marry a man she loved because her 'work' (a thesis on some unspeakably obscure poet) 'must come

---

[8] *Letters III*, 1541–1543.

first'. Apparently More had saved the situation and got the little
fool to the altar alright. . . . He had a good deal of . . . shrewd humour and avuncular playfulness. . . .

But most of our time together was spent in close argument.
You saw at once he was the sort of man who welcomed attacks
on his own favourite beliefs and who was ready to give his whole
attention to what you said without any irrelevant consideration
of who you were. He was very fair and patient in discussion and
talked for truth not victory. And all the time, however abstract the
theme, the homely and human quality—sometimes manifested in
the choice of an illustration, sometimes in the mere twinkle of
his eye—was always in evidence, making one quite sure that his
philosophy had roots in the earth. It is not, I think, what I should
have expected. My impression is that the man was bigger than his
books—there was *more of him*. Anything less like the popular idea
of a 'don' or a 'philosopher' would be hard to find. Perhaps the
extremely rich and flexible voice (he spoke from the chest) had
something to do with it.

With renewed apologies for the inconvenience I must have
caused you by my delay.

TO SISTER PENELOPE, *who had sent Lewis a photo of the head of the
image of the Shroud of Turin: More on what being "in Christ" means;
on the provident arrival of theologian Eric Mascall's* Man: His Origin
and Destiny *and* God-Man *and the delights they and her letter touched
off in him (an emotional peak, to be followed by a trough mentioned in
the next letter).*[9]

9 OCTOBER 1941

I am ashamed of having grumbled. And your act was not that
of a brute—in operation it was more like that of an angel, for (as
I said) you started me on a quite new realisation of what is meant
by being 'in Christ', and immediately after that 'the power which
erring men call chance' put into my hands Mascall's two books in
the *Signpost* series which continued the process.

So I lived for a week end (at Aberystwyth) in one of those
delightful *vernal* periods when doctrines that have hitherto been

[9] *Letters II*, 493–494.

only buried seeds begin actually to come up—like snowdrops or crocuses.[10] I won't deny they've met a touch of frost since (if only things would *last,* or rather if only *we* would!) but I'm still very much, and gladly, in your debt. The only real evil of having read your scripts when I was tired is that it was hardly fair to them and not very useful to you.

I have had to refuse a request from Sister Janet. Will you tell her that the 'wives and oxen'[11] are quite real ones?

I enclose the MS. of *Screwtape.* If it is not a trouble I should like you to keep it safe until the book is printed (in case the one the publisher has got blitzed)—after that it can be made into spills or used to stuff dolls or anything.

Thank you very much for the photo of the Shroud. It raises a whole question on which I shall have to straighten out my thought one of these days.

TO SISTER PENELOPE: *More on her essay "Consider the Dog," mentioned above (24 August 1939); and on the spiritual trough he is in.*[12]

9 NOVEMBER 1941

Thank you so much for the head of Our Lord from the shroud. It has grown upon me wonderfully. I don't commit myself to the genuineness. One can never be quite certain. But the great value is to make one realise that He was a man, and once even a dead man. There is so much difference between a doctrine and a realisation.

I am writing, really, for company, for I'm a sad Ass at the moment. I've been going through one of those periods when one can no longer disguise the fact that movement has been backward not forward. All the sins one thought one had escaped have been back again as strong as ever,

> And all our former pain
> And all our Surgeon's care

---

[10] Cf. Isaiah 35:1–2.
[11] Cf. Luke 14:19–20.
[12] *Letters II,* 494–496.

> Are lost: and all the unbearable, in vain
>   Borne once, is still to bear.[13]

I re-read your essay on the dog Noonie the other night when very tired with great enjoyment. Dogs don't relapse. Cats do, and go wild. I'm a cat.

I've got *Ransom to Venus* and through his first conversation with the 'Eve' of that world: a difficult chapter. I hadn't realised till I came to write it all the *Ave-Eva* business. I may have embarked on the impossible. This woman has got to combine characteristics which the Fall has put poles apart—she's got to be in some ways like a Pagan goddess and in other ways like the Blessed Virgin. But if one can get even a fraction of it into words it is worth doing.

Have you room for an extra prayer? Pray for *Jane* if you have. She is the old lady I call my mother and live with (she is really the mother of a friend)—an unbeliever, ill, old, frightened, full of charity in the sense of alms, but full of uncharity in several other senses. And I can do so little for her.

TO SISTER PENELOPE: *On the inability to advise oneself; on the daily grind of becoming one's true self; on disappointment with oneself; and on spiritual pride. This may be the first reference to what Lewis will later call the "Deeper Magic," articulated again in his letter below to Arthur Greeves, 2 July 1949).*[14]

19 NOVEMBER 1941

Thanks for your kind letters. It was silly to grumble: except that Johnson says 'He that complains acts like a man, like a *social being*,' and it is a curious fact that the advice we can give to others we cannot give to ourselves and truth is more effective through any life rather than our own. Chas. Williams in *Taliessin* is good on this 'No one can live in his own house. My house for my neighbour, his for me.'

I think what really worries me is the feeling (often on waking in the morning) that there's really nothing I so much *dislike* as

---

[13] See Lewis's poem, "Relapse," in *Collected Poems* (London: HarperCollins, 1994).
[14] *Letters II*, 497–498.

religion—that it's all against the grain and I wonder if I can really stand it! Have you ever had this? Does one outgrow it? Of course there's no intellectual difficulty. If our faith is true then that is just what it ought to feel like, until the new man is full-grown. But it's a considerable bore.

What you say about 'disappointed with oneself' is very true— and a tendency to mistake mere disappointment (in which there is much wounded pride and much of a mere sportsman's irritation at breaking a record) for true repentance. I ought to have devoted a *Screwtape* letter to this.

TO PATRICIA THOMSON, *an undergraduate at St. Hugh College, Oxford, who heard Lewis give a sermon on 7 December 1941 (otherwise unknown) that contained an idea which he later developed in "The Shocking Alternative" in* Mere Christianity, *Book II, Chapter 3: "I am trying here to prevent anyone saying the really foolish thing that people say about [Jesus]: 'I'm ready to accept Jesus as a great moral teacher, but I don't accept His claim to be God.' That is the thing we must not say." On the destiny of the virtuous unbeliever.*[15]

8 DECEMBER 1941

When I said it was 'no good' trying to regard Jesus as a human teacher I only meant that it was logically untenable—as you might say 'It's no good trying to maintain that the earth is flat.'

I was saying nothing in that sermon about the destiny of the 'virtuous unbeliever'. The parable of the sheep and the goats suggests that they have a very pleasant surprise coming to them. But in the main, we are not told God's plans about them in any detail. If the Church is Christ's body,—the thing he works through— then the more worried one is about the people outside, the more reason to get *inside* oneself where one can help—you are giving Him, as it were, a new finger. (I assumed last night that I was talking to those who already believed.) If I'd been speaking to those who didn't, of course everything I'd said would be different.

Fear isn't repentance—but it's alright as a *beginning*—much better at that stage than *not* being afraid.

---

[15] *Letters II,* 499–500.

How interested are you? If you care to come and talk about it I expect we could arrange a date. Let me know.

TO PATRICIA THOMSON, *whose fall school term (Michaelmas term) was about to end: On trying to be Christian.*[16]

11 DECEMBER 1941

If you go down to-morrow I am afraid it will be impossible to meet this term. Ring me up or write to me when you come up again and we'll fix a time.

In the meantime, don't let yourself be worried in two incompatible ways. You are wondering whether Christianity is true or false. Remember, if you think it false you needn't bother about all the things in it that seem terrible. If you decide it is true, you needn't worry about not having faith, for apparently you have!

I quite agree any idea of counting up one's good deeds, as if one was in for an exam, is fatal. It was Christianity which first pointed this out. We are not saved 'by merit'. But of all this, when we meet. I suggest George MacDonald's *Phantastes* (Everyman) and *Lilith* and Coventry Patmore's *Poems* and *Rod, Root and Flower* as books that might interest you.

TO BEDE GRIFFITHS: *On Charles Williams; and on the Inklings.*[17]

21 DECEMBER 1941

I'm extremely glad you've got onto my friend Chas. Williams though onto one of his worst books. He is living in Oxford during the war and we made him lecture on Milton to the faculty, so that (would you believe it, remembering the English lectures of your own period) we actually heard a lecture on *Comus* which put the importance where Milton had put it. In fact the lecture was a panegyric of chastity! Just fancy the incredulity with which (at first) an audience of undergraduates listened to something so unheard of. But he beat them in the end.

He is an ugly man with rather a cockney voice. But no one ever thinks of this for five minutes after he has begun speaking.

---

[16] *Letters II*, 500.
[17] *Letters II*, 500–503.

His face becomes almost angelic. Both in public and private he is of nearly all the men I have met the one whose address most overflows with *love*. It is simply irresistible. Those young men and women were lapping up what he said about Chastity before the end of the hour. It's a big thing to have done.

I have seen his impress on the work in the Milton papers when I examined. Fancy an Oxford student, and a girl, writing about Mammon's speech in Book II 'Mammon proposes an ordered state of sin with such majesty of pride that but for the words *live to ourselves* which startle our conscience, we should hardly recognise it as sin, so natural is it to man' (Compare that with the sort of bilge you and I were proud to write in Schools!).

Williams, Dyson of Reading, and my brother (Anglicans) and Tolkien and my doctor, Havard (your Church) are the 'Inklings' to whom my *Problem of Pain* was dedicated. We meet on Friday evenings in my rooms: theoretically to talk about literature, but in fact nearly always to talk about something better. What I owe to them all is incalculable. Dyson and Tolkien were the immediate human causes of my own conversion. Is any pleasure on earth as great as a circle of Christian friends by a good fire?

His stories (I mean Williams) are his best work—*Descent into Hell* and *The Place of the Lion* are the best. I quite agree about what you call his 'affectations'—not that they are affectations, but honest defects of taste. He is largely a self-educated man, labouring under an almost oriental richness of imagination ('clotted glory from Charles' as Dyson called it) which could be saved from turning silly and even vulgar in print only by a severe early discipline which he has never had. But he is a lovely creature. I'm proud of being among his friends.

1942

20 JANUARY 1942

Sorry you're in a trough. I'm just emerging (at least I hope I am) from a long one myself. As for the difficulty of believing it is a trough, one wants to be careful about the word 'believing'. We too often mean by it 'having confidence or assurance as a psychological state'—as we have about the existence of furniture. But that comes and goes and by no means always accompanies intellectual assent, e.g. in learning to swim you believe, and even know intellectually that water will support you long before you feel any real confidence in the fact. I suppose the perfection of faith would make this confidence invariably proportionate to the assent.

In the meantime, as one has learnt to swim only by acting on the assent in the teeth of all instinctive conviction, so we shall proceed to faith only by acting as if we had it. Adapting a passage in the *Imitation* one can say 'What would I do now if I had a full assurance that there was only a temporary trough', and having got the answer, go and do it. I a man, therefore lazy: you a woman, therefore probably a fidget. So it may be good advice to you (though it would be bad to me) not even to try to do in the trough all you can do on the peak.

I have recently been advised by Fr. Adams to abbreviate a prayer for other people which was becoming so long (as my circle widens) as to be irksome. I have done so, but kept the longer one on two days a week. Result, that having ceased to be the rule and become a kind of extra, it ceases to be irksome and is often a

---

[1] *Letters II*, 506–508.

delight. There is danger in making Christianity too much into a 'Law'. Let yourself off something. Relax.

I know all about the despair of overcoming chronic temptations. It is not serious provided self-offended petulance, annoyance at breaking records, impatience *et cetera* doesn't get the upper hand. *No amount* of falls will really undo us if we keep on picking ourselves up each time. We shall of course be very muddy and tattered children by the time we reach home. But the bathrooms are all ready, the towels put out, and the clean clothes are in the airing cupboard. The only fatal thing is to lose one's temper and give it up. It is when we notice the dirt that God is most present to us: it is the very sign of His presence.

The question about Sarah is why she *wants* not to have to ask the good one to make her good. Would it be right (I know so little about children) to point out to her that He *likes* being asked: and that if she *could* be good on her own, taking no notice of Him, that itself wouldn't be good. But ten to one the 2 sticks were primarily a game. . . .

Ransom is having a grand time on Venus at present.

TO MR. H. MORLAND, *who seems to have written Lewis for a reading list on the different atonement theories and other theological and spiritual topics.*[2]

19 AUGUST 1942

The great classical statement of the Anglican position is Hooker's *Laws of Ecclesiastical Polity.* A good modern book is *Essays Catholic and Critical,* edited by Selwyn, Moberley *Atonement and Personality,* though needlessly long and difficult, is good: should be corrected by Aulén *Christus Victor* giving a different kind of theory. If you read Greek, St. Athanasius, *De Incarnatione* is splendid. . . . My own greatest debt is to George MacDonald, specially the three volumes of *Unspoken Sermons* (out of print but often obtainable second hand). Other books you might find helpful are Edwyn Bevan's *Christianity* and Gore's *Jesus Christ,* Bevan's *Symbolism and Belief,* Gore's *Philosophy of the Good Life,* Otto's *Idea of the Holy,* von Hügel's *Eternal Life* and *Essays and Addresses:* and, going further

[2] *Letters II,* 528–529.

back, *Theologia Germanica*, Traherne *Centuries of Meditations*, Lady Julian of Norwich *Revelations of Divine Love*, Boethius *De Consolatione Philosophiae*, Augustine *Confessions* and *De Civitate Dei*.

TO SISTER PENELOPE, *who was in the process of translating St. Athanasius's* The Incarnation of the Word of God: *On gratitude and feelings of gratitude; and on the larger question of whether theoretical questions in the spiritual life are a mask for the reluctance to obey. Tinidril is the naked heroine of* Perelandra.[3]

22 DECEMBER 1942

I have been an unconscionable time answering your last letter, half hoping we might have seen more of St. Athanasius by now. I am so glad the *cognoscenti* approve of it: you will have done a most useful work and, so far as I could judge, done it rather better than well.

Perelandra will reach you, I hope, early in January: I have deterred the artist from putting his idea of Tinidril (you can imagine!) on the cover. I have been very busy with one thing and another: there aren't the days and hours there used to be, are there? The minute hand used to go as the hour hand goes now!

How does one feel thankful? I am thinking of the improvement in the war news, and I don't mean (rhetorically) 'How can one be thankful enough?' but just what I say. It seems to be something which disappears or becomes a mere word the moment one recognises one *ought* to be feeling it. I always tell people not to bother about 'feelings' in their prayers, and above all never to *try* to feel, but I'm a bit puzzled about Gratitude: for if it is not a feeling, what is it?

A funny thing how merely formulating a question awakes the conscience! I hadn't a notion of the answer at the bottom of the last sheet, but now I know exactly what you are going to say: '*Act* your gratitude and let feelings look after themselves.' Thank you. (Do *all* theoretical problems conceal shirkings by the will?)

---

[3] *Letters III*, 1546–1547.

1943

TO MARY NEYLAN, *who had written that she has the flu: On the mercy of having a spiritual director ("our reverend friend").*[1]

31 JANUARY 1943

What frightfully bad luck. And I'm the worst person in the world to write to someone who is feeling weak and listless, not because I have never been in that condition but because I don't myself *dislike* it nearly as much as most people. To lie in bed—to find one's eyes filling with facile tears at the least hint of pathos in one's book—to let the book drop from ones hand as one sinks deeper and deeper into reverie—to forget what you were thinking about a moment ago and *not to mind*—and then to be roused by the unexpected discovery that it is already tea-time—all this I do *not* find disagreeable! ...

I also had a delightful 'anticlimax' with our reverend friend over quite a different matter. They are among the recurrent pleasures of life. What a mercy to have *another's* voice to liberate one from all the endless labyrinths of the *solitary* conscience! ...

Now, go to sleep. Blessings.

TO ARTHUR GREEVES: *On the meaning of interruptions and real life; on the difficulty of being patient; and on expiating through embracing one's own sufferings.*[2]

20 DECEMBER 1943

Things are pretty bad here. Minto's varicose ulcer gets worse and worse, domestic help harder and harder to come by. Sometimes I am very unhappy, but less so than I have often been in what were (by external standards) better times.

The great thing, if one can, is to stop regarding all the unpleasant things as interruptions of one's 'own', or 'real' life. The truth

---

[1] *Letters II,* 550–551.
[2] *Letters II,* 594–596.

is of course that what one calls the interruptions are precisely one's real life—the life God is sending one day by day: what one calls one's 'real life' is a phantom of one's own imagination. This at least is what I see at moments of insight: but it's hard to re-member it all the time—I know your problems must be much the same as mine (with the important difference that mine are of my own making, a very appropriate punishment and, like all God's punishments, a chance for expiation.)

Isn't it hard to *go on* being patient, to go on supplying sympa-thy? One's stock of love turns out, when the testing time comes, to be so very inadequate: I suppose it is well that one should be forced to discover the fact!

I find too (do you?) that hard days drive one back on Nature. I don't mean walks...but little sights and sounds seen at windows in odd moments.

I had a most vivid, tranquil dream about you the other night, just chatting in the old way. Let's hope it will happen sometime. For the rest, I've no news.

1944

30 JANUARY 1944

(1.) I'm afraid I don't know anything about theatrical agencies, nor indeed agencies of any kind. Nor do I know any theatrical people.

(2.) Probably the best *single* book of modern comment on the Bible is *A New Commentary on Holy Scripture* edited by Gore, Goudge and Guillaume, and published by the SPCK ...—a very fat, ugly volume in double columns, but quite readable print. Of course for separate commentaries on particular books of the Bible, their name is legion. The Clarendon Bible (Clarendon Press) is not bad.

(3.) The starting point for interpreting Chas. Williams is *He Came Down from Heaven* (Methuen) where Florence will find some of his main ideas explained directly—i.e., not in imaginative form. If either Florence or you would like a copy of his book on Dante (*The Figure of Beatrice*) I have a spare copy which I would gladly give. It might help.

As for the man, he is about 52, of humble origin (there are still traces of cockney in his voice), ugly as a chimpanzee but so radiant (he emanates more *love* than any man I have ever known) that as soon as he begins talking whether in private or in a lecture he is transfigured and looks like an angel. He sweeps some people quite off their feet and has many disciples. Women find him so attractive that if he were a bad man he could do what he liked either as a Don Juan or a charlatan. He works in the Oxford University Press. In spite of his 'angelic' quality he is also quite an earthly person and when Warnie, Tolkien, he and I meet for our pint in a pub in Broad Street, the fun is often so fast and furious that the company probably thinks we're talking bawdy when in fact we're

---

[1] *Letters III,* 1548–1549.

very likely talking Theology. He is married and, I think, youth-
fully in love with his wife still. That's about all I can think of.

You needn't ask me to pray for you, Arthur—I have done so
daily ever since I began to pray, and am sure you do for me.

TO MRS. PERCIVAL WISEMAN, *who had asked Lewis for the text of one
of his radio talks and to whom Lewis is sending a copy of his sermon,
"The Weight of Glory": On the "purpose" of the death of loved ones;
and on the exchange of intercessions across the barrier of death.*[2]

20 MARCH 1944

I'm afraid the manuscripts of the talks are going straight to the
publisher as soon as the series is over.

Instead I send you a little tract on my views of the future life.
You are quite right to keep clear of the Spiritualists. All that is an
effort to *cancel* death, to go on getting a pale phantom of the same
sort of intercourse with our dear ones which we had when they
and we were members of the same world. But we must *submit* to
death, embrace the cross.

I think the purpose of the separation is to help us to turn what
is merely natural and instinctive affection into real spiritual love
of them in Christ. Not that natural affection isn't good and innocent, but it is merely natural—and therefore must first be crucified
before it can rise again. Those who try to escape the crucifixion fall
in either with charlatans or with delusions from hell: spiritualism
often drives people mad. Of course we should pray for our dead as
I'm sure they do for us.

TO MR. OFFER: *On the human experience of Jesus on the cross; and on
the essential meaning of the two natures of Christ.*[3]

9 MAY 1944

I think I should answer thus.

The words from the Cross 'Why hast thou forsaken me'[4] suggest that Our Lord entered into the human experience to the

---

[2] *Letters II,* 607–608.
[3] *Letters III,* 1550.
[4] Matthew 27:46; Mark 15:34.

degree of complete dereliction and at one point no longer realised His own Deity nor foresaw His own Resurrection.

The gift was never withdrawn. Christ is still Man. Human nature has been taken up into the Divine Nature (see Athanasian Creed) and remains there. Our *bridgehead* is secure.

What do these people *want*? Do they actually visualise Him for 3 hours nailed to a stake—flayed back glued to unplaned wood—Palestinian sun—cloud of insects round head, hands, and feet—the face a mask of bruises, pus, spittle, blood, tears and sweat—the lungs gradually tearing owing to the position—and then complain 'This doesn't hurt enough?' If so . . . !

TO EDITH GATES: *On the love of God as the way to love of neighbor; on how to love God without having the feelings of love; and on how to deal with pride.*[5]

23 MAY 1944

Certainly I cannot love my neighbour properly till I love God. As George MacDonald says in his *Unspoken Sermons* (long out of print but if you can get a 2nd hand copy by any means short of stealing, do! It is beyond price)

> And beginning to try to love his neighbour he finds that this is no more to be reached in itself than the Law was to be reached in itself. As he cannot keep the Law without first rising into the love of his neighbour, so he cannot love his neighbour without first rising higher still. The whole system of the universe works upon this principle—the driving of things upward toward the centre.

On the other hand we have no power to make ourselves love God. The only way is absolute obedience to Him, total surrender. He will give us the 'feeling' if He pleases. But both when He does and when He does not, we shall gradually learn that *feeling* is not the important thing. There is something in us deeper than feeling, deeper even than conscious will. It is rather *being*. When we are *quite* empty of self we shall be filled with Him, for nature

[5] *Letters II*, 616–617.

abhors a vacuum. Of course it is good, as you say, to 'realise' that the source of all our good feelings is God. (That is the right way to deal with pride: not to depreciate the good thing we are tempted to be proud of but to remember where it comes from). But 'realisation' depends on faculties that fail us when we are tired or when we try to use them too often, so we can't depend on it. It is the self you really are and not its reflection in consciousness that matters most.

May I take what is really the closest parallel? No child is begotten without pleasure. But the pleasure is not the cause of life—it is a symptom, something that happens when life is in fact being transmitted. In the same way 'feeling love' is only the echo in consciousness of the real thing which lies deeper.

TO BEDE GRIFFITHS, *with whom Lewis shares an insight from* The Great Divorce *(Chapter 9), which he is writing at the time: On the utter truth of losing one's life to save it (with another word about Charles Williams).*[6]

25 MAY 1944

Thanks for your letter. I too was delighted with our meeting. About the past, and nothing being lost, the point is that 'He who loses his life shall save it'[7] is *totally* true, true on every level. *Everything* we crucify will rise again: *nothing* we try to hold onto will be left us.

I wrote the other day 'Good and evil when they attain their full stature are retrospective. That is why, at the end of all things, the damned will say we were *always* in Hell, and the blessed we have *never* lived anywhere but in heaven.' Do you agree?

You're right about C.W. He has an undisciplined mind and sometimes admits into his theology ideas whose proper place is in his romances. What keeps him right is his *love* of which (and I have now known him long) he radiates more than any man I know.... Continue to pray for me as I do for you.

---

[6] *Letters II*, 617–618.
[7] Matthew 10:39.

TO SISTER PENELOPE, *after Lewis had finished writing* That Hideous Strength *and during the time of the allied armies' successes in the liberation of Europe: A request for prayers for Mrs. Moore; and an insight about persevering in our quest for perfect obedience.*[8]

6 SEPTEMBER 1944

It is on my conscience that I owe you a letter this long time. All sorts of things have happened to me during it. I've finished another book which concludes the Ransom trilogy [*That Hideous Strength*]: the scene is on Earth this time.

I've had an operation for the removal of a piece of shell I got into me in the last war, which, after lying snug and silent like an unrepented sin for 20 years or so, began giving me trouble. How nice modern anaesthetics are compared with the sort I remember from boyhood.

Last of all, and only a few days ago, Jane (you remember my Jane?) has had a slight stroke and lost the power of her left arm. She is in bed and I think will make a full recovery—*this* time. And as usual we are looking, and looking in vain, for domestic help. So have us all in your prayers. . . .

The world has changed since you and I last met: one finds it difficult to keep pace with the almost miraculous mercies we are receiving as a nation. I never in my most sanguine moments dreamed that the invasion of Europe would go quite so well. Query—when Christ tells us to be perfect is it because only He knows how very small an addition to our present efforts would break the enemy's line completely?—that perfection would cost very little more than our actual dithering does? But we're all like the boy who takes nearly, but never quite, enough trouble over his prep. and always just spoils it. Remember me to Mother Maribell and Annie Louise.

---

[8] *Letters II*, 624–625.

TO MARGARET DENEKE: *On the death of her husband, Paul Benecke, Lewis's old history tutor and a Fellow at Magdalen College.*[9]

3 OCTOBER 1944

It will give me great pleasure to come to lunch at one o'clock on Oct. 30th. I will not try to express my sympathy to Miss Benecke when we meet—such things are often merely embarrassing. You, I am sure, will not doubt that she has it.

The gap in College is terrible. Already (and yet it is only a few days) I have twice found myself setting aside a problem 'to ask Benecke about it' and then realised with a pang that there is no more of that. His image haunts every room in Magdalen. I hear his imagined voice again and again: so vividly, when crossing Magdalen bridge this morning, that I almost wondered if there were not some objective reality in the experience. I can hardly explain how his funeral affected me. I have heard that service read in that chapel so often for those who have not believed a word of it and who (had they been alive) would have mocked, that my feeling was almost one of *relief*. Here at last was a dead man not unworthy of the service. In some queer way it enormously strengthened my faith, and before we filed out of chapel I really felt (do not misunderstand me) a kind of joy—a feeling that all was well, just as well as it could be.

I count it among my great good fortunes to have known him. As far as human eyes can judge he was—is—a saint: but oh!, we *still* needed him here so very badly,

TO SISTER PENELOPE: *On a former household servant with severe mental and emotional difficulties.*[10]

21 OCTOBER 1944

Poor 'Muriel', she got odder and odder and the doctors would have put her into an asylum if Jane and I hadn't refused to sign a form. She has now left, and had an operation, and got a job elsewhere. I hope the crisis is tided over. I am almost *sorrier* for her than anyone I have known, because, even if insanity is avoided,

---

[9] *Letters III*, 1552–1553.
[10] *Letters II*, 628.

the temperament seems one that almost precludes any happiness in this world. And the more one tried to be nice the more complications one seemed to introduce. So we must pray for her always.

TO MR. LYELL: *On the meaning of handing one's natural self and appetites over to Christ; on normal self-care, austerity, and lenience; on the kinds of progress; on the parts of the self and the consequences of Adam's sin; and on the goodness of being a body.*[11]

6 DECEMBER 1944

(1) By handing over the natural self to Christ I mean placing it under His orders and trying to will with His will. If a man does that He will usually find that one of the things Christ wills is for him to eat, drink, sleep, *et cetera.* Not always, but usually. You can't tell in advance what He will tell any man to do about the natural appetites. He may tell one man to be very austere, another to be kinder to the flesh than he has been hitherto.

(2) You are quite right. There would be no 'progress' if everyone were living in the Spirit: at least in some senses of the word 'progress'. There might continue to be progress in arts and sciences—why not? But social and economic progress would cease, I expect, because all those problems would solve themselves in the first year or so. Progress means getting nearer to a desired goal and therefore means not being there already. You don't want the London train to go on progressing after it reached London!

(3) The natural self since the Fall consists of body, soul, and spirit all perverted and self centred and at odds with one another. Animalness (the body and what arises from it) is not in itself bad: what is bad is the rebellious *relation* in which it now stands to the other parts. But its rebellion against spirit is less terrible than the spirit's rebellion against God.

(4) By central self or spirit I mean chiefly the Will—the ultimate choosing part. It changes itself by its own actions. By *soul* I mean chiefly the imagination and emotions. New Testament does not use a consistent technical vocabulary. For instance in 'Soul take thine ease *et cetera*'[12] the passage simply means 'Says I to myself'.

---

[11] *Letters II*, 631–632.
[12] Luke 12:19.

I hope this is a bit clearer: but a systematic exposition would have to go far beyond the limits of a letter.

TO ARTHUR GREEVES, *who had disagreed with Lewis on his doctrine of the two natures of Christ.*[13]

11 DECEMBER 1944

I was delighted to hear from you. The statement you read in the papers about the Cambridge professorship was untrue; so far from having accepted it, I haven't even been offered it! Which just shows what newspapers are.

Your view of the divinity of Christ was an old bone of contention between us, wasn't it? But I thought when we last met you had come down on the same side as me. I don't think I can agree that the Churches are empty because they teach that Jesus is God. If so, the ones that teach the opposite, i.e., the Unitarians, would be full, wouldn't they? Are they? It seems to me that the ones which teach the fullest and most dogmatic theory are precisely the ones that retain their people and make converts. While the liberalising and modernising ones lose ground every day. Thus the Roman Catholics are flourishing and growing, and in the C. of E. the 'high' churches are fuller than the 'low'. Not of course that I would accept popularity as a test of truth: only since you introduced it, I must say that as far as it is evidence at all it points the other way.

And in history too. *Your* doctrine, under its old name of Arianism, was given a chance: in fact a very full run for its money for it *officially* dominated the Roman Empire at one time. But it didn't last.

I think the great difficulty is this: if He was *not* God, who or what was He? In *Mat* 28.19 you already get the baptismal formula 'In the name of the Father, the Son, and the Holy Ghost.' Who is this 'Son'? Is the Holy Ghost a man? If not does a man 'send' Him (see *John* 15.26)? In *Col.* 1.12 Christ is 'before all things and by Him all things consist'. What sort of man is this? I leave out the obvious place at the beginning of St. John's Gospel. Take something much less obvious. When He weeps over Jerusalem (Mat.

---

[13] *Letters III*, 1554–1555.

23) why does He suddenly say (v. 34) '*I* send unto you prophets and wise men'? Who could say this except either God or a lunatic? Who is this man who goes about forgiving sins? Or what about *Mark* 2.18–19. What man can announce that simply because he is present acts of penitence, such as fasting, are 'off'? Who can give the school a half holiday except the Headmaster?

The doctrine of Christ's divinity seems to me not something stuck on which you can unstick but something that peeps out at every point so that you'd have to unravel the whole web to get rid of it. Of course you may reject some of these passages as un-authentic, but then I could do the same to yours if I cared to play that game! When it says God can't be tempted I take this to be an obvious truth.[14] God, as God, can't, any more than He can die. He became man precisely to do and suffer what as God he could not do and suffer. And if you take away the Godhead of Christ, what is Christianity all *about*? How can the death of one *man* have this effect for all men which is proclaimed throughout the New Testament?

And don't you think we should allow *any* weight to the fruits of these doctrines? Where are the shining examples of human holiness which ought to come from Unitarianism if it is true? Where are the Unitarian 'opposite numbers' to St. Francis, George Herbert, Bunyan, Geo. MacDonald, and even burly old Dr. Johnson? Where are the great Unitarian books of devotion? Where among them shall I find 'the words of life'?[15] Where have they helped, comforted, and strengthened us?

I'm glad our prayers have been answered and things are a bit better with you. They're pretty bad with us. Minto had a very slight stroke some months ago. Maureen (her husband teaches at Worksop) is going to have a baby and is staying with us. I long to see you again. Remember me to all our friends.

---

[14] James 1:13.
[15] John 6:68.

1945

TO SISTER PENELOPE: *On his domestic difficulties and a lesson to be learned from them. The Latin of* The Imitation of Christ *means "If you wish to be a peacemaker, keep peace in yourself."* [1]

3 JANUARY 1945

Jane [Mrs. Moore] is no worse in body: in mind and spirits sometimes very bad, sometimes better. Pray for us always, we are not a very happy house. More and more I am driven to realise what it says in *The Imitation* 'Si vis alios pacificare, habe pacem in te ipso' and how I fail to carry it out.

TO BEDE GRIFFITHS, *who had mentioned to Lewis that he was thinking of writing a book on the New Creation: On feeling so spared by God in the victory over the Nazis that nothing short of holiness is the only adequate response; and on how thinking about miracles, about the new heavens and the new earth, and about the resurrection of the body has deepened Lewis's appreciation of nature itself. Lewis asks about the chapters of* The Great Divorce, *then being published serially in* The Guardian *newspaper.* [2]

10 MAY 1945

And how did *you* feel on V-Day? I found it impossible to feel either so much sympathy with the people or so much gratitude to God as the occasion demanded. I am sometimes a little awed by the burden of our favours. Every one of us has escaped by a series of Providences, some not far short of miracles: and it seems to me that the sort of life which would be saintly for men less favoured becomes mere minimum decency for us. And how to come up to that standard!

You will remind me that this is precisely the situation we have always been in since our Redemption anyway. True: perhaps one

---

[1] *Letters II, 635–636.*
[2] *Letters II, 647–649.*

of the great [accomplishments] of a worldly deliverance is to bring that other more fully home to one.

I'm interested in what you say about the serial. Do you think the failure to satisfy is due to lack of real *unity* or development? I mean that the dialogues succeed one another arbitrarily and might have come in any other order and might have gone on a longer or shorter time? Spiritual unity I hope it has: but a book needs musical or architectural unity as well.

. . . I too have been very much occupied by the idea of the New Creation. I'm absolutely with you. New heavens and earth—the resurrection of the body—how we have neglected these doctrines and indeed left the romantics and even the Marxists to step into the gap.

I'm working at a book on Miracles at present in which this theme will play a large part. And here's a funny thing. To write a book on miracles, which are in a sense invasions of Nature, has made me realise Nature herself as I've never done before. You don't *see* Nature till you believe in the Supernatural: don't get the full, hot, salty tang of her except by contrast with the pure water from beyond the world. Those who mistake Nature for the All are just those who can never realise her as a *particular creature* with her own flamed, terrible, beautiful individuality. No time to develop this now—but I thought you'd like to know the thoughts I am drunk with.

I hope you will go on with your own idea of a book on the New Creation.

Oremus pro invicem.

In the light of the New Creation all miracles are like *snow-drops*—anticipations of the full spring and high summer which is slowly coming over the whole wintry field of space and time.

The same day Lewis wrote to Griffiths, Thursday, 10 May, Charles Williams suddenly fell ill and was taken to the Radcliffe Infirmary where he was operated on. The following Tuesday, 15 May, Lewis went to the infirmary to call on him before joining the other Inklings at the Bird and Baby pub. He learned that Williams had just died. Lewis wrote later:

I heard of his death at the Infirmary itself, having walked up there with a book I wanted to lend him, expecting this news that day as little (almost) as I expected to die that day myself. It was a Tuesday morning, one of our times of meeting. I thought he would have given me messages to take to the others. When I joined them with my actual message—it was only a few minutes' walk from the Infirmary but, I remember, the very streets looked different—I had some difficulty in making them believe or even understand what had happened.[3]

TO OWEN BARFIELD: *On the sudden death of Charles Williams and the graces this occasioned in Lewis's life.*[4]

18 MAY 1945

Thanks for writing. It has been a very *odd* experience. This, the first really severe loss I have suffered, has (a) Given corroboration to my belief in immortality such as I never dreamed of. It is almost tangible now. (b) Swept away all my old feelings of mere horror and disgust at funerals, coffins, graves *et cetera*. If need had been I think I could have handled *that* corpse with hardly any unpleasant sensations. (c) Greatly reduced my feeling about ghosts. I think (but who knows?) that I should be, tho afraid, more pleased than afraid, if his turned up. In fact, all very curious. Great pain but no mere depression.

Dyson said to me yesterday that he thought what was true of Christ was, in its lower degree, true of all Christians—i.e., they go away to return in a closer form and it is expedient for us that they should go away in order that they may do so. How foolish it is to imagine one can imaginatively foresee what any event will be like! 'Local unique sting' alright of course for I love him (I cannot say more) as much as [I love] you: and yet . . . a sort of brightness and tingling. . . .

To put it in a nutshell—what the idea of death has done to him is nothing to what he has done to the idea of death. Hit it for six: yet it used to rank as a fast bowler!

---

[3] *Preface to Essays Presented to Charles Williams,* ed. C. S. Lewis (Oxford: Oxford University Press, 1947).
[4] *Letters II,* 651–652.

TO MARY NEYLAN, *whose husband has received job security: More on the graces accompanying the death of Charles Williams. Lewis asks if he can dedicate* George MacDonald: An Anthology *to her.*[5]

20 MAY 1945

I think what you say about 'grief being better than estrangement' is very true. I am sorry you should have had this grief. . . .

I also have become much acquainted with grief now through the death of my great friend Charles Williams, my friend of friends, the comforter of all our little set, the most angelic. The odd thing is that his death has made my faith ten times stronger than it was a week ago. And I find all that talk about 'feeling he is closer to us than before' isn't just talk. It's just what it does feel like—I can't put it into words. One seems at moments to be living in a new world. Lots, lots of pain but not a particle of depression or resentment.

By the bye I've finished a selection from Geo. MacDonald (365 extracts) which will come out about Xmas: would you (or not) care to have it dedicated to you? I feel it is rather yours by right as you got more out of him than anyone else to whom I introduced his books. Just let me know.

And why should you assume I'm too occupied to see you? Friday mornings in term are bad, but alright in Vac: and Friday afternoons in both. I should like a visit (with a week's notice) whenever you find one convenient.

Excuse this paper. It may be less blotched than yours but yours did at least begin life as a real piece of note paper! I'm so glad Dan has got his job made permanent. Blessings!

TO FLORENCE (MICHAL) WILLIAMS, *the widow of Charles Williams: A letter of condolence.*[6]

22 MAY 1945

Thank you for your most kind letter. We all knew that your marriage was one in a thousand. I think you will not be offended if I tell you this; that whenever Charles disagreed with anything

---

[5] *Letters II,* 652–653.
[6] *Letters II,* 653–654.

we had said about women in general, it was a common turn of raillery to reply 'Oh Charles!—of course he's in love, so his opinions on that subject are worthless!'

I feel, in my degree, as you do. My friendship is not ended. His death has had the very unexpected effect of making death itself look quite different. I believe in the next life ten times more strongly than I did. At moments it seems almost tangible. Mr. Dyson, on the day of the funeral, summed up what many of us felt, 'It is not blasphemous', he said 'To believe that what was true of Our Lord is, in its less degree, true of all who are in Him. They go away in order to be *with* us in a new way, even closer than before.' A month ago I would have called this silly sentiment. Now I know better. He seems, in some indefinable way, to be all around us now. I do not doubt he is doing and will do for us all sorts of things he could not have done while in the body. Of course this expects no answer. God bless you.

TO SISTER PENELOPE, *who had written Lewis of having successfully laid hands for healing on a crippled dog: On praying for animals; and on what he was learning from the death of Charles Williams.*[7]

28 MAY 1945

I was intensely interested in the story of your healing of the little dog. I don't see why one shouldn't. Perhaps indeed those to whom God allows a gift in this way should confirm their own faith in it by practising on beasts for in one way they may be easier to heal than men. Although they cannot have faith in Him (I suppose) they certainly have faith in us, which is faith in Him at one remove: and there is no sin in them to impede or resist. I am glad it happened. . . .

. . . The little book will be called *The Great Divorce* and will appear about August. *That Hideous Strength* is due in July. The Miracle book is finished but will not come out till next year.

Jane is up and down: very liable, I'm afraid, to fits of really bad jealousy—she can't bear to see other people doing the work. Pray for her, dear Sister.

---

[7] *Letters II,* 656–657.

TO ANNE RIDLER, *the poet, who had published an obituary of Charles Williams: On what he was learning from the death of Charles Williams.*[8]

3 JUNE 1945

I envy you parts of your obituary. You get in very essential points which I had missed—his scepticism and his way of converting the other person's mere stammer into great truth. . . .

It is an interesting fact that everyone almost who has spoken or written to me about his death says something different of him and all true. One feels curiously *un*-depressed, do you find? It has increased enormously one's faith in the next life and I can't help feeling him all over the place. I can't put it into words: I never knew the death of a good man could itself do so much good. I don't mean there isn't pain, pain in plenty: but not dull, sullen, sickening, drab, resentful pain.

TO ROGER LANCELYN GREEN, *who had sent Lewis the manuscript of his latest tale: A letter of blessing and wounding, encouragement and challenge, with a diagnosis of spiritual disease and a prescription to read Charles Williams's novel.*[9]

16 SEPTEMBER 1945

I have now read *The Wood That Time Forgot* and this is what I think. The general *narrative power* is excellent: i.e., on the question whether you have in general the story-telling talent, you may (in my opinion) set your mind at rest. I read it on a railway journey and it carried me as far as Bletchley (which was at chapter VII) without a single flagging of interest. I particularly admired the transition from the natural to the supernatural part. This went just gradually enough to solicit one's faith and by the right stages. I thank you for giving me the authentic thrill: as you did several times. . . .

Now for a matter which I would not mention if it were not that you and I (obviously) can converse with the freedom of patients in the same hospital. None of these faults is purely *literary*. The talent is certain: but you have a sickness in the soul. You are

---

[8] *Letters II*, 658–659.
[9] *Letters II*, 670–672. See Lewis's letter of 28 June 1949, below.

much too much *in* that enchanted wood yourself—and perhaps with no very powerful talisman round your neck. You are in love with your own heroine—which is author's incest and always spoils a book. I know all about it because I've been in the wood too. It took me years to get out of it: and only after I'd done so did re-enchantment begin. If you try to stay there the wood will die on you—and so will you!

Have you read C. Williams's *Descent into Hell*? If not, do so at once (I can lend you a copy). May I show the MS to Tolkien? My brother has read it and likes it very much.

TO ARTHUR GREEVES: *On the meaning of the incarnation; and on how God might reconstruct in eternity Lewis's selfish uncle, Augustus Hamilton, from the goodness that his uncle possessed.*[10]

26 DECEMBER 1945

I am sorry to see that it was October last when you wrote to me. But real correspondence (i.e., with my personal friends) is almost impossible in term time now.

You ask me . . . 'Surely God has always been the same loving and heavenly Father and it was the *interpretation* of God that Christ revealed.' I see what you mean but the question is to me very difficult to answer. On the one hand something really *new* did happen at Bethlehem: not an interpretation but an *event*. God became Man. On the other hand there must be a sense in which God, being outside time, is changeless and nothing ever 'happens' to Him. I think I should reply that the event at Bethlehem was a novelty, a change to the maximum extent to which any event is a novelty or change: but that *all* time and *all* events in it, if we could see them all at once and fully understand them, are a definition or diagram of what God eternally is.

But that is quite different from saying that the incarnation was simply an interpretation, or a change in *our* knowledge. When Pythagoras discovered that the square on the hypotenuse was equal to the sum of the squares on the other two sides he was discovering what had been just as true the day before though no one knew it. But in 50 BC the proposition 'God is Man' would *not*

---

[10] *Letters II*, 692–695.

have been true in the same sense in which it was true in 10 AD because though the union of God and Man in Christ is a timeless fact, in 50 BC we hadn't yet got to that bit of time which defines it. I don't know if I make myself clear. . . .

We got news of Uncle Gussie's death yesterday. A difficult man to think of from that point of view. He was, as far as one can see, a very selfish man who yet succeeded in avoiding all the usual consequences of selfishness: that is, he was not at all a bore, had no self-pity, was not jealous, and seemed to be as happy as the day was long. I think he illustrates the enormous difference between selfishness and self-centredness. He had plenty of the first: he pursued his own interests with very little regard to other people. But he had none of the second. I mean, he loved outside himself. His mind was not occupied with himself but with science, music, yachting *et cetera*. That was the good element and it was (as I think all good elements are) richly rewarded in this life. Let's hope and pray that it will carry him through where he is now. It may be the little spark of innocence and disinterestedness from which the whole man can be reconstructed.

There's all the difference in the world between a fire that has gone out and one that is *nearly* out. The latter, with skilful treatment, can always be coaxed back to life. It is rather a terrible thing that some people who try really hard to be unselfish yet have in them that terrible self-centredness which he was free from.

1946

TO MR. N. FRIDAMA, *who seems to have asked Lewis about the steps in his conversion to Christianity: On the Calvinist doctrine of double predestination.*[1]

15 FEBRUARY 1946

I was baptised in the Church of Ireland (same as Anglican). My parents were not notably pious but went regularly to church and took me. My mother died when I was a child.

My Christian faith was first undermined by the attitude taken towards *Pagan* religion in the notes of modern editors of Latin and Greek poets at school. They always assumed that the ancient religion was pure error: hence, in my mind, the obvious question 'Why shouldn't ours be equally false?' A theosophical Matron at one school helped to break up my early beliefs, and after that a 'Rationalist' tutor to whom I went finished the job. I abandoned all belief in Christianity at about the age of 14, though I pretended to believe for fear of my elders. I thus went thro' the ceremony of Confirmation in total hypocrisy. My beliefs continued to be agnostic, with fluctuation towards pantheism and various other sub-Christian beliefs, till I was about 29.

I was brought back (a.) By Philosophy. I still think [Bishop George] Berkeley's proof for the existence of God is unanswerable. (b.) By increasing knowledge of medieval literature. It became harder and harder to think that all those great poets and philosophers were wrong. (c.) By the strong influence of 2 writers, the Presbyterian George MacDonald and the Roman Catholic, G. K. Chesterton. (d.) By argument with an Anthroposophist [Owen Barfield]. He failed to convert me to his own views (a kind of Gnosticism) but his attack on my own presuppositions smashed the ordinary pseudo-'scientific' world-picture forever.

On Calvinism. Both the statement that our final destination is already settled and the view that it still may be either Heaven or

---

[1] *Letters II*, 702–703.

Hell, seem to me to imply the ultimate reality of Time, which I don't believe in. The controversy is one I can't join on either side for I think that in the real (Timeless) world it is meaningless. In great haste.

TO BEDE GRIFFITHS: *On the sources of his early atheism, on the importance of the doctrine of the Fall, on the danger of worry, and on living in the present moment.*[2]

20 DECEMBER 1946

No. I don't think I feel like you 'disillusioned'. I think that though I am emotionally a fairly cheerful person my actual judgement of the world has always been what yours now is and so I have not been disappointed. The early loss of my mother, great unhappiness at school, and the shadow of the last war and presently the experience of it, had given me a very pessimistic view of existence. My atheism was based on it: and it still seems to me that *far* the strongest card in our enemies' hand is the actual course of the world: and that, quite apart from particular evils like wars and revolutions. The inherent 'vanity' of the 'creature',[3] the fact that life preys on life, that all beauty and happiness is produced only to be destroyed—this was what stuck in my gullet. . . .

I still think the argument from design the weakest possible ground for Theism, and what may be called the argument from un-design the strongest for Atheism.

Of course my error was in asking how I knew the universe to be so bad: whence came the light which discovered this darkness, the straight by which I judged this crookedness?

Hence the very important part which the Fall (both human and angelic) has played in my thought since I became a Christian. When you say that nothing here . . . has a value in itself, that everything has a value in relation to God, I couldn't agree with you more. And I often, like you, think that all the valuable future may lie with the Christened Chinaman. But one mustn't assume burdens that God does not lay upon us.

---

[2] *Letters II,* 746–748.
[3] Romans 8:20.

It is one of the evils of rapid diffusion of news that the sorrows of *all* the world come to us every morning. I think each village was meant to feel pity for *its own* sick and poor whom it can help and I doubt if it is the duty of any private person to fix his mind on ills which he cannot help. (This may even become an *escape* from the works of charity we really *can* do to those we know).

A great many people (not you) do now seem to think that the mere state of being *worried* is in itself meritorious. I don't think it is. We must, if it so happens, give our lives for others: but even while we're doing it, I think we're meant to enjoy Our Lord and, in Him, our friends, our food, our sleep, our jokes, and the birds song and the frosty sunrise.

As about the distant, so about the future. It is very dark: but there's usually light enough for the next step or so. Pray for me always.

1947

TO MRS. FRANK L. JONES: *On the meaning of the doctrine of the two natures of Christ and the significance of Gethsemane and the Cross (with a postscript on avoiding ideological psychiatrists).*[1]

23 FEBRUARY 1947

(1.) The doctrine that Our Lord was God and man does *not* mean that He was a human body which had God instead of the normal human soul. It means that a real man (human body *and* human soul) was in Him so united with the 2nd Person of the Trinity as to make one Person: just as in you and me a complete anthropoid animal (animal body *and* animal 'soul' i.e., instincts, sensations *et cetera*) is so united with an immortal rational soul as to be one person. In other words, if the Divine Son had been removed from Jesus what would have been left would have been not a corpse but a living man.

(2.) This human soul in Him was unswervingly united to the God in Him in that which makes a personality one, namely Will. But it had the feelings of any normal man: hence could be tempted, could fear *et cetera*. Because of these feelings it could pray 'if it be possible, let this cup pass from me':[2] because of its perfect union with His Divine Nature it unswervingly answered 'Nevertheless, not as I will but as thou wilt.'[3] The Matthew passages...make clear this unity of will [and] give in addition the human feelings.

(3.) God could, had He pleased, have been incarnate in a man of iron nerves, the Stoic sort who lets no sigh escape Him. Of His great humility He chose to be incarnate in a man of delicate sensibilities who wept at the grave of Lazarus[4] and sweated blood in Gethsemane.[5] Otherwise we should have missed the great

---

[1] *Letters II, 764–766.*
[2] Matthew 26:39.
[3] Matthew 26:39.
[4] John 11:35.
[5] Luke 22:44.

lesson that it is by his *will* alone that a man is good or bad, and that *feelings* are not, in themselves, of any importance. We should also have missed the all important help of knowing that He has faced all that the weakest of us face, has shared not only the strength of our nature but every weakness of it except sin. If He had been incarnate in a man of immense natural courage, that would have been for many of us almost the same as His not being incarnate at all.

(4.) The prayer recorded in Matthew is much too short to be long enough for the disciples to go to sleep! They record the bit they heard before they fell asleep.

(5.) It is probable that all the gospels are based on acts and sayings which the disciples deliberately learned by heart: a much surer method even now than transmission by writing: still more so among people whose memories were uninfected by too many books and whose books were only manuscripts. But this is guess work. With all good wishes....

Keep clear of psychiatrists unless you know that they are also Christians. Otherwise they start with the assumption that your religion is an illusion and try to 'cure' it: and this assumption they make not as professional psychologists but as amateur philosophers. Often they have never given the question any serious thought.

TO BEDE GRIFFITHS, *who had informed Lewis that he had just been appointed prior (second in command) of his monastery: On the danger of trying to anticipate future difficulties and of living in the future.*[6]

15 APRIL 1947

I offer you my congratulations on your new office: my prayers you know you already have. There will certainly, as you anticipate, be a cross somewhere in it, but one mustn't assume crosses any more than consolations. You remember in the *Imitation [of Christ],* 'The devil does not mind in the least whether he snares us by true or false pictures of the future.' In my experience the cross seldom comes where it is anticipated.

---

[6] *Letters II,* 770. For more about what Lewis called "terror-pictures of the future" and about living in the present moment, see *SL,* Letters V and XV.

TO PHYLLIS ELINOR SANDEMAN, *who had written Lewis of her attachment to the home that had been in her family for six hundred years: On the possessiveness of the natural loves.*[7]

31 JUNE 1947

I think that about Houses the answer is this. Nothing rises again which has not died. The natural and possessive love for a house *if* it has been crucified, if it has become disinterested, if it has submitted to sacrifice, will rise again: i.e., the love for a house *you were willing to give up* will rise again. The wilful, grasping love will not—or only rise as a horror.

About the house itself, if the love rises, then all that is necessary to bless it will, I believe, be there. It may not be very like what you would now call 'a house': but you'll see *then* that it was what you really meant by the house.

But the whole point is that you can *keep* forever only what you *give up:* beginning with the thing it is hardest to give up—one's self. What you grab you lose: what you offer freely and patiently to God or your neighbour, you will have. (Your heavenly library will contain only the books you have given or lent! And the dirty thumb marks on the latter will have turned into beautiful marginal decorations—I'm joking of course, but to illustrate a serious principle).

Loving dogs more than children is a misfortune not a sin. *Acting* on that superior love for dogs—i.e., sacrificing the interests of the humans in your household to the animals—is a sin. I think myself that animals which have acquired a personality from living with us will probably be restored: but I can only repeat what I said on this point in *The Problem of Pain* (chapter on *Animal Pain*).

Remember, all this is only my guess. I'm not inspired, very far from it. All good wishes.

---

[7] *Letters II,* 788–789.

TO ARTHUR GREEVES, *who had taken issue with "Miracles of the New Creation," Miracles, Chapter 16, especially the last three paragraphs: On the physical reality of our resurrected bodies; on God's use of the physical in the sacraments; and on how God is no way limited by the sacraments.*[8]

19 AUGUST 1947

I agree that we don't know what a spiritual body is. But I don't like *contrasting* it with (your words) 'an actual, physical body'. This suggests that the spiritual body would be the opposite of 'actual'—i.e., some kind of vision or imagination. And I do think most people imagine it as something that *looks* like the present body and isn't really there. Our Lord's eating the boiled fish[9] seems to put the boots on that idea, don't you think? I suspect the distinction is the other way round—that it is something compared with which our present bodies are half real and phantasmal.

When I say that certain graces are 'offered' us only through certain physical acts I mean that is the ordinary public offer certified by scripture and supported by unbroken Christian experience. I don't of course (heaven forbid!) mean to limit what God may please to do in secret and special ways. In fact 'offer' is the operative word. No doubt He gives more than He offers: but the offer was as I describe.

TO FRANCIS USHERWOOD: *On the relationship between God's sovereignty and our free will; and on the meaning of luck.*[10]

9 SEPTEMBER 1947

No, I am sure God has not forced B to give A the job. God's action would consist, I believe, in arranging all the circumstances so that A came at the right moment *et cetera*—i.e., in presenting B with the *situation,* on which then his free will worked. Ordinary people regard life as a mixture of 'luck' and free will. It is the part usually called 'luck' by which, on my view, God answers prayers.

---

[8] *Letters III,* 1573–1574.
[9] John 21:12–13.
[10] *Letters II,* 801–802.

TO RHONA BODLE, *a New Zealander who came to live in England from 1947 to 1952 to learn how to educate deaf children and who, having read his three books of BBC radio talks, had written Lewis about her doubts about the divinity of Christ: On trying too hard to believe and to feel; on trusting God and working with the light one has and obeying God first and foremost; on the various kinds of conversion; and on the Christian life as rowing a boat (face toward the Helmsman, back toward the future, body dedicated to rowing). This is the first of fourteen letters from Lewis to Bodle in this collection.*[11]

31 DECEMBER 1947

I think it possible that what is keeping you from belief in Christ's Divinity is your apparently strong desire to believe. If you don't think it true why do you *want* to believe it? If you *do* think it true, then you believe it already. So I would recommend less anxiety about the whole question. You believe in God and trust Him. Well, you can trust Him about this. If you go on steadily praying and attempting to obey the best light He had given you, can you not rely on Him to guide you into any further truth He wishes you to know? Or even if He leaves you all your life in doubt, can't you believe that He sees that to be the best state for you?

I *don't* mean by this that you should cease to study and make enquiries: but that you should make them not with frantic desire but with cheerful curiosity and a humble readiness to accept whatever conclusions God may lead you to. (But always, all depends on the steady attempt to obey God all the time. 'He who *does* the will of the Father shall know of the doctrine.')[12]

As for books, the very best popular defence of the full Christian position I know is G. K. Chesterton's *The Everlasting Man.* Mascall's *The God-Man* might also help.

It is only fair to tell you that my impression is that you are in fact very much nearer to belief in Christ than you suppose: and that if you really face the opposite view tranquilly (and why be afraid of it unless you already know in your bones that the Christian view is true) you will find you don't really believe it—i.e., don't really believe that all you have got out of the books you mention

---

[11] *Letters II*, 823–824.
[12] John 7:17.

is based on an illusion—which, if an illusion *at all,* must be a most blasphemous and horrible one. Conversions happen in all sorts of different ways: some sharp and catastrophic (like St. Paul, St. Augustine, or Bunyan) some very gradual and intellectual (like my own). No good predicting how God will deal with one: He has His own way with each of us. So don't worry. Continue all your efforts. You are being *steered* by Another: you've only got to row—and therefore the future journey is behind your back.

I'm pretty sure where you'll land, myself, and you will then wonder how you ever doubted it. But you needn't keep looking over your shoulder too often. Keep your eye on the Helmsman, keep your conscience bright and your brain clear and believe that you are in good hands. (No one can *make* himself believe anything and the effort does harm. Nor make himself *feel* anything, and that effort also does harm. What *is* under our own control is action and intellectual inquiry. Stick to that.) All good wishes.

1948

TO RHONA BODLE: *On when to pray and how to pray, with or without pleasant feelings and emotions; on prayer as our gift to God of our will and on good feelings as a gift from God; and on training oneself to meditate.*[1]

3 JANUARY 1948

I very much doubt if I'm good enough at prayer myself to advise others. First thing in the morning and last thing at night are good times but I don't find that they are the best times for one's main prayer. I prefer sometime in the early evening, before one has got sleepy—but of course it depends on how your day is mapped out.

'Grudging' though a nuisance need not depress us too much. It is the act of *will* (perhaps strongest where there is some disinclination to contend against) that God values, rather than the state of our emotions—the act being what we give Him, the emotions what He gives us (usually, I think, indirectly through the state of our body, health *et cetera,* though there are direct kindlings from Him too. There are *presents,* to be given thanks for but never counted on).

Of course it is very difficult to keep God only before one for more than a few seconds. Our minds are in ruins before we bring them to Him and the rebuilding is gradual. It may help to *practice* concentration on other objects twice a week quite apart from one's prayer: i.e., sit down looking at some physical object (say, a flower) and try for a few minutes to attend exclusively to it, *quietly* (never impatiently) rejecting the train of thought and imagination which keep starting up. All good wishes.

---

[1] *Letters II,* 826.

TO DON GIOVANNI CALABRIA, *who had sent Lewis the Litany of Humility composed by Cardinal Merry del Val: On the danger of being too aware of global worries and of forgetting to help Christ in the people close at hand; on the dignity to which God raises human beings when they receive Holy Communion; and on Lewis's besetting temptations against humility.*[2]

27 MARCH 1948

I was glad to receive your letter—so full (as is your wont) of Charity.

Everywhere things are troubling and uneasy—wars and rumours of war: perhaps not the final hour but certainly times most evil.

Nevertheless, the Apostle again and again bids us 'Rejoice'.[3]

Nature herself bids us do so, the very face of the earth being now renewed, after its own manner, at the start of Spring.

I believe that the men of this age (and among them you Father, and myself) think too much about the state of nations and the situation of the world. Does not the author of *The Imitation* warn us against involving ourselves too much with such things?

We are not kings, we are not senators. Let us beware lest, while we torture ourselves in vain about the state of Europe, we neglect either Verona or Oxford.

In the poor man who knocks at my door, in my ailing mother, in the young man who seeks my advice, the Lord Himself is present: therefore let us wash His feet.

I have always believed that Voltaire, infidel though he was, thought aright in that admonition of his to cultivate your own garden: likewise William Dunbar (the Scottish poet who flourished in the 15th century) when he said

Man, please thy Maker and be merry;
This whole world rate we at a penny!

Tomorrow we shall celebrate the glorious Resurrection of Christ. I shall be remembering you in the Holy Communion.

---

[2] *Letters II*, 842–843.
[3] Philippians 4:4.

Away with tears and fears and troubles! United in wedlock with the eternal Godhead Itself, our nature ascends into the Heaven of Heavens. So it would be impious to call ourselves 'miserable'. On the contrary, Man is a creature whom the Angels—were they capable of envy—would envy. Let us lift up our hearts! 'At some future time perhaps even these things it will be a joy to recall.'[4]

For the Litany composed by Cardinal Merry many thanks. You did not know, did you, that all the temptations against which he pours forth these prayers I have long been exceeding conscious of? [*From the longing to be thought well of, deliver me, Jesus, . . . from the fear of being rejected, deliver me, Jesus, . . .*] *Touché*, you pink me!

Let us pray for each other always. Farewell.

TO RHONA BODLE: *More advice along the lines just given, with a word of consolation about how God holds us fast; on remedies for the overfamiliarity of some parts of scripture; and on patience with the process of intellectual conversion.*[5]

22 JUNE 1948

Splendid! As long as you keep in your present way—holding fast to God, whether the Incarnation can be accepted or not—you can't go wrong. Because, you see, it is not really you who are holding fast to Him but He to you: and He will bring you to wherever He wants.

I should try St. John's Gospel and the non-Pauline epistles if the first three gospels are deadened with familiarity. But why worry? (I don't mean 'Why read and think?': that's obviously right.) You are wondering if the Incarnation is true. Well, if it's not true God doesn't want you to believe it. If you are worried by not (or not yet) believing it, then you must in your heart of hearts believe it to be true, for who could be so worried at not believing an error!

Your own argument, that you at any rate have come to know God only thro' Christ is a very strong one: and I don't mind betting you will come to the Christian belief in the end. But don't read with a determination to do so. Take the books naturally as you would any other serious books. And get out of your head

---

[4] Virgil, Aeneid, I, 203.
[5] *Letters II*, 857.

expressions like 'theological problem', 'dogma' et cetera. You are an adult student reading some very interesting ancient records, with God to guide you. Let them and Him work. And don't get fussed and don't demand quick returns. All is obviously going pretty well.

1949

TO RHONA BODLE: *A letter of encouragement on the verge of her conversion.*[1]

10 FEBRUARY 1949

I doubt whether I, or anyone else, needs to interfere. The route you are following at present seems to be the right one. Adding to Pascal's 'if you had not found me you would not seek me' (a sentence I have long loved), the very obvious further step 'And if I had not drawn you, you would not have found me,' and seeing both in the light of Our Lord's words 'No man cometh to me unless the Father have drawn him'[2]—well, it is pretty clear that you are being conducted. 'Follow-my-leader' is a good enough guide now. Thinking as you now do of Christ you will not be able for long to set aside the sayings which proclaim Him to be more than man ('Before Abraham was I AM'[3]—'I AM and hereafter ye shall see the Son of Man *et cetera*'[4]—'Thy sins are forgiven thee'[5]—'I am the Vine').[6]

I didn't listen in (I never do) to the discussion you mention: but I quite agree that people are far too concerned about the 'modern' man and this-that-and-the-other man. Why not, as you say, just *man*? You are always in my prayers.

TO RHONA BODLE, *to whom Lewis sent his sermon "Transposition" with this letter—found in* The Weight of Glory and Other Addresses.[7]

15 MARCH 1949

(1) I wonder if the first one in this volume would help at all. (2) Have you ever thought what a rum thing *your own* incarnation is?

---

[1] *Letters II,* 915–916.
[2] John 14:6.
[3] Ibid., 8:58.
[4] Matthew 26:64.
[5] ibid., 9:5.
[6] John 15:1.
[7] *Letters II,* 926.

TO MARY NEYLAN, *whose daughter Sarah, Lewis's goddaughter, was being confirmed and receiving her first holy communion: On Lewis's respect for a parent's right to read something an adult writes to an underage child.*[8]

3 APRIL 1949

The enclosed is a desperate attempt to do what I am very ill qualified for. After writing it it occurred to me that I might have said all the things that you (knowing Sarah) might know to be particularly disastrous. So I thought you'd better vet it before passing it on. I'm so clumsy.

Blessings on all three—and I'm sorry I can't come. But I'd only have behaved like an ass if I had!

TO SARAH NEYLAN: *On why old people may appear to be awkward around young people; on not expecting, counting on, or demanding good feelings connected with holy activities; and on doing only the things we ought to do, the things we've got to do, and the things we like doing.*[9]

3 APRIL 1949

I am sorry to say that I don't think I shall be able to be at your confirmation on Saturday. For most men Saturday afternoon is a free time, but I have an invalid lady to look after and the weekend is the time when I have no freedom at all, and have to try to be Nurse, Kennel-Maid, Wood-cutter, Butler, House-maid and Secretary all in one. I had hoped that if the old lady were a little better than usual and if all the other people in the house were in good tempers I might be able to get away next Saturday. But the old lady is a good deal worse than usual and most of the people in the house are in bad tempers. So I must 'stick to the ship'.

If I *had* come and we had met, I am afraid you might have found me very shy and dull. (By the way, always remember that old people can be quite as shy with young people as young people

---

[8] *Letters III*, 1585–1586.
[9] This letter is accidentally missing from the *Collected Letters* but is printed in *Letters of C. S. Lewis*, edited, with a memoir, by W. H. Lewis (London: Bles, 1966; New York: Harcourt, Brace and World, 1966), 215–216; revised and enlarged by Walter Hooper (San Diego: Harcourt Brace, 1988), 390–391.

can be with old. This explains what must seem to you the idiotic way in which so many grown-ups talk to you.) But I will try to do what I can by a letter.

I think of myself as having to be two people for you. (1) The real, serious, Christian godfather (2) The fairy godfather. As regards (2) I enclose a bit of the only magic (a very dull kind) which I can work. Your mother will know how to deal with the spell. I think it will mean one or two, or even five, pounds for you now, to get things you want, and the rest in the Bank for future use. As I say, it is a dull kind of magic and a really good godfather (of type 2) would do something much more interesting: but it is the best an old bachelor can think of, and it is with my love.

As for No 1, the serious Christian godfather, I feel very unfit for the work—just as you, I dare say, may feel very unfit for being confirmed and for receiving the Holy Communion. But then an angel would not be really fit and we must all do the best we can. So I suppose I must try to give you advice. And the bit of advice that comes into my head is this: don't expect (I mean, don't *count on* and don't *demand*) that when you are confirmed, or when you make your first Communion, you will have all the *feelings* you would like to have. You may, of course: but also you may not. But don't worry if you don't get them. They aren't what matter. The things that are happening to you are quite real things whether you feel as you would wish or not, just as a meal will do a hungry person good even if he has a cold in the head which will rather spoil the taste. Our Lord will give us right feelings if He wishes—and then we must say Thank you. If He doesn't, then we must say to ourselves (and Him) that He knows best. This, by the way, is one of the very few subjects on which I feel I do know something. For years after I had become a regular communicant I can't tell you how dull my feelings were and how my attention wandered at the most important moments. It is only in the last year or two that things have begun to come right—which just shows how important it is to keep on doing what you are told.

Oh—I'd nearly forgotten—I have *one* other piece of advice.

Remember that there are only three kinds of things anyone need ever do. (1) Things we *ought* to do (2) Things we've *got* to do (3) Things we *like* doing. I say this because some people seem to spend so much of their time doing things for none of the three reasons, things like reading books they don't like because other people read them. Things you ought to do are things like doing one's school work or being nice to people. Things one has got to do are things like dressing and undressing, or household shopping. Things one likes doing—but of course I don't know what you like. Perhaps you'll write and tell me one day.

Of course I always mention you in my prayers and will most especially on Saturday. Do the same for me.

TO RHONA BODLE, *who had written to him about a Jewish student who wanted to learn about Jesus: On modern translations of the New Testament; on real Christianity and real Judaism; and on respecting the secularity of public schools.*[10]

28 MAY 1949

Knox is better literature than Moffatt but he has to translate the Vulgate not the Greek. This really makes very little difference but the Rabbi will make play with it so she'd better have Moffatt.

I also suggest G.K. Chesterton's *Everlasting Man*. And can't she counter-attack if the Rabbi doesn't believe in miracles? If he doesn't believe in the signs and wonders in Egypt, or the passage of the Red Sea, or the miracles of Elijah, then quite clearly he is not holding the real Jewish faith. She is quite entitled to say 'If you want me to remain a Jewess send me a real Jew not a Jewish Modernist.' And as I don't think they'll be able to find her one, she can then ask how it is that there are still real Christians and no real Jews.

I quite agree with you about not using one's job for propaganda: but once the pupil raises the question I think one has a free hand. . . .

If they do find her a *real* Jew then the battle moves onto a different front: but, I think, half their weapons would be gone.

TO RHONA BODLE, *who had written Lewis about the wordless resolution of her doubts about the divinity of Christ: On the nature of religious language and of poetry.*[11]

---

[10] *Letters II,* 941.
[11] *Letters II,* 947.

24 JUNE 1949

Welcome home! And thank you for writing to tell me: this has been a wonderful week, for I have just heard that my oldest friend is to be baptised on Saturday.

No, one can't put these experiences into words: though all writing is a continual attempt to do so. Indeed, in a sense, one can hardly put anything into words: only the simplest colours have names, and hardly any of the smells. The simple physical pains and (still more) the pleasures can't be expressed in language. I labour the point lest the devil should hereafter try to make you believe that what was wordless was therefore vague and nebulous. But in reality it is just the clearest, the most concrete, and the most indubitable realities which escape language: not because *they* are vague but because language is. What goes easily into words is precisely the abstract—thought about 'matter' (not apples or snuff), about 'population' (not actual babies), and so on. Poetry I take to be the continual effort to bring language back to the actual.

God bless you: mention me sometimes in your prayers.

TO BEDE GRIFFITHS, *after Lewis's hospitalization: On the necessity for the purification of faith and of the motives for faith; on the good news about so many of Lewis's friends, especially Owen Barfield, becoming Christians; on the fate of the virtuous unbelievers and the possibility of vicarious faith; and a window into Lewis's own practice of intercessory prayer.*[12]

27 JUNE 1949

I have just emerged from the Acland (*streptococcus*) and my future plans are uncertain —I mean, for the Vacation. I might possibly be able to look you up but doubt if it is possible.

I think the fact that you and I both at the time of our conversions had the feeling that we might be taking part in a Christian Renaissance is a disadvantage to us. It may even imply a drop of mere, what class shall I call it?, Vogue, Movementism, Historicism, Worldliness, in our then state of mind which has to be brought to a painful crisis before it can be cured. In so far as our Faith to any degree at all (even .0001%) leaned on hopes of some

---

[12] *Letters II, 948.*

speedy triumph for Christendom (for which we have no Promise) it was not real Faith. It is not for us to know the times and the seasons.[13] My own *feelings* move up and down.

I think a glance at my correspondence would cheer you up: letter after letter from recent converts, by ones and by twos, often (which is most helpful) married couples with children. Of [course] it amounts to nothing by the standards of world statistics. But are they the right standards? I sometimes have a feeling that the big mass-conversions of the Dark Ages, often carried out by force, were all a false dawn, and the whole work has to be done over again. As for the virtuous heathen, we are told that Our Lord is the saviour 'of all men' though 'specially of those that believe'.[14] As there is certainly vicarious suffering is there not also vicarious faith?

Oh, by the way, Barfield was baptised last Saturday: have him in your prayers.

I have two lists of names in my prayers, those for whose conversion I pray, and those for whose conversion I give thanks. The little trickle of *transferences* from List A to List B is a great comfort. At any rate 'Fear not, little flock.'[15]

TO ARTHUR GREEVES: *On the meaning of innocent human suffering; on the relationship between human free will and God's will; and on his brother's alcoholism.*[16]

6 JULY 1949

I think the view you express in your letter is the same I hold, and indeed I fancy I have stated it in print. I do not hold that God 'sends' sickness or war in the sense in which He sends us all good things. Hence in Luke xiii.16 Our Lord clearly attributes a disease not to the action of His Father but to that of Satan. I think you are quite right. All suffering arises from sin.

---

[13] Acts 1:7: "And he said unto them, It is not for you to know the times or the seasons, which the Father hath put in his own power."

[14] 1 Timothy 4:10.

[15] Luke 12:32.

[16] *Letters II*, 956–957. For more on the meaning of innocent human suffering, see Chapters 6 and 7 in *The Problem of Pain* (San Francisco: HarperOne, 2001).

The sense in which it is also God's will seems to me twofold (a) The one you mention: that God willed the free will of men and angels in spite of His knowledge that it could lead in some cases to sin and then to suffering: i.e., He thought Freedom worth creating even at that price. It is like when a mother allows a small child to walk on its own instead of holding it by her hand. She knows it may fall but learning to walk on one's own is worth a few falls. When it does fall this is in one sense contrary to the mother's will: but the general situation in which falls are possible *is* the mother's will. (In fact, as you and I have so often said before 'in one way it is, in another way it isn't'!)

(b) The world is so made that the sins of one inflict suffering on another. Now I don't think God allows this to happen at random. I think that if He knew that the suffering entailed on innocent A by the sins of B would be (in the deep sense and the long run) *bad* for A, He would shield A from it. And in that sense I think it is sometimes God's will that A should go through this suffering. The supreme case is the suffering that our sins entailed on Christ. When Christ saw that suffering drawing near He prayed (Luke xxii.42) 'If thou be willing, remove this cup from me: nevertheless not my will but thine.' This seems to me to make it quite clear that the crucifixion was (in the very qualified sense which I've tried to define) God's will. I do not regard myself as disagreeing with you, but as holding the same view with a few necessary complications which you have omitted.

Warnie is now definitely better as far as this bout is concerned: but we dare not assume that it is the last. As long as there was no one but him to leave in charge at the Kilns and as long as he is a dipsomaniac it *seems* impossible for me to get away for more than a very few days: but I don't doubt at all that if it is good for us both (I mean, you and me) to meet and have some happiness together it will all be arranged in ways we can't now foresee.

I've just finished re-reading *War and Peace*. The great beauty of *long* books is that however often you read them there are still large tracts you have forgotten.

TO ARTHUR GREEVES: *On his brother's admission to an Oxford hospital, for treatment of alcoholism; and on the meaning of vicarious suffering, or what Lewis will call, in* The Lion, the Witch and the Wardrobe, *the "Deeper Magic," mentioned above in his letter to Sister Penelope, 19 November 1941.*

2 JULY 1949

Thanks for your most kind and comforting letter—like a touch of a friend's hand in a dark place. For it is much darker than I feared. W's trouble is to be called 'nervous insomnia' in speaking to Janie and others; but in reality (this for your private ear) it is Drink. This bout started about ten days ago. Last Sunday the doctor and I begged him to go into a nursing home (that has always effectively ended previous bouts) and he refused. Yesterday we succeeded in getting him in; but alas, too late. The nursing home has announced this morning that he is out of control and they refuse to keep him. Today a mental specialist is to see him and he will be transferred, I hope for a *short* stay, to what is called a hospital but is really an asylum. Naturally there is no question of a later Irish jaunt for me this year. A few odd days here and there in England is the best I can hope for.

Don't imagine I doubt for a moment that what God sends us must be sent in love and will all be for the best if we have grace to use it so. My *mind* doesn't waver on this point; my *feelings* sometimes do. That's why it does me good to hear what I believe repeated in your voice—it being the rule of the universe that others can do for us what we cannot do for ourselves and one can paddle every canoe *except* one's own. That is why Christ's suffering *for us* is not a mere theological dodge but the supreme case of the law that governs the whole world; and when they mocked him by saying, 'He saved others, himself he connot save,'[17] they were really uttering, little as they knew it, the ultimate law of the spiritual world.

---

[17] Matthew 27:42; Mark 15:31.

TO ARTHUR GREEVES: *On praying "thy will be done on earth as it is in Heaven"; on not being able to come to Ireland for a vacation with Arthur; and on the problem of alcoholism.*[18]

27 JULY 1949

Good, I'm glad we are really agreed. The one thing I forgot to say in my other letter (and I think you will agree with it too) is that we make a great mistake by quoting 'thy will be done' without the rest of the sentence 'on earth *as it is in Heaven'*.[19] That is the real point, isn't it? Not merely submission but a prayer that we may be enabled to do God's will *as* (in the same way as) angels and blessed human spirits do it, with alacrity and delight like players in an orchestra responding spontaneously to the conductor.

I don't think I can make a second attempt to get to County Down. Warnie himself is going away (without me) soon and of course I must be on duty then. I'm taking a few short trips (long week ends) instead: there's a difference between that and any Irish holiday long enough to be worth taking. But I have (faint) hopes of another year. He has been completely tee-total now since he came out of hospital. If only he could keep it up! Perhaps he will. I had thought, like you, that 'others depending on us' might be an incentive, but you see this broke down as soon as it was tried. I think it would work with an ordinary temptation, but not with what is really a recurrent obsession—i.e., almost as much a medical as a moral problem. If we could get a 12 months' clean bill of health from him I should feel much freer.

The whole affair has done at least this good that it has made us write to one another again! If you call this scrawl writing—my hand has gone all to pot. God bless you.

TO MISS BRECKENRIDGE: *On the problem in prayer of God's foreknowledge; and on the Fall and evolution.*[20]

---

[18] *Letters II,* 960.
[19] Matthew 6:10.
[20] *Letters II,* 962.

1 AUGUST 1949

Don't bother about the idea that God 'has known for millions of years exactly what you are about to pray'. That isn't what it's like. God is hearing you *now*, just as simply as a mother hears a child. The difference His timelessness makes is that this *now* (which slips away from you even as you say the word *now*) is for Him infinite. If you must think of His timelessness at all, don't think of Him *having* looked forward to this moment for millions of years: think that to Him you are always praying this prayer. But there's really no need to bring it in. You have gone into the Temple ('one day in Thy court is better than a thousand')[21] and found Him, as always, there. That is all you need to bother about.

There is *no* relation of any importance between the Fall and Evolution. The doctrine of Evolution is that organisms have changed, sometimes for what we call (biologically) the better... quite often for what we call (biologically) the worse.... The doctrine of the Fall is that at one particular point one species, Man, tumbled down a moral cliff. There is neither opposition nor support between the two doctrines.... Evolution is not only not a doctrine of *moral* improvements, but of biological changes, some improvements, some deteriorations.

TO MARY VAN DEUSEN, *an American who had asked Lewis to write a book on prayer, a request that made more sense as more and more correspondents needed direction in prayer. This is the first of thirty-four letters from Lewis to her in this collection.*[22]

9 AUGUST 1949

Thanks for your very interesting letter of the 3rd.

I don't feel I could write a book on Prayer: I think it would be rather 'cheek' of my part.

All good wishes.

---

[21] Psalm 84:10.
[22] *Letters II*, 965.

TO "MRS. LOCKLEY," *a woman whose husband had taken a mistress ("Lockley" is the pseudonym Lewis's brother gave her in his edition of his brother's correspondence; he later forgot her actual name): Lewis tells her that he has confided her situation to his spiritual director; he affirms the graces she has received—charity, submission to God's will, and the avoidance of indulged jealousy—and cautions her to keep remembering that these graces are gifts; and he draws a salutary moral about being patient with God even when God appears not to be answering our prayers. This is the first of his five letters to her in this collection.*[23]

2 SEPTEMBER 1949

Apparently I was mistaken in thinking that to condone the infidelity and submit to the arrangement your husband suggests would be *wrong*. My adviser of course says that it is impossible to him to 'give a fair ruling without knowing more of the parties'. But with that reservation he suggests (1) Mrs. A should refuse to have intercourse with her husband, otherwise carry on, completely ignoring the mistress. (2) Mr. A must never mention the mistress in his house nor when he has seen her, nor should he let Mrs. A or anyone else have any suspicion when or where he meets the mistress. I can't myself quite see the point of No. 2, and I take it that anyway it is impracticable. . . .

On the actual practical arrangements I don't feel that I—an elderly bachelor and the most amateurish of theologians—can be useful. Where I *might* help, on the internal and spiritual problems for yourself, you obviously do not need my help. All the things I would have said to most women in your position (about charity, submission to God's will, and the poisonous nature of indulged jealousy, however just the case) you clearly know already. I don't think it can do you any harm to know that you have these graces, provided you know that they are *Graces*, gifts from the Holy Spirit, and not your own merits. God, who foresaw your tribulation, has specially armed you to go through it, not without pain but without strain; not a case of 'tempering the wind to the shorn lamb' but of giving the lamb a coat proportional to the wind. On all *that* side you have only to go on as you are

---

[23] *Letters II*, 975–976.

doing. And you certainly needn't worry at all about there being any material for psychotherapy in you. . . .

One point in your story looms large in my mind—the fatal consequences of your husband's lack of faith in you when he did not get those letters. For this is just how *we* also might desert God. If nothing, or nothing we recognise comes through, we imagine He has let us down and reject Him, perhaps at the very moment when help was on its way. No doubt your husband may have been readier to desert you because a quite different temptation had already begun. But then that applies to the God–Man situation also.

TO "MRS. LOCKLEY": *On the appropriateness of sharing her marital crisis with him and of her refusing her husband's request for sexual intercourse.*[24]

6 SEPTEMBER 1949

Telling these things to someone you approach as a consultant is no more disloyalty than revealing one's body to a doctor is indecent exposure. With a trained confessor this, as it were, *disinfectant* situation would be even more so.

I don't think the arrangement the old man suggested is 'dishonest'. I think his advice turns on the fine but important distinction between *enduring* a situation which is some one else's fault and *sanctioning* it in a way which makes one an accessory. After all, your husband has no right to have it both ways and you have no duty (or right) to make him feel as if he had. It would do him no harm to realise that this affair is *just as much* adultery as if it were 'furtive visits to a prostitute'.

TO DON GIOVANNI CALABRIA: *On Lewis's own vice of acedia (indolence); on his fright at having been delirious; and on refraining from worry about matters beyond our ability to change.*[25]

10 SEPTEMBER 1949

I have just found in my desk the letter which you so kindly wrote at Easter this year. I think I have sent no reply: nothing could be less civil than this silence of mine, nothing less human.

---

[24] *Letters II*, 977.
[25] *Letters II*, 978–979.

I acknowledge my fault, I ask pardon. But I do not wish you to believe either that your memory has fallen from my mind or that your name has fallen from my daily prayers. For nothing else was responsible for it except the perpetual labour of writing and (lest I should seem to exonerate myself too much) a certain Accidia, an evil disease and, I believe, of the Seven Deadly Sins that one which in me is the strongest—though few believe this of me.

From a brief illness, God be thanked, I am recovered. I had what the doctors once used to call in English 'tonsillitis': but now by a more splendid name, 'streptococcus'. Fever laid on me a heavy hand and for some hours I was delirious . . . oh how well has your poet written of the lost souls who 'have lost the good of the intellect': for what torture is more dreadful than that? For while the mind is alienated from us, to ourselves we seem to toil away with much effort of thought, to knit together syllogisms, to treat of the most subtle questions—not knowing, however, what it is we are thinking about. The *working* of the mind is there, but not its *work*.

In this island we are troubled by a severe drought. About other nations I say nothing. For what is required of me unless more and more to hold fixed in my heart our Lord's words: 'Ye shall hear of wars and rumours of wars. See that ye be not troubled'?[26]

Farewell, my Father; and of your fatherly charity cease not to make mention of me before our common Lord (true God and the only true Man—for all we others, since the Fall of Adam, are but half men).

TO "MRS. LOCKLEY": *On infidelity as breaking a promise; on the Christian concept of marriage as sacrament and as mystical union with Christ; reliance and dependence on God, a daily spiritual exercise; and on the danger of being too curious about people's private lives.*[27]

12 SEPTEMBER 1949

I don't think your objection to 'setting yourself up as a judge' is cowardly. It may spring from the fact that you are the injured party and have a very proper conviction that the plaintiff cannot also be on the Bench. I also quite realise that he didn't feel the sin

---

[26] Matthew 24:6.
[27] *Letters II*, 979–980.

as a Christian would: but he must, as a man, feel the dishonour of breaking a promise. After all constancy in love thunders at him from every love-song in the world, quite apart from our mystical conception of marriage. . . .

As you say, the thing is to rely *only* on God. The time will come when you will regard all this misery as a small price to pay for having been brought to the dependence. Meanwhile (don't I know) the trouble is that relying on God has to begin all over again every day as if nothing had yet been done. . . .

The reason why I am saddled with many people's troubles is, I think, that I have no natural curiosity about private lives and am therefore a good subject. To anyone who (in *that* sense) enjoyed it, it would be a dangerous poison.

TO "MRS. LOCKLEY": *On the problems of pains and the problems of pleasures.*[28]

22 SEPTEMBER 1949

The intellectual problem (why children lose one or both parents in this way and other ways) is no harder than the problem why some women lose their husbands. In each case, no doubt, what we regard as a mere hideous interruption and curtailment of life is really the *data,* the concrete situation on which life is to be built. . . . When the *data* are of the kind we naturally like (wealth, health, good fathers or husbands) of course we tend not to notice that they are data or limitations at all. But we're told that they are: and what seem to us the easiest conditions may really be the hardest ('How hardly shall they that have riches' *et cetera*).[29]

TO "MRS. LOCKLEY": *On the unreliability of introspection.*[30]

27 SEPTEMBER 1949

Yes, yes, I know. The moment one asks oneself 'Do I believe?' all belief seems to go. I think this is because one is trying to turn round and look *at* something which is there to be used and work

---

[28] *Letters II,* 982–983.
[29] Mark 10:23.
[30] *Letters II,* 983.

from—trying to take out one's eyes instead of keeping them in the right place and seeing *with* them. I find that it happens about other matters as well as faith. In my experience only very robust pleasures will stand the question, 'Am I really enjoying this?' Or attention—the moment I begin thinking about my attention (to a book or a lecture) I have *ipso facto* ceased attending. St. Paul speaks of 'Faith actualised in Love'.[31] And 'the heart is deceitful':[32] you know better than I how very unreliable introspection is. I should be much more alarmed about your progress if you wrote claiming to be overflowing with Faith, Hope and Charity.

TO RHONA BODLE, *who seems to have suggested that Lewis is proud to have been successful in his prayers for her: On how all our prayers of intercession are really Christ's own prayers; and on Williams's doctrine of co-inherence—we are truly members of one another.*[33]

24 OCTOBER 1949

Pish! There's nothing to be proud about. The whole situation is that of being lent a dignity that doesn't belong to me—the child being allowed to give the penny to the bus conductor, the dog being given the newspaper to carry home.

Or, looked at another way, the really efficacious intercession is Christ's, and yours is *in* His, as you are *in* Him, since you became part of His 'body', the Church. Read Charles Williams on Co-inherence in almost any of his later books or plays (*Descent of the Dove, Descent into Hell, The House of the Octopus*).

TO RHONA BODLE: *On praying for the dead; and on how God uses our prayers.*[34]

26 OCTOBER 1949

I have never seen any more difficulty about praying for the dead than for the living, and it is quite clear that God wishes us to do that. How He uses, or why He should use, our prayers, I

---

[31] Galatians 5:6.
[32] Jeremiah 17:9.
[33] *Letters II*, 988.
[34] *Letters II*, 989–990.

do not pretend to say, but I am attracted by Pascal's saying that 'God has instituted prayer to lend to his creatures the dignity of Causality.'

I wonder whether this sonnet which I wrote years ago, though not a very good poem, makes clear what I think. It is the fact that II Kings xix.32 and Herodotus give these different accounts of the mysterious fading away of a great army!—

The Bible says Sennacherib's campaign was foiled
By an angel: but Herodotus declares, by mice—
Innumerably nibbling all one night they toiled
To eat away his bow-strings as warm wind eats ice.

But muscular archangels, I suggest, employed
Six little jaws to labour at each slender string
And by their aid (weak masters though they be) destroyed
The smiling-lipped Assyrian, cruel-bearded king.

No stranger that Omnipotence should choose to need
Small helps than great! Not strange, then, if His action lingers
Till men have prayed, and suffers our weak prayers indeed
To move as very muscles His delaying fingers,

Who, in His longanimity and love for our
Small dignities, holds back awhile His eager power.[35]

TO RHONA BODLE: *A list of spiritual books.*[36]

3 NOVEMBER 1949

I'm very ill qualified to give you a list. What about Kirk's *Vision of God*, E. L. Mascall's *The God-Man*, and Charles Williams' *The Descent of the Dove*? But I really just don't know the literature. Old books I expect I've mentioned before: *The Imitation*, Hilton's *Scale of Perfection*, Anon, *Theologica Germanica*, Traherne, *Centuries of Meditations*, Lady Julian, *Revelations of Divine Love*.

---

[35] See *Poems*.
[36] *Letters II*, 993–994.

TO RHONA BODLE, *who had written Lewis of her upcoming confirmation: On not expecting remarkable sensations connected to holy activities.*[37]

9 NOVEMBER 1949

Congratulations. You are daily in my prayers.

Caveat [let her beware!]—don't count on any remarkable sensations, either at this or your first (or fifty first) Communion. God gives these or not as He pleases. Their presence does not prove that things are especially well, nor their absence that things are wrong. The intention, the obedience, is what matters.

TO WARFIELD M. FIROR, *an American surgeon and a benefactor of the Lewis household during the time of postwar austerities: On aging; on the need for continual vigilance about the regrowth of old vices and the need to welcome the renewal of old joys; on the peace of God as something more real than sensible realities; and on the entanglements of worldly attachments and the severity with which God has to deal with them.*[38]

5 DECEMBER 1949

I knew I should provoke (and deserve) a smile by my references to old age. But what counts is not the age so much as the prospect; not the mileage travelled or ahead, but the view from this bend in the road. I grudged the passing years in childhood because they were bringing me nearer to School and I thought that to be a schoolboy would be much less pleasant than to be a child. And as it turned out, I was quite right. I did not grudge them as a young man because I thought having a job and acquiring a reputation would be nicer than wishing and hoping for them. I was right again. But don't let me pursue a useless and querulous line of thought.

Yes, I *have* thought (though with no background of biology like yours) about rhythm and recuperation: perhaps, in my thought, more strictly *renewal* —the way things come back, changed, yet the same. We are all only too familiar with this in the case of sins or diseases which we hoped we had left behind. How terribly like a malignant tumour a vice is—the big, drastic operation which

[37] *Letters II*, 994.
[38] *Letters II*, 1005–1008.

one screws oneself to face, the apparent cure, and then, remorse-
lessly, gradually, the return—

> And all our former pain
> And all our surgeon's care
> Are lost, and all the unbearable (in vain
> Borne once) is still to bear.[39]

(This is at least as true of mental vices as of those we loosely
call bodily.) But it does work with the good things as well. At any
moment something may sink an artesian well right down into
one's pent self and old joy, even old power, may come rushing up.
That is why I think that *Resurrection* (what ever it exactly means) is
so much profounder an idea than mere immortality. I am sure we
don't just 'go on'. We really die and are really built up again.

Now this—though I didn't foresee the fact till this minute—
links up with what you were saying about the Peace of God.
(By the way, I don't think 'incomprehensible' in the [Athana-
sian] Creed or 'passing comprehension'[40] mean what is usually
thought. It doesn't mean, I am told, simply *unintelligible,* like a
book in an unknown tongue. It means not thinkable-out, not
capable of being fully summed up or intellectually mastered). I
am sure you are right, that is power. Our idea of peace expresses
only the negative results of it: the exclusion of care, haste, fear *et
cetera* but not the positive thing that excludes them. So someone
who had never bathed might think of a swim only as absence of
clothes, absence of solidity in touch with one, *et cetera:* but not
what really counts, the cool, yielding embrace of the water. But
(here comes the connection with what I was saying, and also the
rub) does it not come exactly in proportion as we have, in some
sense, *died.*

I am concerned about that at present, chiefly as a result of reading William Law. It's all there in the New Testament, though.
'Dying to the world'—'the world is crucified to me and I to the
world'.[41] And I find I haven't begun: at least not if it means (and

---

[39] See Lewis's letter above to Sister Penelope, 9 November 1941.
[40] Philippians 4:7.
[41] Galatians 6:14.

can it mean less) than a steady and progressive disentangling of all one's motives from the merely natural or this-worldly objects: like training a creeper to grow up one wall instead of another. I don't mean disentangling from things wrong in themselves, but, say, from the very pleasant evening which we hope to have over one of your hams to-morrow night, or from gratification at my literary success. It is not the things, nor even the pleasure in them, but the fact that in such pleasures my heart, or so much of my heart, lies. Or to put it in a fantastic form—if a voice said to me (and one I couldn't disbelieve) 'you shall never see the face of God, never help to save a neighbour's soul, never be free from sin, but you shall live in perfect health till the age of 100, very rich, and die the most famous man in the world, and pass into a twilight consciousness of a vaguely pleasant sort forever'—how much would it worry me? How much compared with another war? Or even with an announcement that I should have to have all my teeth out? You see? And what right have I to expect the Peace of God while I thus put my whole heart, at least all my strongest wishes, in the world which he has warned me against?

Well, thank God (for there is still part of me, a tiny little infantine voice somewhere amidst all the strong, confident *natural* voices, which can just thank Him, or perhaps only thank Him for being able to wish to thank Him) we shall not be left to the world. All His terrible resources (but it is we who force him to use them) will be brought against us to detach us from it —insecurity, war, poverty, pain, unpopularity, loneliness. We must be taught that this tent is not home. And, by Jove, how terrible it would be if all suffering, including death itself, were *optional,* so that only a very few voluntary ascetics ever even attempted to achieve the end for which we are created. *A propos*—dare we gloss the text 'Strait is the way and few there be that find it'[42] by adding 'And that's why most of you have to be bustled and badgered into it like sheep—and the sheep-dogs have to have pretty sharp teeth too'! I hope so.

---

[42] Matthew 7:14.

1950

TO MARY VAN DEUSEN, *who had asked Lewis about what was required and what was optional as far as sacraments, church attendance, and the like were concerned: On the necessity of both private and public prayer; on God's rejoicing in our differences; on the meaning of membership, our common life in the Body of Christ—"complementing and helping and receiving one another"; on the reality of spiritual and physical healings; and on relying on obedience rather than feeling.*[1]

7 DECEMBER 1950

(1.) To the best of my knowledge the Episcopalian Church in America is exactly the same as the Anglican Church.

(2.) The only rite which we know to have been instituted by Our Lord Himself is the Holy Communion ('Do this in remembrance of me'[2]—'If you do not eat the flesh of the Son of Man and drink His blood, ye have no life in you'[3]). This is an order and must be obeyed. The other services are, I take it, traditional and might lawfully be altered. But the New Testament does not envisage solitary religion: some kind of regular assembly for worship and instruction is everywhere taken for granted in the Epistles. So we must be regular practising members of the Church.

Of course we differ in temperament. Some (like you—and me) find it more natural to approach God in solitude: but we must go to church as well. Others find it easier to approach Him through the services: but they must practice private prayer and reading as well. For the Church is not a human society of people united by their natural affinities but the Body of Christ in which all members however different (and He rejoices in their differences and by no means wishes to iron them out) must share the common life, complementing and helping and receiving one another precisely by their differences. (Re-read 1st Corinthians 12 and meditate on

---

[1] *Letters III*, 68–69.
[2] Luke 22:19; I Corinthians 11:24.
[3] John 6:53.

it. The word translated *members* would perhaps be better translated *organs*).

If people like you and me find much that we don't naturally like in the public and corporate side of Christianity all the better for us: it will teach us humility and charity towards simple low-brow people who may be better Christians than ourselves. I naturally *loathe* nearly all hymns: the face, and life, of the charwoman in the next pew who revels in them, teach me that good taste in poetry or music are *not* necessary to salvation.

(3.) I am not clear *what* question you are asking me about spiritual healing. That this gift was promised to the Church is certain from Scripture. Whether any instance of it is a real instance, or even (as might happen in this wicked world) fraud, is a question only to be decided by the evidence in that particular case. And unless one is a doctor one is not likely to be able to judge the evidence. Very often, I expect, one is not called upon to do so. Anything like a sudden *furore* about it in one district, especially if accompanied by a publicity campaign on modern commercial lines, would be to me suspect: but even then I might be wrong. On the whole, my attitude would be that any claim *may* be true, and that it is not my duty to decide whether it is.

'Regular but cool' in Church attendance is no bad symptom. Obedience is the key to all doors: *feelings* come (or don't come) and go as God pleases. We can't produce them at will and mustn't try.

TO SHELDON VANAUKEN, *a young, American ex-naval officer who was pursuing a graduate degree in history in Oxford, whose wife and he had begun to read Lewis's books and who had now begun the correspondence with Lewis that would become the book,* A Severe Mercy: On the *psychological doctrine of wish fulfillment; on our deep desire for privacy and no interference; on the real history of religion; on which of the great world religions are believable; on the alternative between Christianity and Hinduism; and on the Tao.*[4]

---

[4] *Letters III,* 70–72. Vanauken's side of the correspondence is found in his book, published by Harper and Row, 1977.

14 DECEMBER 1950

My own position at the threshold of Christianity was exactly the opposite of yours. You wish it were true: I strongly hoped it was *not*. At least, that was my conscious wish: you may suspect that I had unconscious wishes of quite a different sort and that it was these which finally shoved me in. True: but then I may equally suspect that under your conscious wish that it were true, there lurks a strong unconscious wish that it were not. What this works out to is that all that modern stuff about concealed wishes and wishful thinking, however useful it may be for explaining the origin of an error which you already know to be an error, is perfectly useless in deciding which of two beliefs is the error and which is the truth. For (a.) One never knows all one's wishes, and (b.) In very big questions, such as this, even one's conscious wishes are nearly always engaged on both sides.

What I think you can say with certainty is this: the notion that everyone *would like* Christianity to be true, and that therefore all atheists are brave men who have accepted the defeat of all their deepest desires, is simply impudent nonsense. Do you think people like Stalin, Hitler, Haldane, Stapledon (a corking good writer, by the way) would be pleased on waking up one morning to find that they were not their own masters, that they had a Master and a Judge, that there was nothing ever in the deepest recesses of their thoughts about which they could say to Him 'Keep out. Private. This is *my* business'? Do you? *Rats!* Their first reaction would be (as mine was) rage and terror. And I very much doubt whether even you would find it *simply* pleasant. Isn't the truth this: that it would gratify some of our desires (ones we feel in fact pretty seldom) and outrage a great many others? So let's wash out all the Wish business. It never helped anyone to solve any problem yet.

I don't agree with your picture of the history of religion— Christ, Buddha, Mohammed and others elaborating an original simplicity. I believe Buddhism to be a simplification of Hinduism and Islam to be a simplification of Christianity. Clear, lucid, transparent, simple religion (Tao *plus* a shadowy, ethical god in the background) is a late development, usually arising among highly educated people in great cities. What you really start with is ritual, myth, and mystery, the death and return of Balder or Osiris, the dances, the initiations, the sacrifices, the divine kings. Over against that are the Philosophers, Aristotle or Confucius, hardly religious at all.

The only two systems in which the mysteries and the philosophies come together are Hinduism and Christianity: there you get both Metaphysics and Cult (continuous with the primeval cults). That is why my first step was to be sure that one or other of these had the answer. For the reality can't be one that appeals *either* only to savages *or* only to high brows. Real things are like that (e.g., matter is the first most obvious thing you meet—milk, chocolates, apples, and also the object of quantum physics).

There is no question of just a crowd of disconnected religions. The choice is between (a.) The materialist world picture: which I *can't* believe. (b.) The real archaic primitive religions: which are not moral enough. (c.) The (claimed) fulfilment of these in Hinduism. (d.) The claimed fulfilment of these in Christianity. But the weakness of Hinduism is that it *doesn't* really join the two strands. Unredeemably savage religion goes on in the village: the Hermit philosophises in the forest: and neither really interferes with the other. It is only Christianity which compels a high brow like me to partake in a ritual blood feast, and also compels a central African convert to attempt an enlightened universal code of ethics.

Have you tried Chesterton's *The Everlasting Man*? The best popular apologetic I know.

Meanwhile, the attempt to practice the *Tao* is certainly the right line. Have you read the *Analects* of Confucius? He ends up by saying 'This is the Tao. I do not know if any one has ever kept it.' That's significant: one can really go direct from there to the *Epistle to the Romans*.

I don't know if any of this is the least use. Be sure to write again, or call, if you think I can be of any help.

TO SHELDON VANAUKEN: *On why there is no demonstrable proof, but only reasonable probability, of Christianity; on the slow belief in life after death; more on wish fulfillment; and on God as the only object of total humility. Lewis had just finished creating the character Puddleglum in*

The Silver Chair *and would soon return to these themes in his paper to the Socratic Club, "Obstinacy in Belief."*[5]

23 DECEMBER 1950

I do not think there is a *demonstrative* proof (like Euclid) of Christianity, nor of the existence of matter, nor of the good will and honesty of my best and oldest friends. I think all three are (except perhaps the second) far more probable than the alternatives. The case for Christianity in general is well given by Chesterton: and I tried to do something in my *Broadcast Talks*.

As to *why* God doesn't make it demonstratively clear: are we sure that He is even interested in the kind of Theism which would be a compelled logical assent to a conclusive argument? Are *we* interested in it in personal matters? I demand from my friend a trust in my good faith which is *certain* without demonstrative proof. It wouldn't be confidence at all if he waited for rigorous proof. Hang it all, the very fairy-tales embody the truth. Othello believed in Desdemona's innocence when it was proved: but that was too late. Lear believed in Cordelia's love when it was proved: but that was too late. 'His praise is lost who stays till all commend.' The magnanimity, the generosity which will trust on a reasonable probability, is required of us. But supposing one believed and was wrong after all? Why, then you would have paid the universe a compliment it doesn't deserve. Your error would even so be more interesting and important than the reality. And yet how could that be? How could an idiotic universe have produced creatures whose mere dreams are so much stronger, better, subtler than itself?

Note that life after death, which still seems to you the essential thing, was itself a *late* revelation. God trained the Hebrews for centuries to believe in Him without promising them an after-life: and, blessings on Him, he trained me in the same way for about a year. It is like the disguised prince in a fairy tale who wins the heroine's love *before* she knows he is anything more than a woodcutter. What would be a bribe if it came first had better come last.

---

[5] *Letters III*, 74–76. "Obstinacy in Belief" is found in *The World's Last Night and Other Addresses* (New York: Harcourt, Brace & World, 1960), 13–30.

It is quite clear from what you say that you have *conscious* wishes on both sides. And now, another point about *wishes*. A wish may lead to false beliefs, granted. But what does the existence of the wish suggest? At one time I was much impressed by Arnold's line 'Nor does the being hungry prove that we have bread.' But, surely, though it doesn't prove that one particular man will get food, it *does* prove that there is such a thing as food? I.e., if we were a species that didn't normally eat, wasn't designed to eat, would one feel hungry?

You say the Materialist universe is 'ugly'. I wonder how you discovered that? If you are really a product of a materialistic universe, how is it you don't feel at home there? Do fish complain of the sea for being wet? Or if they did, would that fact itself not strongly suggest that they had not always been, or would not always be, purely aquatic creatures? Notice how we are perpetually *surprised* at Time. ('How time flies! Fancy John being grown-up and married? I can hardly believe it!') In heaven's name, why? Unless, indeed, there is something in us which is *not* temporal.

Total Humility is not in the Tao because the Tao (as such) says nothing about the object to which it would be the right response: just as there is no law about railways in the acts of Queen Elizabeth. But from the degree of respect which the Tao demands for ancestors, parents, elders, and teachers, it is quite clear what the Tao *would* prescribe towards an object such as God.

But I think you are already in the meshes of the net! The Holy Spirit is after you. I doubt if you'll get away!

TO SISTER PENELOPE: *On the consequences of Mrs. Moore going into a nursing home; and on cheerful insecurity rather than worry.*[6]

30 DECEMBER 1950

Yours was a cheering letter which warmed my heart (I wish it would have warmed my fingers too: as it is they will hardly form the letters!)....

Our state is thus: my 'mother' has had to retire permanently into a Nursing Home. She is in no pain but her mind has almost completely gone. What traces of it remain seem gentler and more

---

[6] *Letters III,* 78–79.

placid than I have known it for years. Her *appetite* is, oddly, enormous. I visit her, normally, every day, and am divided between a (rational?) feeling that this process of gradual withdrawal is merciful and even beautiful, and a quite different feeling (it comes out in my dreams) of horror.

There is no denying—and I don't know why I should deny to you—that our domestic life is both more physically comfortable and more psychologically harmonious for her absence. The expense is of course very severe and I have worries about that. But it would be very dangerous to have no worries—or rather no *occasions* of worry. I have been feeling that very much lately: that *cheerful insecurity* is what Our Lord asks of us. Thus one comes, late and surprised, to the simplest and earliest Christian lessons!

...I am glad to hear your inner news. Mine, too, is I think (but who am I to judge?) fairly good. *Oremus pro invicem* [Let us pray for each other].

1951

TO MARY VAN DEUSEN: *More on faith healing; on petitionary prayer and its efficacy; on all personal prayer being united to Christ's perpetual prayer and to the Church's prayer; and on praying for people one dislikes.*[1]

5 JANUARY 1951

Whether any individual Christian who attempts Faith Healing is prompted by genuine faith and charity or by spiritual pride is, I take it, a question we cannot decide. That is between God and him. Whether the cure occurs in any given case is clearly a question for the doctors. I am speaking now of healing by some *act*, such as anointing or laying on of hands. *Praying* for the sick—i.e., praying simply, without any overt act is unquestionably right and indeed we are commanded to pray for all men.[2] And *of course* your prayers can do real good.

Needless to say, they don't *do* it either as a medicine does or as magic is supposed to do: i.e., automatically. Prayer is Request—like asking your employer for a holiday or asking a girl to marry one. God is free to grant the request or not: and if He does you cannot prove scientifically that the thing would not have happened anyway. Just as the boss might (for all you know) have given you a holiday even if you hadn't asked. (Cynical people of my sex will tell one that if a girl has determined to marry you, married you would have been whether you asked her or not!) Thus one can't establish the efficacy of prayer by statistics as you might establish the connection between pure milk and fewer cases of tuberculosis. It remains a matter of faith and of God's personal action: it would become a matter of demonstration only if it were impersonal or mechanical.

When I say 'personal' I do not mean private or individual. All our prayers are united with Christ's perpetual prayer and are part

---

[1] *Letters III*, 81–82. See Lewis's essay, "The Efficacy of Prayer" in *The World's Last Night and Other Addresses,* 3–11.
[2] I Timothy 2:1.

of the Church's prayer. (In praying for people one dislikes I find it very helpful to remember that one is joining in *His* prayer for them.)

TO SHELDON VANAUKEN, *who had asked whether he should continue with his postgraduate work in history or study theology: On the danger of combining one's vocation with one's spiritual interest.*[3]

5 JANUARY 1951

We must ask three questions about the probable effect of your research subject to something more theological.

(1.) Would it be better for your immediate enjoyment? Answer, probably but not certainly, Yes.

(2.) Would it be better for your academic career? Answer, probably No. You would have to make up in haste a lot of knowledge which could not be very easily digested in the time.

(3.) Would it be better for your soul? I don't know. I think there is a great deal to be said for having one's deepest spiritual interest distinct from one's ordinary duty as a student or professional man.

St. Paul's *job* was tent-making. When the two coincide I should have thought there was a danger lest the natural interest in one's job and the pleasures of gratified ambition might be mistaken for spiritual progress and spiritual consolation: and I think clergymen sometimes fall into this trap.

Contrariwise, there is the danger that what is boring or repellent in the job may alienate one from the spiritual life. And finally someone has said 'None are so unholy as those whose hands are cauterised with holy things': sacred things may become profane by becoming matters of the job. You *now* want truth for her own sake: how will it be when the same truth is also needed for an effective footnote in your thesis? In fact, the change might do good or harm. I've always been glad myself that Theology is not the thing I earn my living by. On the whole, I'd advise you to get on with your tent-making. The performance of a *duty* will probably teach you quite as much about God as academic Theology would do. Mind, I'm not certain: but that is the view I incline to.

---

[3] *Letters III,* 82–83..

TO SHELDON VANAUKEN: *More on the nature and discernment of voca-tion.*[4]

Look: the question is not whether we should bring God into our work or not. We certainly should and must: as MacDonald says 'All that is not God is death.' The question is whether we should simply (a.) Bring Him in in the dedication of our work to Him, in the integrity, diligence, and humility with which we do it or also (b.) Make His professed and explicit service our job. The A vocation rests on all men whether they know it or not: the B vocation only on those who are specially called to it. Each vocation has its peculiar dangers and peculiar rewards. Naturally, I can't say which is yours.

When I spoke of danger to your academic career on a change of subject I was thinking chiefly of *time*. If you can get an extra year, it would be another matter. I was not at all meaning that 'intellectual history' involving Theology would *in itself* be aca-demically a bad field of research.

I shall at any time be glad to see, or hear from you.

TO "MRS. LOCKLEY": *On the spiritual danger of happiness and unhap-piness; on the temptation to disbelieve; on the devil's hyperactivity when growth in holiness is near—near the altar, conversion, and the like; and on the varied reception of the first Narnian Chronicle.*[5]

How right you are: the great thing is to stop thinking about happiness. Indeed the best thing about happiness itself is that it liberates you from thinking about happiness—as the greatest pleasure that money can give us is to make it unnecessary to think about money. And one sees why we have to be taught the 'not thinking' when we lack as well as when we have. And I'm sure that, as you say, you will 'get through somehow in the end'.

Here is one of the fruits of unhappiness: that it forces us to think of life as something to go *through*. And out at the other end.

---

[4] *Letters III*, 84–86
[5] *Letters III*, 93. "Mrs. Lockley" is a pseudonym for a lady who has not yet been identified.

If only we could steadfastly do that while we are happy, I suppose we should need no misfortunes. It is hard on God really. To how few of us He *dare* send happiness because He knows we will forget Him if He gave us any sort of nice things for the moment. . . .

I *do* get that sudden feeling that the whole thing is hocus pocus and it now worries me hardly at all. Surely the mechanism is quite simple? Sceptical, incredulous, materialistic *ruts* have been deeply engraved in our thought, perhaps even in our physical brains by all our earlier lives. At the slightest jerk our thought will flow down those old ruts. And notice when the jerks come. Usually at the precise moment when we might receive Grace. And if you were a devil would you not give the jerk just at those moments? I think that all Christians have found that he is very active near the altar or on the eve of conversion: worldly anxieties, physical discomforts, lascivious fancies, doubt, are often poured in at such junctures. . . . But the Grace is not frustrated. One gets *more* by pressing steadily on through these interruptions than on occasions when all goes smoothly. . . .

I am glad you all liked 'The Lion'. A number of mothers, and still more, schoolmistresses, have decided that it is likely to frighten children, so it is not selling very well. But the real children like it, and I am astonished how some *very* young ones seem to understand it. I think it frightens some adults, but very few children.

TO VERA MATHEWS, *whose father had just died: On how death matters and on the good that comes from the dead to the living after the death; and on the great dignity and comicality in each of us, to be revealed and appreciated only in heaven.*[6]

27 MARCH 1951

I have just got your letter of the 22nd containing the sad news of your father's death. But, dear lady, I hope you and your mother are not really 'trying to pretend it didn't happen'. It does happen, happens to all of us, and I have no patience with the high minded people who make out that it 'doesn't matter'. It matters a great

---

[6] *Letters III*, 103–104.

deal, and very solemnly. And for those who are left, the pain is not the whole thing. I feel very strongly (and I am not alone in this) that some good comes from the dead to the living in the months or weeks after the death. I think I was much helped by my own father after his death: as if our Lord welcomed the newly dead with the gift of some power to bless those they have left behind; His *birthday* present. Certainly, they often seem just at that time, to be very near us. God bless you all and give you grace to receive all the good in this, as in every other event, is intended you.

My brother joins me in great thanks for all your kindnesses, and especially on behalf of dear little comical Victor Drewe—our barber, as you know. When he cut my hair last week he spoke in the most charming way of his wife who has just been ill and (he said) 'She looks so pretty, Sir, so pretty, but terribly frail.' It made one want to laugh and cry at the same time—the lover's speech, and the queer little pot-bellied, grey-headed, unfathomably *respectable* figure. You don't misunderstand my wanting to laugh, do you? We shall, I hope, all enjoy one another's funniness openly in a better world.

TO WARFIELD M. FIROR, *who seems to have shared with Lewis three rules for the spiritual life: On the death of Mrs. Moore; on the difficulty of keeping rested; on obedience to God's plan for the day; and on the difficulty of maintaining stable "inner weather."*[7]

27 MARCH 1951

Your letter came to cheer a rather grim day. I have never known a spring like this: the sun has hardly appeared since last October and this morning a thin mixture of rain and snow is falling. My own household is lucky because we have *a* wood, and therefore *wood* (what a valuable idiom) for fires: there is hardly any coal in England. The worst of a wood fire—delightful to eye and nose—is that it demands continual attention. But this is a trifle: many people have to spend most of their leisure at the cinema because it is the only warm place. (I hardly ever go myself. Do you? It seems to me an astonishingly ugly art. I don't mean 'ugly'

[7] *Letters III,* 104–106.

in any high flying moral or spiritual sense, but just disagreeable to the eye—crowded, unrestful, inharmonious.)

There has been a great change in my life owing to the death of the old lady I called my mother. She died without apparent pain after many months of semi-conscious existence, and it would be hypocritical to pretend that it was a grief to us.

Of your three rules I heartily agree with the first and the third. The second ('keep rested' sounds at first as if our obedience to it must very often depend on many factors outside our control. I can think of some in whose ears it would sound like a cruel mockery. But I suspect that you have a reply. Do you mean that there is a kind of rest which 'no man taketh from us'[8] and which can be preserved even in the life of a soldier on active service or of a woman who works behind a counter all day and then goes home to work and mend and wash? And no doubt there is: but it doesn't always include rest for the legs.

'His plan for the day'—yes, that is all important. And I keep losing sight of it: in days of leisure and happiness perhaps even more than in what we call 'bad' days.

The whole difficulty with me is to keep control of the mind and I wish one's earliest education had given one more training in that. There seems to be a disproportion between the vastness of the soul in one respect (i.e., as a mass of ideas and emotions) and its smallness in another (i.e., as central, controlling ego). The whole inner weather changes so completely in less than a minute. Do you read George Herbert—

If what my soul doth feel sometimes
    My soul might always feel—

He's a good poet and one who helped to bring me back to the Faith.

My brother and all other ham-eating beneficiaries (should I call us Hamsters?) join me in good wishes. All blessings.

---

[8] John 16:22.

TO SHELDON VANAUKEN, *who had told Lewis he now believed in Christ: On learning to pray and choosing a denomination, while expecting a hellish counterattack.*[9]

17 APRIL 1951

My prayers are answered. No: a glimpse is not a vision. But to a man on a mountain road by night, a glimpse of the next three feet of road may matter more than a vision of the horizon. And there must perhaps always be just enough lack of demonstrative certainty to make free choice possible: for what could we do but accept if the faith were like the multiplication table?

There will be a counter attack on you, you know, so don't be too alarmed when it comes. The enemy will not see you vanish into God's company without an effort to reclaim you. Be busy learning to pray and (if you have made up your mind on the denominational question) get confirmed.

Blessings on you and a hundred thousand welcomes. Make use of me in any way you please: and let us pray for each other always.

TO MARY VAN DEUSEN, *who had mentioned her married daughter Genia's emotional distress and Chad Walsh's book,* C.S. Lewis: Apostle to the Skeptics: *On the relative ease in discerning right from wrong and the relative difficulty in discerning the better or best; and on Lewis's own domestic troubles. The "different trouble" is his brother's alcoholism.*[10]

18 APRIL 1951

Thanks for your letter of the 7th. I have just returned from a holiday and the time since has been spent in writing about 40 letters with my own hand: so much for Ivory Towers.

I also find your question very difficult in my own life. What is right we usually know, or it is our own fault if we don't: but what is prudent or sensible we often do not. Is it part of the scheme that we should ordinarily be left to make the best we can of our own

---

[9] *Letters III*, 106.
[10] *Letters III*, 107–108.

very limited and merely probable reasonings? I don't know. Or
would guidance even on these points be more largely given if we
had early enough acquired the regular habit of seeking it?

How terrible your anxiety about your daughter must have
been. She shall have her place in my prayers, such as they are.

Walsh didn't know much about my private life. Strictly between ourselves, I have lived most of it (that is now over) in a
house would was hardly ever at peace for 24 hours, amidst senseless wranglings, lyings, backbitings, follies, and *scares*. I never
went home without a feeling of terror as to what appalling situation might have developed in my absence. Only now that it is
over (though a different trouble has taken its place) do I begin to
realise quite how bad it was.

God bless you all.

TO MISS BRECKENRIDGE: *On forgiveness of ourselves; and on the mystics' commonsense disregard of mystical phenomena.*[11]

19 APRIL 1951

I think that if God forgives us we must forgive ourselves. Otherwise it is almost like setting up ourselves as a higher tribunal
than Him.

Many religious people, I'm told, have physical symptoms like
the 'prickles' in the shoulder. But the best mystics set no value on
that sort of thing, and do not set much on visions either. What
they seek and get is, I believe, a kind of direct experience of
God, immediate as a taste or colour. There is no *reasoning* in it,
but many would say that it is an experience of the intellect—the
reason resting in its enjoyment of its object.

TO MARY VAN DEUSEN: *On not burdening oneself with any unnecessary cares; on love of country; on ordering the natural loves; and on divine
love.*[12]

---

[11] *Letters III,* 109.
[12] *Letters III,* 118–119.

25 MAY 1951

About your idea that error in upbringing might be partly responsible for Genia's trouble, does any trained psychologist agree with you? From what I hear such people say I should very much doubt whether it could have had any 'depth' effect. Do not burden yourself with any *unnecessary* cares: I suspect you are not at all to blame. I pray for Genia every night.

About loving one's country, you raise two different questions. About one, about there seeming to be (now) no *reason* for loving it, I'm not at all bothered. As MacDonald says 'No one loves because he sees reason, but because he loves.'

Or say there are two kinds of love: we love wise and kind and beautiful people because we need them, but we love (or try to love) stupid and disagreeable people because they need us. This second kind is the more divine, because that is how God loves us: not because we are lovable but because He is love, not because He needs to receive but because He delights to give.

But the other question (*what* one is loving in loving a country) I do not find very difficult. What I feel sure of is that the personifications used by journalists and politicians have very little reality. A treaty between the governments of two countries is not at all like a friendship between two people: more like a transaction between two people's lawyers.

I think love for one's country means chiefly love for people who have a good deal in common with oneself (language, clothes, institutions) and is in that way like love of one's family or school: or like love (in a strange place) for anyone who once lived in one's home town. The familiar is in itself a ground for affection. And it is good: because any *natural* help towards our spiritual duty of loving is good and God seems to build our higher loves round our merely natural impulses—sex, maternity, kinship, old acquaintance, *et cetera*. And in a less degree there are similar grounds for loving other nations—historical links and debts for literature *et cetera* (hence we all reverence the ancient Greeks). But I would distinguish this from the talk in the papers. Mind you, I'm in considerable doubt about the whole thing. My mind tends to move in a world of individuals not of societies.

TO SISTER PENELOPE, *who had written him of her latest translation: On Lewis's state of ease; and on his realizing that he had never understood the real meaning of forgiveness (a realization that came to him on April 25th—see the letter below to Don Giovanni Calabria, 26 December 1951).*[13]

5 JUNE 1951

My love for George MacDonald has not extended to most of his poetry. I have naturally made several attempts to like it. Except for the *Diary of An Old Soul* it won't (so far as I'm concerned) do. . . .

I'm very glad to hear the work is 'roaring' . . . and I much look forward to seeing the results. As for me I specially need your prayers because I am (like the pilgrim in Bunyan) travelling across 'a plain called Ease'. Everything without, and many things within, are marvellously well at present. Indeed (I do not know whether to be more ashamed or joyful at confessing this) I realise that until about a month ago I never really believed (though I thought I did) in God's forgiveness. What an ass I have been both for not knowing and for thinking I knew. I do not feel that one must never say one believes or understands anything: any morning a doctrine I thought I already possessed may blossom into this new reality. . . . But pray for me always, as I do for you.

TO GENIA GOELZ, *the married daughter of Mary Van Deusen, who seems to have shared with Lewis some of her theological questions and her quandary about which denomination to join: On distinguishing the fact of the virgin birth of Jesus Christ from any scientific explanation of it; similarly, on the fact of the physical resurrection of Christ; and on what she should do while she is discerning her denominational choice—read the New Testament, pray for guidance, obey her conscience, seek God "with cheerful seriousness," and submit to the beginnings of her "treatment."*[14]

13 JUNE 1951

(1) I think you are confusing the Immaculate Conception with the Virgin Birth. The former is a doctrine peculiar to the Roman

---

[13] *Letters III*, 123–124.
[14] *Letters III*, 126–127.

Catholics and asserts that the mother of Jesus was born free of original sin. It does not concern us at all.

(2) The Virgin Birth is a doctrine plainly stated in the Apostle's Creed that Jesus had no physical father, and was not conceived as a result of sexual intercourse. It is not a doctrine on which there is any dispute between Presbyterians as such and Episcopalians as such. A few individual Modernists in both these churches have abandoned it; but Presbyterianism or Episcopalianism in general, and in actual historical instances, through the centuries both affirm it. The exact details of such a miracle—an exact point at which a supernatural force enters this world (whether by the creation of a new spermatazoon, or the fertilisation of an ovum without a spermatozoa, or the development of a foetus without an ovum) are not part of the doctrine. These are matters in which no one is obliged and everyone is free, to speculate. *Your* starting point about this doctrine will not, I think, be to collect the opinions of individual clergymen, but to read Matthew Chap. I and Luke I and II.

(3) Similarly, your question about the resurrection is answered in Luke XXIV. This makes it clear beyond any doubt that what is claimed is *physical* resurrection. (All Jews except Sadducees already believed in spiritual revival—there would have been nothing novel or exciting in that.)

(4) Thus the questions that you raise are not questions at issue between real Presbyterians and real Episcopalians at all for both these claim to agree with Scripture. Neither church, by the way, seems to be very intelligently represented by the people you have gone to for advice, which is bad luck. I find it very hard to advise in your choice. At any rate the programme, *until* you can make up your mind, is to read your New Testament (preferably a modern translation) intelligently. Pray for guidance, obey your conscience, in small as well as great matters, as strictly as you can.

(5) Don't bother much about your feelings. When they are humble, loving, brave, give thanks for them: when they are conceited, selfish, cowardly, ask to have them altered. In neither case are they *you,* but only a thing that happens to you. What matters is your intentions and your behaviour. (I hope all of this is not very dull and disappointing. Write freely again if I can be of any use to you.)

P. S. Of course God does not consider you hopeless. If He did He would not be moving you to seek Him (and He obviously is). What is going on in you at present is simply the beginning of the *treatment*. Continue seeking with cheerful seriousness. Unless He wanted you, you would not be wanting Him.

TO MARY VAN DEUSEN: *On God's providential arrangement of what appears to us to be coincidence; on accepting suffering and offering it to God on behalf of others; and on our membership with one another in the body of Christ (what Charles Williams called "co-inherence").* [15]

12 SEPTEMBER 1951

It is very remarkable (or would be if we did not know that God arranges things) that you should write about our vicarious sufferings when another correspondent has recently written on the same matter.

I have not a word to say against the doctrine that Our Lord suffers in all the sufferings of His people (see Acts IX.6) or that when we willingly accept what we suffer for others and offer it to God on their behalf, then it may be united with His sufferings and, in Him, may help to their redemption or even that of others whom we do not dream of. So that it is not in vain: though of course we must not count on seeing it work out exactly as we, in our present ignorance, might think best. The key text for this view is *Colossians* I.24. Is it not, after all, one more application of the truth that we are all 'members of one another'? [16] I wish I had known more when I wrote the *Problem of Pain*.

God bless you all. Be sure that Grace flows into you and out of you and through you in sorts of ways, and no faithful submission to pain in yourself or in another will be wasted.

TO DON GIOVANNI CALABRIA: *On our ability to love and think about and pray for one another across the divide of death. Lewis's word cogitationes should be translated as "thoughts," rather than "meditations."* [17]

---

[15] *Letters III*, 134–135.
[16] Romans 12:5.
[17] *Letters III*, 136–137.

13 SEPTEMBER 1951

I was moved with unaccustomed joy by your letter and all the more because I had heard you were ill; sometimes I feared lest you had perhaps died.

But never in the least did I cease from my prayers for you; for not even the River of Death ought to abolish the sweet intercourse of love and meditations.

Now I rejoice because I believe (although you keep silent about your health—do not condemn the body: *Brother Ass*, as St. Francis said!) I believe you are well or at least better.

I am sending you my tale [*Out of the Silent Planet*] recently translated into Italian in which, frankly, I have rather played than worked. I have given my imagination free rein yet not, I hope, without regard for edification—for building up both my neighbour and myself. I do not know whether you will like this kind of trifle. But if you do not, perhaps some boy or girl will like it from among your 'good children'.

For myself, after a long succession of minor illnesses (I do not know their Italian names) I am now better.

I salute the fiftieth anniversary of your priesthood with congratulations, prayers and blessings. Farewell. May we always pray for one another both in this world and in the world to come.

TO MRS. JESSUP, *who seems to have written Lewis about the difficulties of being in a marriage in which one of the spouses is a Christian and one is not: On the slow process of being remade and how difficult we must be to live with after conversion as before; and on not concealing but not flaunting our conversion.*[18]

15 OCTOBER 1951

I agree with everything you say (except that I should publish anything on the subject: a bachelor is not the man to do it—there is such an obvious answer to anything he says!).

Our regeneration is a slow process. As Charles Williams says there are three stages: (1.) The Old Self on the Old Way. (2.) The Old Self on the New Way. (3.) The New Self on the New Way.

---

[18] *Letters III*, 141–142.

After conversion the Old Self can of course be just as arrogant, importunate, and imperialistic about the Faith as it previously was about any other interest. I had almost said 'Any other Fad'—for just as the loveliest complexion turns green in a green light, so the Faith itself may have at first all the characteristics of a Fad and we may be as ill to live with as if we had taken up Nudism or Psychoanalysis or Pure Wool Clothing. You and I, clearly, both know all about that: one makes blunders.

About obedience, the principle is clear. Obedience to man is limited by obedience to God and, when they really conflict, must go. But of course that gives one very little guidance about particulars. The converted party must pray: I suppose it is not often necessary to pray *in the presence* of the other! Especially if the converted party is the woman, who usually has the house to herself all day. Of course there must be no *concealment,* in the sense that if the question comes up one must say frankly that one does pray. But there is a difference between not concealing and *flaunting.* For the rest (did I quote this before?) MacDonald says 'the time for *speaking* seldom arrives, the time for *being* never departs.' Let you and me pray for each other.

TO DON GIOVANNI CALABRIA: *On Lewis's great joy that he now believed in the forgiveness of sins with his whole heart; and on the danger of too much sadness over our sinfulness. The phrase Lewis uses, mistranslated "Lift up our hearts," in* Letters III, *is* Sursum corda, *the opening dialogue to the Preface of the Eucharistic Prayer in the liturgies of the Christian Church, dating back to the third century.*[19]

26 DECEMBER 1951

Thank you for the letter which I have received from you today and I invoke upon you all spiritual and temporal blessings in the Lord.

As for myself, during the past year a great joy has befallen me. Difficult though it is, I shall try to explain this in words. It is astonishing that sometimes we believe that we believe what, really, in our heart, we do not believe.

---

[19] *Letters III,* 151–152.

For a long time I believed that I believed in the forgiveness of sins. But suddenly (on St. Mark's day) this truth appeared in my mind in so clear a light that I perceived that never before (and that after many confessions and absolutions) had I believed it with my whole heart.

So great is the difference between mere affirmation by the intellect and that faith, fixed in the very marrow and as it were palpable, which the Apostle wrote was *substance*.[20]

Perhaps I was granted this deliverance in response to your intercessions on my behalf!

This emboldens me to say to you something that a layman ought scarcely to say to a priest nor a junior to a senior. (On the other hand, *out of the mouths of babes:*[21] indeed, as once to Balaam, out of the mouth of an ass!)[22] It is this: you write much about your own sins. Beware (permit me, my dearest Father, to say beware) lest humility should pass over into anxiety or sadness. It is bidden us to 'rejoice and always rejoice'.[23] Jesus has cancelled the hand-writing which was against us.[24] Lift up your hearts!

Permit me, I pray you, these stammerings. You are ever in my prayers and ever will be.

---

[20] Hebrews 11:1.

[21] Psalm 8:2; Matthew 21:16.

[22] Numbers 22:24–31.

[23] Philippians 4:4.

[24] Colossians 2:14–245.

1952

TO MARY VAN DEUSEN: *On feeling frightened that life is going too well; on suffering; on the danger in believing that any particular suffering is a punishment; on all pain as contrary to God's will; on the fate of unbelievers and our responsibility to them; and on the meaning of Christ's descent into hell.*[1]

31 JANUARY 1952

How singular! In the last year my life also became much 'better' and, just like you, I often feel a little frightened. We must both distinguish (a.) The bad Pagan feeling that the gods don't like us to be happy...(b.) The good Christian caution lest we become soft and self-indulgent and cease to recognise one's dependence on God.

That suffering is not *always* sent as a punishment is clearly established for believers by the book of Job and by John IX. 1–4. That it *sometimes* is, is suggested by parts of the Old Testament and Revelation. It would certainly be most dangerous to assume that any given pain was penal. I believe that all pain is contrary to God's will, absolutely but not relatively. When I am taking a thorn out of my finger (or a child's finger) the pain is 'absolutely' contrary to my will: i.e., if I could have chosen a situation without pain I would have done so. But I *do* will what caused pain, relatively to the given situation: i.e., granted the thorn I prefer the pain to leaving the thorn where it is. A mother smacking a child would be in the same position: she would rather cause it this pain than let it go on pulling the cat's tail, but she would like it better if no situation which demands a smack had arisen.

On the heathen, see I Tim. IV 10.[2] Also in Matt, XXV 31–46 the people don't sound as if they were believers. Also the doctrine of Christ's descending into Hell* and preaching to the dead: would that would be outside time, and include those who died

---

[1] *Letters III,* 162–163.
[2] I Timothy 4:10.

long after Him as well as those who died before He was born as Man. I don't think we know the details: we must just stick to the view that (a.) All justice and mercy will be done, (b) But that nevertheless it is our duty to do all we can to convert unbelievers. All blessings.

*I.e., Hades, the land of the dead: not Gehenna, the land of the lost.

TO GENIA GOELZ, *who had decided to be baptized an Episcopalian: On the joys and distresses of being an adult convert.*[3]

29 FEBRUARY 1952

Dear *Mrs.* Goelz (or may I, being old, and bold, and avuncular, say dear Genia?

I learn from *Mrs.* Van Deusen that you are 'taking the plunge'. As you have been now for so long in my prayers, I hope it will not seem intrusive to send my congratulations. Or I might say condolences and congratulations. For whatever people who have never undergone an adult conversion may say, it is a process not without its distresses. Indeed, they are the very sign that it is a true initiation. Like learning to swim or to skate, or getting married, or taking up a profession. There are cold shudderings about all these processes. When one finds oneself learning to fly *without* trouble one soon discovers (usually. There *are* blessed exceptions where we are allowed to take a real step without that difficulty), by waking up, that it was only a dream.

All blessings and good wishes.

TO MARY VAN DEUSEN: *On the blessing an uncongenial pastor can be.*[4]

29 FEBRUARY 1952

I have written to Genia. Your news is very good. In a way it is [a] good sign, isn't it?, that the Rector should *not* be a person she particularly likes. I will indeed continue my prayers for her. With love to all.

---

[3] *Letters III,* 169.
[4] *Letters III,* 169–170.

TO GENIA GOELZ, *who had asked Lewis for a prayer in her struggle to believe: Lewis's prayer for a daily increase in obedience and faith.*[5]

18 MARCH 1952

Don't bother at all about that question of a person being 'made a Christian' by baptism. It is only the usual trouble about words being used in more than one sense. Thus we might say a man 'became a soldier' the moment that he joined the army. But his instructors might say six months later 'I think we have made a soldier of him'. Both usages are quite definable, only one wants to know which is being used in a given sentence. The Bible itself gives us one short prayer which is suitable for all who are struggling with the beliefs and doctrines. It is: 'Lord I believe, help Thou my unbelief.'[6] Would something of this sort be any good?: Almighty God, who art the Father of lights and who has promised by thy dear Son that all who do thy will shall know thy doctrine:[7] give me grace so to live that by daily obedience I daily increase in faith and in the understanding of thy Holy Word, through Jesus Christ our Lord. Amen.

TO MARY VAN DEUSEN: *On the value of a fixed form of public worship; on the difficulty of extemporaneous public worship; and on the relationship between liturgical prayer and private prayer.*[8]

1 APRIL 1952

The advantage of a fixed form of service is that we know what is coming. *Extempore* public prayer has this difficulty: we don't know whether we can mentally join in it until we've heard it—it might be phoney or heretical. We are therefore called upon to carry on a *critical* and a *devotional* activity at the same moment: two things hardly compatible. In a fixed form we ought to have 'gone through the motions' before in our private prayers: the rigid form really sets our devotions *free*.

---

[5] *Letters III,* 172.
[6] Mark 9:24.
[7] John 7:17.
[8] *Letters III,* 177–178.

I also find the more rigid it is, the easier it is to keep one's thoughts from straying. Also it prevents any service getting too completely eaten up by whatever happens to be the preoccupation of the moment (a war, an election, or what not). The *permanent* shape of Christianity shows through. I don't see how the *extempore* method can help becoming provincial and I think it has a great tendency to direct attention to the minister rather than to God.

TO DON GIOVANNI CALABRIA: *On the death of his spiritual director, Father Adams; and on his prayer for Christian unity.*[9]

14 APRIL 1952

You were and are much in my prayers and thank you for your letters. And do you pray for me, especially at present when I feel very much an orphan because my aged confessor and most loving father in Christ has just died. While he was celebrating at the altar, suddenly, after a most sharp but (thanks be to God) very brief attack of pain, he expired; and his last words were, 'I come, Lord Jesus.' He was a man of ripe spiritual wisdom—noble minded but of an almost childlike simplicity and innocence. . . .

'That they all may be one'[10] is a petition which in my prayers I never omit. While the wished-for unity of doctrine and order is missing, all the more eagerly let us try to keep the bond of charity: which, alas, your people in Spain and ours in Northern Ireland do not.

Farewell, my Father.

TO "MRS. LOCKLEY," *who had asked if she could, as a Christian, divorce her adulterous husband: On divorce and remarriage; and on divorce as an act of charity toward the children of the adulterous relationship.*[11]

13 MAY 1952

In Bishop Gore's *The Sermon on the Mount* . . . I find the view that Christ forbade 'divorce in such a sense as allowed re-marriage'. The question is whether He made an exception by allowing divorce

---

[9] *Letters III,* 181–182.
[10] John 17:21.
[11] *Letters III,* 188–189.

in such a sense as allowed re-marriage when the divorce was for adultery. In the Eastern Church re-marriage of the innocent party is allowed: not in the Roman. The Anglican bishops at Lambeth in 1888 denied re-marriage to the guilty party, and added that 'there has always been a difference of opinion in the Church as to whether Our Lord meant to forbid re-marriage of the innocent party in a divorce'.

It would seem then that the only question is whether you can divorce your husband in such a sense as would make you free to re-marry. I imagine that nothing is further from your thoughts. I believe that you are free as a Christian woman to divorce him especially since the refusal to do so does harm to the innocent children of his mistress: but that you must (or should) regard yourself as no more free to marry another man than if you had not divorced him. But remember I'm no authority on such matters, and I hope you will ask the advice of one or two sensible clergymen of our own Church.

Our own Vicar whom I have just rung up, says that there *are* Anglican theologians who say that you must not divorce him. His own view was that in doubtful cases the Law of Charity should always be the over-riding consideration, and in a case such as yours charity directs you to divorce him.

TO GENIA GOELZ, *who had just been confirmed as an Episcopalian and who, in the first fervor of her conversion, had challenged Fred Hoyle, the Cambridge astronomer: On the need to expect that the first excitement of being a Christian will be replaced by the hard work of believing without the support of one's feelings; and on temptations to pride and the need to temper one's enthusiasms with discipline.*[12]

15 MAY 1952

Thanks for your letter of the 9th. All our prayers are being answered and I thank God for it. The only (possibly, not necessarily) unfavourable symptom is that you are just a trifle too excited. It is quite right that you should feel that 'something terrific' has happened to you (It has) and be 'all glowy'. Accept these sensations with thankfulness as birthday cards from God, but remember that

[12] *Letters III,* 191–192.

they are only greetings, not the real gift. I mean, it is not the sensations that are the real thing. The real thing is the gift of the Holy Spirit which can't usually be—perhaps not ever—experienced as a sensation or emotion. The sensations are merely the response of your nervous system. Don't depend on them. Otherwise when they go and you are once more emotionally flat (as you certainly will be quite soon), you might think that the real thing had gone too. But it won't. It will be there when you can't feel it. May even be most operative when you can feel it least.

Don't imagine it is all 'going to be an exciting adventure from now on'. It won't. Excitement, of whatever sort, never lasts. This is the push to start you off on your first bicycle: you'll be left to [do] lots of dogged *pedalling* later on. And no need to be depressed about it either. It will be good for your spiritual leg muscles. So enjoy the push while it lasts, but enjoy it as a treat, not as something normal.

Of course, none of us have 'any right' at the altar. You might as well talk of a non-existent person 'having a right' to be created. It is not *our* right but God's free bounty. An English peer said, 'I like the order of the Garter because it has no dam' nonsense about *merit*.' Nor has Grace. And we must keep on remembering that as a cure for Pride.

Yes, pride is a perpetual, nagging temptation. Keep on knocking it on the head but don't be too worried about it. As long as one knows one is proud one is safe from the worst form of pride.

If Hoyle answers your letter, then let the correspondence drop. He is not a great philosopher (and none of my scientific colleagues think much of him as a scientist), but he is strong enough to do some harm. You're not David and no one has told you to fight Goliath! You've only just enlisted. Don't go off challenging enemy champions. Learn your drill. I hope this doesn't sound all like cold water! I can't tell you how pleased I was with your letter.

TO BEDE GRIFFITHS: *On the workings of grace in the lives of those who are homosexual.*[13]

---

[13] *Letters III*, 195.

28 MAY 1952

The stories you tell about two [homosexuals] belong to a terribly familiar pattern: the man of good will, saddled with an abnormal desire which he never chose, fighting hard and time after time defeated. But I question whether in such a life the successful operation of Grace is so tiny as we think. Is not this continued avoidance either of presumption or despair, this ever renewed struggle, itself a great triumph of Grace? Perhaps more so than (to human eyes) equable virtue of some who are psychologically sound.

I am glad you think Jane Austen a sound moralist. I agree. And not platitudinous, but subtle as well as firm.

TO MARY VAN DEUSEN: *On psychiatry as a science and as a philosophy; on why strangers can be advisers when one's self and family members cannot; and on another dimension of vicariousness (Lewis was referring here to "The Practice of Substituted Love," a chapter in Charles Williams's* He Came Down from Heaven).[14]

10 JUNE 1952

I think psychiatry is like surgery: i.e., the thing is in itself essentially an infliction of wounds but may, in good hands, be necessary to avoid some greater evil. But it is more tricky than surgery because the personal philosophy and character of the operator come more into play. In setting a broken ankle all surgeons would agree as to the proper position to which the bones should be restored, because anatomy is an exact science. But all psychiatrists are not agreed as to the proper shape of the soul: where their ideas of that proper shape are based on a heathen or materialistic philosophy, they may be aiming at a shape *we* should strongly disapprove. One wants a Christian psychiatrist. There are a few of these, but nothing like enough.

If I can successfully say to Genia what you have often said in vain, that is not because of any quality in me but depends on a general (and at first sight cruel) law: we can *all* 'take' from a stranger what we can't 'take' from our own parents. I listen with profit to

---

[14] *Letters III,* 199–200.

elderly friends saying the very same things which I neglected or even resented when my father said them. Nay more: I can obey advice from others which I have often given myself in vain. I suppose this is one aspect of the *vicariousness* of the universe: Charles Williams's view that every one can help to paddle every one else's canoe better than his own. We must bear one another's burdens because that is the only way the burdens can get borne: and 'He saved others, himself He cannot save'[15] is a fundamental law.

Yes: 'things' continue almost alarmingly 'better' with me. God bless you all.

TO GENIA GOELZ: *On the reality of our individuality in the body of Christ; and on the five sources of discernment: the scripture, the church, Christian friends, books, and meditation.*[16]

20 JUNE 1952

Thanks for yours of the 10th. I would prefer to combat the 'I'm special' feeling not by the thought 'I'm no more special than anyone else' but by the feeling 'Everyone is as special as me.' In one way there is no difference, I grant, for both remove the speciality. But there is a difference in another way. The first might lead you to think, 'I'm only one of the crowd like anyone else'. But the second leads to the truth that there isn't any crowd. No one is like anyone else. All are 'members' (organs) in the Body of Christ.[17] All different and all necessary to the whole and to one another: each loved by God individually, as if it were the only creature in existence. Otherwise you might get the idea that God is like the government which can only deal with the people as the mass.

About confession, I take it that the view of our Church is that everyone may use it but none is obliged to. I don't doubt that the Holy Spirit guides your decisions from within when you make them with the intention of pleasing God. The error would be to think that He speaks *only* within whereas, in reality, He speaks also through Scripture, the Church, Christian friends, books *et cetera*.

---

[15] Mark 15:31.
[16] *Letters III,* 204–205.
[17] I Corinthians 12:27.

TO RHONA BODLE: *On the magnificence of her work with deaf children.*[18]

22 JUNE 1952

It was a great joy to hear from you again. You have been daily in my prayers for a long time and, needless to say, will remain. I shall be grateful for a place in yours.

The work you are engaged in is a magnificent one (much in my mind because, as it falls out, I've just been reading Helen Keller's book): hard, no doubt, but you can never be attacked by the suspicion that it is not worth doing. There are jolly few professions of which we can say that. The translation of great stories into a limited vocabulary will, incidentally, be a wonderful discipline: you will learn a lot about thought and language in general before you are done. I hope you will sometimes let me know how you get on. God bless you.

TO MARY VAN DEUSEN, *who seems to have mentioned a commendation from a Kemper Hall concerning acceptable rituals and devotions that another person, P. A. Wolfe, has criticized strongly: On the use of incense and the praying of the Hail Mary; and on how to deal with difficult people. Lewis's "new trouble" is his brother's alcoholism.*[19]

26 JUNE 1952

Incense and Hail Marys are in quite different categories. The one is merely a question of ritual: some find it helpful and others don't, and each must put up with its absence or presence in the church they are attending with cheerful and charitable humility.

But Hail Marys raise a *doctrinal* question: whether it is lawful to address devotions to any *creature*, however holy. My own view would be that a *salute* to any saint (or angel) cannot in itself be wrong any more than taking off one's hat to a friend: but that there is always some danger lest such practices start one on the road to a state (sometimes found in Roman Catholics) where the Blessed Virgin Mary is treated really as a deity and even becomes the centre of the religion. I therefore think that such salutes are better avoided. And if the Blessed Virgin is as good as the best

---

[18] *Letters III,* 207.
[19] *Letters III,* 209–210.

mothers I have known, she does not *want* any of the attention which might have gone to her Son diverted to herself.

It seems, nevertheless, quite clear that the Spirit of God is, or is more strongly with Kemper Hall than with P. A. Wolfe. In him you describe a type I know. I think we may accept it as a rule that whenever a person's religious conversation dwells chiefly, or even frequently, on the faults of other people's religions, he is in a bad condition. The fact that he shakes your faith is significant. Pray *for* him but not, I should say, *with* him. If he insists on talking religion to you ask him for positive things: ask him to tell you what he knows of God.

All blessings. My 'new trouble' is still there: but I have much to be thankful for.

TO MISS REIDY, *who had misunderstood the point of Lewis's poem, "The Pilgrim's Problem": On blaming the map for our being lost.*[20]

28 JUNE 1952

The point was that as foolish people on a walk, when by their own errors they are off the course, think the map was wrong, so, when we do not find in ourselves the fruits of the Spirit which all our teachers promise, it is not that the promise was false, but that we have failed to use the Grace we have been given. The 'map' can be found in almost any Christian teaching.

TO DON GIOVANNI CALABRIA: *On hope and joy even in evil times; and on love and tending to our work while we await the return of the Lord.*[21]

14 JULY 1952

Thank you, dearest Father, both for the tracts of your Congregation and for your letter dated July 7th.

The times we live in are, as you say, grave: whether 'graver than all others in history' I do not know. But the evil that is closest always seems to be the most serious: for as with the eye so with the heart, it is a matter of one's own perspective. However, if our times are indeed the worst, if That Day is indeed now ap-

---

[20] *Letters III,* 210. For the poem, see *Collected Poems* (London: HarperCollins, 1994).
[21] *Letters III,* 213–214.

proaching, what remains but that we should rejoice because our redemption is now nearer and say with St. John: 'Amen; come quickly, Lord Jesus.'[22]

Meanwhile our only security is that The Day may find us working each one in his own station[23] and especially (giving up dissensions) fulfilling that supreme command that we love one another.[24]

Let us ever pray for each other.

Farewell: and may there abide with you and me that peace which no one can take from us.[25]

TO MARY VAN DEUSEN: *On changing one's style of prayer; on continuing an old friendship with someone who does not share one's spiritual values; and on the freedom of the will and predestination.*[26]

14 JULY 1952

I think you are perfectly right to change your manner of prayer from time to time and I should suppose that all who pray seriously do thus change it. One's needs and capacities change and also, for creatures like us, excellent prayers may 'go dead' if we use them too long. Whether one should use written prayers composed by other people, or one's own words or own wordless prayer, or in what proportion one should mix all three, seems to me entirely a question for each individual to answer from his own experience.

I myself find prayers without words the best, *when* I can manage it, but I can do so only when least distracted and in best spiritual and bodily health (or what I think *best*). But another person might find it quite otherwise.

Your question about old friendships where there is no longer spiritual communion is a hard one. Obviously it depends very much on what the other party wants. The great thing in friendship as in all other forms of love is, as you know, to turn from the demand to *be* loved (or helped or answered) to the wish to love (or help or answer). Perhaps in so far as one does this one also discov-

---

[22] Revelation 22:20.
[23] Luke 12:35–38.
[24] John 13:34.
[25] John 16:22.
[26] *Letters III*, 237–238.

ers how much love one should spend on the sort of friends you mention. I don't think a decay in one's desire for mere 'society' or 'acquaintance' or 'the crowd' is a bad sign. (We mustn't take it as a sign of one's increasing spirituality of course: isn't it merely a natural, neutral, development as one grows older?)

All that Calvinist question—Free-Will and Predestination, is to my mind undiscussable, insoluble. Of course (say us) if a man repents God will accept him. Ah yes, (say they) but the fact of his repenting shows that God has already moved him to do so. This at any rate leaves us with the fact that in *any concrete case* the question never arrives as a practical one. But I suspect it is really a *meaningless* question. The difference between Freedom and Necessity is fairly clear on the bodily level: we know the difference between making our teeth chatter on purpose and just finding them chattering with cold. It begins to be less clear when we talk of human love (leaving out the erotic kind). 'Do I like him because I choose or because I must?'—there are cases where this has an answer, but others where it seems to me to mean nothing. When we carry it up to relations between God and Man, has the distinction perhaps become nonsensical? After all, when we are most free, it is only with a freedom God has given us: and when our will is most influenced by Grace, it is still *our will*. And if what *our will* does is not 'voluntary', and if 'voluntary' does not mean 'free', what are we talking about? I'd leave it all alone. Blessings.

TO MRS. JOHNSON, *who had asked Lewis thirteen questions: On the nature of purgatory; on the efficacy of the prayers to false gods or to a poorly conceived God; on the salvation of unbelievers (Lewis had finished the story of Emeth in* The Last Battle *the previous March); on how to read the Bible; on the commandment not to murder; on capital punishment; on revenge; on pacifism; on the presence in heaven of our earthly beloved; and on the story of his barber.*[27]

8 NOVEMBER 1952

I am returning your letter with the questions in it numbered so that you'll know which I am answering.

---

[27] *Letters III*, 245–248.

(1.)[28] Some call me *Mr.* and some *Dr.* and I not only don't care but usually don't know which.

(2.)[29] Distinguish (A) A second chance in the strict sense, i.e., a new earthly life in which you could attempt afresh all the problems you failed at in the present one (as in religions of Re-Incarnation). (B) Purgatory: a process by which the work of redemption continues, and first perhaps begins to be noticeable after death. I think Charles Williams depicts B, not A.

(3.)[30] We are never given any knowledge of 'What would have happened if...'

(4.)[31] I think that every prayer which is sincerely made even to a false god or to a very imperfectly conceived true God, is accepted by the true God and that Christ saves many who do not think they know Him. For He is (dimly) present in the *good* side of the inferior teachers they follow. In the parable of the Sheep and Goats (Matt. XXV 31 and following) those who are saved do not seem to know that they have served Christ. But of course our anxiety about unbelievers is most usefully employed when it leads us not to speculation but to earnest prayer for them and the attempt to be in our own lives such good advertisements for Christianity as will make it attractive.

(5.)[32] It is Christ Himself, not the Bible, who is the true word of God. The Bible, read in the right spirit and with the guidance of good teachers will bring us to Him. When it becomes really necessary (i.e., for our spiritual life, not for controversy or curiosity) to know whether a particular passage is rightly translated or is Myth (but of course Myth specially chosen by God from among countless Myths to carry a spiritual truth) or history, we shall no doubt be guided to the right answer. But we must not use the Bible (our fathers too often did) as a sort of Encyclopedia out of which texts (isolated from their context and not read without

[28] Her question: "What is your correct title?" (Her list of questions is in the Wade Center.)
[29] Her question: "Do people get another chance after death? I refer to Charles Williams."
[30] Her question: "What would happen if I had died an atheist?"
[31] Her question: "What happens to Jews who are still waiting for the Messiah?"
[32] Her question: "Is the Bible infallible?"

188 • YOURS, JACK

attention to the whole nature and purport of the books in which they occur) can be taken for use as weapons.

(6.) *Kill* means *murder*. I don't know Hebrew: but when Our Lord quotes this commandment he uses Gk *phoneuseis* (murder)[33] not *apoktenein* (kill).[34]

[(7.)][35] The question of what you would 'want' is off the point. Capital punishment might be wrong though the relations of the murdered man wanted him killed: it might be right though they did not want this. The question is whether a Christian nation ought or ought not to put murderers to death: not what passions interested individuals may feel.

(8.)[36] There is no doubt at all that the natural impulse to 'hit back' must be fought against by the Christian whenever it arises. If one I love is tortured or murdered my desire to avenge him must be given no quarter. So far as nothing but this question of retaliation comes in 'turn the other cheek' *is* the Christian law. It is, however, quite another matter when the neutral, public authority (*not* the aggrieved person) may order killing of either private murderers or public enemies in mass. It is quite clear that our earliest Christian writer, St. Paul, approved of capital punishment—he says the 'magistrate' bears and should bear 'the sword'.[37] It is recorded that the soldiers who came to St. John Baptist asking, 'What shall we do?'[38] were *not* told to leave the army. When Our Lord Himself praised the Centurion[39] He never hinted that the military profession was in itself sinful. This has been the general view of Christendom. Pacifism is a very recent and local variation. We must of course respect and tolerate Pacifists, but I think their view erroneous.

---

[33] Πονεύσειζ as in Matthew 19:18.
[34] Αποκτειναι as in John 8:37.
[35] Her question: "If a thief killed Eileen would I be wrong to want him to die?"
[36] Her question: "Is killing in self defense all right?"
[37] Romans 13:4.
[38] Luke 3:14.
[39] Matthew 8:10.

(9.)[40] The symbols under which Heaven is presented to us are
(a) a dinner party,[41] (b) a wedding,[42] (c) a city,[43] and (d) a concert.[44]
It would be grotesque to suppose that the guests or citizens or
members of the choir didn't know one another. And how can love
of one another be commanded in this life if it is to be cut short
at death?

(10.)[45] Whatever the answer is, I'm sure it is not that ('erased
from the brain'). When I have learnt to love God better than my
earthly dearest, I shall love my earthly dearest better than I do
now. In so far as I learn to love my earthly dearest at the expense
of God and *instead* of God, I shall be moving towards the state in
which I shall not love my earthly dearest at all. When first things
are put first, second things are not suppressed but increased. If
you and I ever come to love God perfectly, the answer to this
tormenting question will then become clear, and will be far more
beautiful than we could ever imagine. We can't have it now.

(11.)[46] Thanks very much: but I haven't a sweet tooth.

(12.)[47] Not that I know of: but I'm the last person who would
know.

(13.)[48] There is a poor barber whom my brother and I sometimes help. I got up one day intending to go to him for a hair-cut
preparatory to going to London. Got a message putting off London engagement and decided to postpone hair-cut. Something,
however, kept on nagging me to stick to it—'Get your hair cut.'
In the end, said 'Oh damn it, I'll go.'

---

[40] Her question: "Will we recognise our loved ones in Heaven?"
[41] Matthew 22:4.
[42] Matthew 22:2–12; Luke 12:36.
[43] Hebrews 11:16; 12:22.
[44] Revelation 5:8–14.
[45] Her question: "If Wayne didn't go to Heaven I wouldn't want to either.
Would his name be erased from my brain?"
[46] Her question: "Do you like sweets?"
[47] Her question: "Are you handsome?"
[48] Her request: "Tell me the story about the barber." See the letter above to Vera
Mathews, 27 March 1951.

TO MARY WILLIS SHELBURNE, *who had become a Roman Catholic: On the closeness in the body of Christ of those who are at the heart of their own denomination; on how close we are to real believers in any religion rather than to the modernists within them; and on prayer as the most reliable work we can do for Christian reunion.*[49]

10 NOVEMBER 1952

It is a little difficult to explain how I feel that though you have taken a way which is not for me I nevertheless can congratulate you—I suppose because your faith and joy are so obviously increased. Naturally, I do not draw from that the same conclusions as you—but there is no need for us to start a controversial correspondence!

I believe we are very near to one another, but not because I am at all on the Rome-ward frontier of my own communion. I believe that, in the present divided state of Christendom, those who are at the heart of each division are all closer to one another than those who are at the fringes. I would even carry this beyond the borders of Christianity: how much more one has in common with a *real* Jew or Muslim than with a wretched liberalising, occidentalised specimen of the same categories.

Let us by all means pray for one another: it is perhaps the only form of 'work for re-union' which never does anything but good. God bless you.

TO MRS. D. JESSUP, *who had written Lewis about her domestic crisis: On the need to persevere through spiritual aridity and even desolation as a normal experience, even for Jesus, while not rejecting consolation when God gives it; and on Lewis's lack of interest in public affairs.*[50]

13 NOVEMBER 1952

Yes, of course I will—for all six of you. I am very sorry to hear that your (temporal) news is so grim. Your spiritual news is perhaps better than you think. You seem to have been dealing with the dryness (or 'the wall' as you well name it) in the right way. Everyone has experienced it or will.

---

[49] *Letters III*, 248–249.
[50] *Letters III*, 251–252.

It is clearly what George MacDonald meant when he said 'Have pity on us for the *look of things,* When desolation stares us in the face. Although *the serpent-mask have lied before,* It fascinates the bird.'

It is very important to remember that Our Lord experienced it to the full, twice—in Gethsemane when He sweated blood, and next day when he said 'Why hast thou forsaken me?'[51] We are not asked to go anywhere where he has not gone before us. The *shining* quality may come back when we least expect it, and in circumstances which would seem to an outside observer (or to ourselves) to make it most impossible. (We must not reject it, as there is an impulse to do, on the ground that we *ought,* in the conditions, to be miserable.)

What is most re-assuring to me, and most moving, is your sane and charitable recognition that others have as great, or worse, trials: one of those things which no one else can decently say to the sufferer but which are invaluable when he says them to himself. And of course there was no 'conceit' or 'selfishness' in your writing to me: are we not all 'members of one another'?[52] (I can't reply about Eisenhower. I am no politician. I should suppose that the diverse views of his election taken in England depend entirely on the different ways in which our own political parties think they can make capital out of it. As you know public affairs seem to me much less important than private—in fact important only in so far as they affect private affairs.)

You are quite right (though not in the way you meant) when you say I needn't 'work up' sympathy with you! No, I needn't. I have had enough experiences of the crises of family life, the terrors, despondencies, hopes deferred, and wearinesses. The trouble is that things go on *so long,* isn't it? And one gets so tired of trying! No doubt it will all seem short when looked at from eternity. But I needn't preach to you. You're doing well: scoring pretty good marks! Keep on. Take it hour by hour. Don't add the past and the future to the present load more than you can help. God bless you all.

---

[51] Matthew 27:46; Mark 15:34.
[52] Romans 12:5.

TO MRS. D. JESSUP: *On the necessity to thank God when God answers prayers; and on remembering the times when God answers prayers.*[53]

17 NOVEMBER 1952

Thanks be to God for your good news. There is a comic, but also charming, contrast between the temperance with which you bore a great fear and the wild excess of your apologies for a wholly imaginary offence in writing that letter. You did perfectly right and there is nothing whatever for me to forgive. And I should be very sorry if you carried out your threat (made, I know, from the best motives) of never writing to me again. *You* are not the kind of correspondent who is a 'nuisance': if you were you would not be now thinking you *are* one—That kind never does.

But don't send me any newspaper cuttings. I never believe a word said in the papers. The real history of a period (as we always discover a few years later) has very little to do with all that, and private people like you and me are never allowed to know it while it is going on. Of course you will all remain in my prayers. I think it very wrong to pray for people while they are in distress and then not to continue praying, now with thanksgiving, when they are relieved.

Many people think their prayers are never answered because it is the answered ones that they forget. Like the others who find proof for a superstition by recording all the cases in which bad luck has followed a dinner with 13 at table and forget all the others where it hasn't. God bless you. Write freely whenever you please.

TO MARY VAN DEUSEN: *On the difference between wordless prayer and the practice of the presence of God (the spirituality of the seventeenth century Carmelite, Brother Lawrence of the Resurrection); on loving others too much; and on what time of day to pray.*[54]

25 NOVEMBER 1952

No, by wordless prayer I didn't mean the practice of the Presence of God. I meant the same mental act as in verbal prayer

---

[53] *Letters III*, 251–252.
[54] *Letters III*, 253.

only without the words. The Practice of the Presence is a much higher activity. I don't think it matters much whether an absolutely uninterrupted recollection of God's presence for a whole lifetime is possible or not. A much more frequent and prolonged recollection than we have yet reached certainly *is* possible. Isn't that enough to work on? A child learning to walk doesn't need to know whether it will ever be able to walk 40 miles in a day: the important thing is that it *can* walk to-morrow a little further and more steadily than it did to-day.

I don't think we are likely to give *too much* love and care to those we love. We might put in active care in the form of assistance when it would be better for them to act on their own: i.e., we might be busybodies. Or we might have too much 'care' for them in the sense of *anxiety*. But we never love anyone too much: the trouble is always that we love God, or perhaps some other *created* being, too little.

As to the 'state of the world' if we have time to hope and fear about it, we certainly have time to pray. I agree it *is* very hard to keep one's eyes on God amid all the daily claims and problems. I think it wise, if possible, to move one's main prayers from the last-thing-at-night position to some earlier time: give them a better chance to infiltrate one's other thoughts.

TO PHYLLIS ELINOR SANDEMAN, *who had sent Lewis a copy of her book,* Treasure on Earth: A Country House at Christmas. *Page 83 tells the story of how she, as an unhappy little girl, takes refuge in a dark gallery: "But almost at once, breaking in upon her grief with a gentle but increasing pressure, she seemed to detect a sympathy in the surrounding atmosphere as if unseen presences thronging about her were offering their love and consolation."*[55]

10 DECEMBER 1952

I have read *Treasure on Earth* and I don't believe you have any notion how good it is. You have done a most difficult thing.... I've never seen the hushed internal excitement of a child on Christmas Eve better done. That is something we can all recognise. . . .

---

[55] *Letters III,* 261–263.

The only page that I can't enter into at all is p. 83. I can't conceive not being afraid, as a child, of those unseen presences. I should have behaved like little Jane Eyre in the Red Room when she dried her tears for fear a ghostly voice should awake to comfort her. One would rather be scolded by a mortal than comforted by a ghost.

You will notice when you re-read your book in a different mood that it doesn't really give the impression of a very happy childhood. Ecstatic, yes: shot through with raptures and tingling delights, but not very secure, not very consoled. And that, I believe, is absolutely true: I fancy *happy* childhoods are usually forgotten. It is not settled comfort and heartsease but momentary joy that transfigures the past and lets the eternal quality show through. (I sometimes eat parsnips because their taste, which I dislike, reminds me of my prep-school, which I disliked: but those two dislikes don't in the least impair the strange job of 'being reminded'.)

One could go on meditating on these things indefinitely—Very many thanks for the book: it is that rare thing (rare at our age) a present one really likes. The illustrations are good too, as much of them as the coarse printing and paper has not murdered, but don't believe anyone who says you draw better than you write. The reverse is true. With much gratitude and all good wishes.

1953

TO DON GIOVANNI CALABRIA: *On the need for a book on prayer for beginners.*[1]

I invite your prayers about a work which I now have in hand. I am trying to write a book about private prayers for the use of the laity, especially for those who have been recently converted to the Christian faith and so far are without any sustained and regular habit of prayer. I tackled the job because I saw many no doubt very beautiful books written on this subject of prayer for the religious but few which instruct tyros and those still babes (so to say) in the Faith. I find many difficulties nor do I definitely know whether God wishes me to complete this task or not.

Pray for me, my Father, that I neither persist, through overboldness, in what is not permitted to me nor withdraw, through too great timidity, from due effort: for he who touches the Ark without authorization[2] and he who, having once put his hand to the plough, draws it back are both lost.[3]

Both you and your Congregation are in my daily prayers. While we are in the Way, this is our only intercourse: be it granted to us, I pray, hereafter, to meet in our True Country face to face.

TO DON GIOVANNI CALABRIA: *On Lewis's "problem with petitionary prayer" (see the letter above to his brother, 3 March 1940).*[4]

14 JANUARY 1953

I send you many heartfelt thanks for your charity in being willing to meditate on my proposed little book and pray for it. I take your opinion as a good sign.

---

[1] *Letters III*, 275–276.
[2] I Chronicles 13:9–10.
[3] Luke 9:62.
[4] *Letters III*, 279–281.

And now, my dearest friend, hear what difficulty leaves me in most doubt. Two models of prayer seem to be put before us in the New Testament which are not easy to reconcile with each other.

One is the actual prayer of the Lord in the Garden of Gethsemane ('if it be possible[5] . . . nevertheless, not as I will but as Thou wilt').[6]

The other, though, is in Mark XI 24. 'Whatsoever you ask believing that you shall receive you shall obtain' (and observe that in the place where the version has, in Latin, *accipietis*—and our vernacular translation, similarly, has the *future* tense, 'shall receive'—the Greek text has the *past* tense ἐλάβετε = *accepistis*—which is very difficult).

Now the question: How is it possible for a man, at one and the same moment of time, *both* to believe most fully that he *will* receive *and* to submit himself to the Will of God—Who perhaps is refusing him?

How is it possible to say, simultaneously, 'I firmly believe that Thou wilt give me this', *and,* 'If Thou shalt deny me it, Thy will be done'? How can one mental act both exclude possible refusal and consider it? I find this discussed by none of the Doctors.

Please note: it creates no difficulty for me that God sometimes does not will to do what the faithful request. This is necessary because He is wise and we are foolish: but why in Mark XI 24, does He promise to do everything (whatsoever) we ask in full faith? Both statements are the Lord's; both are among what we are required to believe. What should I do?

TO MARY VAN DEUSEN, *who had asked Lewis to advise her about becoming a member of the Associates of Holy Cross, the lay group attached to the Order of the Holy Cross, a Benedictine Anglican monastic order: On not joining a group unless God clearly inspires such as the only or best way to do or receive good; and on the optional but helpful practice of private confession of sins to a priest.*[7]

---

[5] Matthew 26:39; Mark 14:35.
[6] Luke 22:42
[7] *Letters III,* 285–286.

26 JANUARY 1953

Thank you for your letter of the 17th and the wholly delightful photographs. I am glad things are still Fine. I've never thought of becoming an Associate of anything myself and feel difficulty about advising. You mention externals—what Associates have to do and that they have asked you to become one—but say nothing about the motives in your own mind either for or against it. They are the real point, aren't they? I don't think one ought to join an Order, however much one might like it or however nice the people who have asked you—unless one thinks that God especially presses one to do so as the only, or the best, way of doing some good to others or receiving some good oneself. And if one does think that, then I suppose one must join however much one disliked it and however nasty the particular inviters were! It is not as if it were a club! Why not try living according to their Rule for a bit *without* joining them and seeing what it is like for a person such as you in circumstances such as yours?

Confession, of course, you can have without joining anything. I think it is a good thing for most of us and use it myself.

That is very good news about really good people beginning to go into government jobs, and at a sacrifice. I have always thought of how that the greatest of all dangers to your country is the fear that politics were not in the hands of your best types and that this, in the long run, might prove ruinous. A change in that, the beginning of what might be called a *volunteer* aristocracy, might have incalculable effects. More power to your myriad elbows!

TO RHONA BODLE: *On the need to read/present the Gospels with some commentary/teaching; and on learning/teaching how to love people one doesn't like.*[8]

9 FEBRUARY 1953

Thanks for your interesting letter of February 1st which arrived to-day. It is difficult to one, who, like me, has no experience, to give an opinion of these problems, which, I see, are very intricate. The story about the girl who had reached the age of 16 under Christian

---

[8] *Letters III*, 291–292.

teachers without hearing of the Incarnation is an eye-opener. For ordinary children (I don't know about the Deaf) I don't see any advantage in presenting the Gospels without some doctrinal comment. After all, they weren't written for people who did not know the doctrine, but for converts, already instructed, who now wanted to know a bit more about the life and saying of the Master. No ancient sacred books were intended to be read without a teacher: hence the Ethiopian comment in the Acts says to St. Philip, 'How *can* I understand unless someone tells me?'[9]

Could the bit—and I think there must be *something*—about people I don't like come in as a comment on the *Forgive* clause in the Lord's Prayer?[10]

TO DON GIOVANNI CALABRIA: *On the way a good Christian friendship transcends so many differences and reveals how all human beings are related in the old Adam and the new Adam; on Lewis's daily prayer for Christian unity; on the difference between "Post-Christian man" and "pre-Christian man"; and on Lewis's continuing question about petitionary prayer (see the letter above to Don Giovanni Calabria, 14 January 1953).*[11]

17 MARCH 1953

I was delighted, as always, by your letter.

It is a wonderful thing and a strengthening of faith that two souls differing from each other in place, nationality, language, obedience and age should have been thus led into a delightful friendship; so far does the order of spiritual beings transcend the material order.

It makes easier that necessary doctrine that we are most closely joined together alike with the sinner Adam and with the Just One, Jesus, even though as to body, time and place we have lived so differently from both. This unity of the whole human race exists: would that there existed that nobler union of which you write. No day do I let pass without my praying for that longed-for consummation.

---

9 Acts 8:31.
10 Matthew 6:12.
11 *Letters III*, 305–306.

What you say about the present state of mankind is true: indeed, it is even worse than you say.

For they neglect not only the law of Christ but even the Law of Nature as known by the Pagans.[12] For now they do not blush at adultery, treachery, perjury, theft and the other crimes which I will not say Christian Doctors, but the Pagans and the Barbarians have themselves denounced.

They err who say 'the world is turning pagan again'. Would that it were! The truth is that we are falling into a much worse state.

'Post-Christian man' is not the same as 'pre-Christian man'. He is as far removed as virgin is from widow: there is nothing in common except want of a spouse: but there is a great difference between a spouse-to-come and a spouse lost.

I am still working on my book on Prayer.

About this question which I submitted to you, I am asking all theologians: so far in vain.

Let us ever pray for each other, my Father.

TO VERA GEBBERT, *who had told Lewis of her pregnancy and of her having read Isaiah 66:9 from the Bible she kept open on her dining table: On not wishing to be pregnant.*[13]

23 MARCH 1953

Your first story (about mistaking [your pregnancy] for sea-sickness) is one of the funniest I ever heard. In our country there are usually alterations of shape which would throw grave doubts on the sea-sick hypothesis! . . . but no doubt you manage things better in America. Any way, congratulations and encouragements. As to wishing it had not happened, one can't help momentary wishes: guilt begins only when one embraces them. You can't help their knocking at the door, but one mustn't ask them in to lunch. And no doubt you have many feelings on the other side. I am sure you felt as I did when I heard my first bullet, 'This is War: this is what Homer wrote about.' For, all said and done, a woman who has never had a baby and a man who has never

---

[12] Romans 2:14–15.
[13] *Letters III,* 310–312.

been either in a battle or a storm at sea, are, in a sense, rather *outside*—haven't really 'seen life'—haven't *served*. We will indeed have you in our prayers.

Now as to your other story, about Isaiah 66? It doesn't really matter whether the Bible was open at that page thru' a miracle or through some (unobserved) natural cause. We think it matters because we tend to call the second alternative 'chance.' But when you come to think of it, there can be no such thing as chance from God's point of view. Since He is omniscient His acts have no consequences which He has not foreseen and taken into account and intended. Suppose it was the draught from the window that blew your Bible open at Isaiah 66. Well, that current of air was linked up with the whole history of weather from the beginning of the world and you may be quite sure that the result it had for you at that moment (like all its other results) was intended and allowed for in the act of creation. 'Not one sparrow,'[14] you know the rest. So *of course* the message was addressed to you. To suggest that your eye fell on it *without* this intention, is to suggest that you could take Him by surprise. Fiddle-de-dee! This is not Predestination: your will is perfectly free: but all physical events are adapted to fit in as God sees best with the free actions He knows we are going to do. There's something about this in *Screwtape*.[15]

Meanwhile, *courage*! Your moments of nervousness are not your real self, only medical phenomena. All blessings.

TO CORBIN SCOTT CARNELL, *who had asked for further explanation of the first note Lewis had written in* Miracles, *Chapter 15, about the historicity of various books of the Bible: On the kinds of inspired literature in the Bible.*[16]

5 APRIL 1953

I am myself a little uneasy about the question you raise: there seems to be almost equal objection to the position taken up in my footnote and to the alternative of attributing the same kind and degree of historicity to all the books of the Bible. You see, the

---

[14] Matthew 10:29.
[15] *The Screwtape Letters* (San Francisco: HarperOne, 2001), Letter 27.
[16] *Letters III*, 318–319.

question about Jonah and the great fish does not turn simply on intrinsic probability. The point is that the whole *Book of Jonah* has to me the air of being a moral romance, a quite different *kind* of thing from, say, the account of King David or the New Testament narratives, not *pegged,* like them, into any historical situation.

In what sense does the Bible 'present' this story 'as historical'? Of course it doesn't *say* 'This is fiction': but then neither does Our Lord *say* that His Unjust Judge, Good Samaritan, or Prodigal Son are fiction. (I would put *Esther* in the same category as Jonah for the same reason.) How does a denial, or doubt, of their historicity lead logically to a similar denial of New Testament miracles?

Supposing (as I think is the case) that sound critical reading reveals different *kinds* of narrative in the Bible, surely it would be illogical to conclude that these different kinds should all be read in the same way? This is not a 'rationalistic approach' to miracles. Where I doubt the historicity of an Old Testament narrative I never do so on the ground that the miraculous *as such* is incredible. Nor does it deny 'a unique sort of inspiration': allegory, parable, romance, and lyric might be inspired as well as chronicle. I wish I would direct you to a good book on the subject, but I don't know one. With all good wishes.

TO MARY VAN DEUSEN: *On the confession of sins to a priest—its optionality and its usefulness in feeling forgiven and in growing in self-knowledge.*[17]

6 APRIL 1953

I think our official view of confession can be seen in the form for the Visitation of the Sick where it says 'Then shall the sick person be moved (i.e., advised, prompted) to make a ... Confession ... if he feel his conscience troubled with any weighty matter.' That is, where Rome makes Confession compulsory for all, we make it permissible for any: not 'generally necessary' but profitable. We do not doubt that there can be forgiveness without it. But, as your own experience shows, many people do not *feel* forgiven, i.e., do not effectively 'believe in the forgiveness of sins', without it. The quite enormous advantage of coming really to

---

[17] *Letters III,* 320.

believe in forgiveness is well worth the horrors (I agree, they *are* horrors) of a first confession.

Also, there is the gain in self-knowledge: most of [us] have never really faced the facts about ourselves until we uttered them aloud in plain words, calling a spade a spade. I certainly feel I have profited enormously by the practice. At the same time I think we are quite right not to make it generally obligatory, which would force it on some who are not ready for it and might do harm.

As for conduct of services, surely a wide latitude is reasonable. Has not each kind—the very 'low' and the very 'high'—its own value?

I don't think I owe Genia a letter, and I think advice is best kept till it is asked for. Of course she, and you, are always in my prayers. I think she is of the impulsive type, but one must beware of meddling.

TO MARY VAN DEUSEN: *More on the question of her joining a religious order (see the letter above to Mary Van Deusen, 26 January 1953); and on discerning when, whom, and how to evangelize.*[18]

7 APRIL 1953

I don't think gratitude is a relevant motive for joining an Order. Gratitude might create a state of mind in which one became aware of a vocation: but the vocation would be the proper reason for joining. They themselves would surely not wish you to join *without* it? You can show your gratitude in lots of other ways.

Is there in this Order, even for lay members such as you would be, not something like a noviciate or experimental period? If so, that would be the thing, wouldn't it? If not, I think I can only repeat my previous suggestion of undergoing a sort of unofficial noviciate by living according to the Rule for 6 months or so and seeing how it works. Most of it is the things you probably do anyway and are things we ought to do. (The only one I'm doubtful about is the 'special intention' clause in No. 3. I'm not quite sure what the theological implications are.) The question is whether the fact of being compelled to it by a vow would act as a useful support or be a snare and a source of scruples: I don't think I can

---

[18] *Letters III*, 321–322.

tell you the answer to that. Is the vow irrevocable or can you contract out again?

About putting one's Christian point of view to doctors and other unpromising subjects I'm in great doubt myself. All I'm clear about is that one sins if one's real reason for silence is simply the fear of looking a fool. I suppose one is right if one's reason is the probability that the other party will be repelled still further and only confirmed in his belief that Christians are troublesome and embarrassing people to be avoided whenever possible. But I find it a dreadfully worrying problem. (I am quite sure that an importunate bit of evangelisation from a comparative stranger would *not* have done me any good when *I* was an unbeliever.)

TO MARY WILLIS SHELBURNE: *On the difficulty of thinking and talking about the doctrine of Trinity, especially the Holy Spirit.*[19]

17 APRIL 1953

I'm not quite so shocked as you by the story of Charles and Mary. If even adult and educated Christians in trying to think of the Blessed Trinity have to guard constantly against falling to the heresy of Tritheism, what can we expect of children. And 'another of whom he was not quite sure' is perhaps no bad *beginning* for a knowledge about the Holy Ghost....

I'd sooner pray for God's mercy than for His justice on my friends, my enemies, and myself.

TO ELSIE SNICKERS: *On the origin of sin, not in the reason but in the will; on forgiving and excusing; on the difference between psychotherapy and spiritual direction; and on the suitability and timing of the study of psychology.*[20]

18 MAY 1953

No. I don't think sin is completely accounted for by faulty reasoning nor that it can be completely cured by re-education. That view ... overlook[s] the (to me) obviously central fact that our *will* is not necessarily determined by our *reason*. If it were, then, as you

[19] *Letters III*, 323.
[20] *Letters III*, 329–331.

say, what are called 'sins' would not be sins at all but only mistakes, and would require not repentances but merely correction.

But surely daily experience shows that it is just not so. A man's reason sees perfectly clearly that the resulting discomfort and inconvenience will far outweigh the pleasure of the ten minutes in bed. Yet he stays in bed: not at all because his reason is deceived but because desire is stronger than reason. A woman knows that the sharp 'last word' in an argument will produce a serious quarrel which was the very thing she had intended to avoid when that argument began and which may permanently destroy her happiness. Yet she says it: not at all because her reason is deceived but because the desire to score a point is at the moment stronger than her reason. People—you and I among them—constantly choose between two courses of action the one which we know to be the worse: because, at the moment, we *prefer* the gratification of our anger, lust, sloth, greed, vanity, curiosity or cowardice, not only to the known will of God but even to what we know will make for our own real comfort and security. If you don't recognise this, then I must solemnly assure you that either [you] are an angel, or else are still living in 'a fool's paradise': a world of illusion.

Of course it is true that many people are so mis-educated or so psychopathic that their freedom of action is very much curtailed and their responsibility therefore very small. We cannot remember that too much when we are tempted to judge harshly the acts of other people whose difficulties we don't know. But we know that some of *our own acts* have sprung from evil *will* (proud, resentful, cowardly, envious, lascivious or spiteful will) although we knew better, and that what we need is not—or not *only*—re-education but repentance, God's forgiveness, and His Grace to help us to do better next time. Until one has faced this fact one is a child.

And it is not the function of psychotherapy to make us face *this*. Its work is the non-moral aspects of conduct. You must not go to the psychologists for *spiritual* guidance. (One goes to the dentist to cure one's toothache, not to teach one in what spirit to bear it if it cannot be cured: for that you must go to God and God's spokesmen.)

For this reason I am rather sorry that you have taken Psychology as a subject for your academic course. A continued interest in it on the part of those who have had psychotherapeutic treatment is usually, I think, not a good thing. At least, not until a long interval has elapsed and their *personal* interest in it, the interest connected with *their own case,* has quite died away. At least that is how it seems to me. All blessings.

TO RHONA BODLE, *who had written to Lewis of her frustration over being forbidden to teach religion in New Zealand schools: On the vocation of being a Christian teacher in a secular school.*[21]

20 MAY 1953

The restraints imposed on you by 'secular education' are, no doubt, very galling.[22] But I wonder whether secular education will do us all the harm the secularists hope. Secular *teachers* will. But Christian teachers in secular schools may, I sometimes think, do more good precisely because they are *not* allowed to give religious instruction in class. At least I think that, as a child, I should have been very allured and impressed by the discovery—which must be made when questions are asked—that the teacher believed firmly in a whole mass of things he wasn't allowed to teach! Let them give us the charm of mystery if they please.

It was very nice to hear from you again. All blessings on you and your work.

TO MARY WILLIS SHELBURNE: *On the need for the laity to focus on the faults of the laity and not of the clergy.*[23]

30 MAY 1953

Yes, we are always told that the present wide-spread apostasy must be the fault of the clergy, not of the laity. If I were a parson I should always try to dwell on the faults of the clergy: being a layman, I think it more wholesome to concentrate on those of the laity. I am rather sick of the modern assumption that, for all

---

[21] *Letters III,* 331–332.
[22] Bodle said of this letter: "I had explained that in N.Z. government schools religion instruction cannot be given by teachers. I was feeling frustrated. The principal did, however, allow me to take classes after school for any children who wanted to come."
[23] *Letters III,* 333.

events, 'WE', the people, are never responsible: it is always our rulers, or ancestors, or parents, or education, or anybody but precious 'US', WE are apparently perfect and blameless. Don't you believe it. Nor do I think the Church of England holds out many attractions to the worldly. There is more real poverty, even actual want, in English vicarages than there is in the homes of casual labourers.

TO HILA NEWMAN, *an eleven-year-old girl who had sent Lewis her drawings and a letter of appreciation for the first three Chronicles of Narnia: On Lewis's care not to decode the Chronicles of Narnia.*[24]

3 JUNE 1953

Thank you so much for your lovely letter and pictures. I realised at once that the coloured one was not a particular scene but a sort of line-up like what you would have at the very end if it was a play instead of stories. *The [Voyage of the] DAWN TREADER* is *not* to be the last: There are to be 4 more, 7 in all. Didn't you notice that Aslan said nothing about Eustace not going back? I thought the best of your pictures was the one of Mr. Tumnus at the bottom of the letter.

As to Aslan's other name, well I want you to guess. Has there never been anyone in *this* world who (1.) Arrived at the same time as Father Christmas. (2.) Said he was the son of the Great Emperor. (3.) Gave himself up for someone else's fault to be jeered at and killed by wicked people. (4.) Came to life again. (5.) Is sometimes spoken of as a Lamb (see the end of the *Dawn Treader*). Don't you really know His name in this world? Think it over and let me know your answer!

Reepicheep in your coloured picture has just the right perky, cheeky expression. I love real mice. There are lots in my rooms in College but I have never set a trap. When I sit up late working they poke their heads out from behind the curtains just as if they were saying, 'Hi! Time for *you* to go to bed. We want to come out and play.'

[24] *Letters III*, 334–335.

TO MARY VAN DEUSEN: *On minding one's own business except when asked; and on St. Paul's teaching on the strong and the weak in the Letter to the Romans, Chapter 14.*[25]

8 JUNE 1953

Yes, I think your position is the right one. If one is asked for advice, then, and then only, one has to have an opinion about the exact rule of life which would suit some other Christian. Otherwise, I think the rule is to mind one's own business.

St. Paul goes further than this: it may even be proper at times to adopt practices which you yourself think unnecessary, and which *are* unnecessary to you, if your difference on such points is a stumbling-block to the Christians you find yourself among. Hence, you see, other Christians' practices concern us, when at all, as a ground for concessions on our part, not for interference or complacent assertion that our way is best. This is in *Romans* chap XIV: read the chapter and meditate on it. I am very glad you have seen the real point.

TO MARY VAN DEUSEN: *On the need to trust that God has reasons for answering prayers for healing with an apparent "no"; and on the safety, ease, and beauty that religious practices provide on the obedient climb up the staircase of grace.*[26]

29 JUNE 1953

I never know what to say in cases like that of the sick child's mother whom you mention. There seems plenty of evidence that God does sometimes, in answer to prayer, heal in miraculous fashion: sometimes, it would appear, not. No doubt there are very good reasons for both.

I wouldn't quite say that 'religious Practices help the search for truth' for that might imply that they have no further use when the Truth has been found. I think about the practices what a wise old priest said to me about a 'rule of life' in general—'It is not a stair but a bannister' (or rail or balustrade—I don't know what you call it in America), i.e., it is, not the thing you ascend by but it is a protective

---

[25] *Letters III,* 335–336.
[26] *Letters III,* 342.

against falling off and a help-up. I think thus we ascend. The stair is God's grace. One's climb from step to step is obedience. Many different kinds of bannisters exist, all legitimate. It is possible to get up without any bannisters, if need be: but no one would willingly build a staircase without them because it would be less safe, more laborious, and a little lacking in beauty.

TO MARY WILLIS SHELBURNE: *A reflection on the coronation of Queen Elizabeth II—on the tragic splendor of being human.*[27]

10 JULY 1953

You know, over here people did *not* get that fairy-tale feeling about the coronation. What impressed most who saw it was the fact that the Queen herself appeared to be quite overwhelmed by the sacramental side of it. Hence, in the spectators, a feeling of (one hardly knows how to describe it)—awe—pity—pathos—mystery. The pressing of that huge, heavy crown on that small, young head becomes a sort of symbol of the situation of *humanity* itself: humanity called by God to be His vice-gerent and high priest on earth, yet feeling so inadequate. As if He said 'In my inexorable love I shall lay upon the dust that you are glories and dangers and responsibilities beyond your understanding'. Do you see what I mean? One has missed the whole point unless one feels that we have all been crowned and that coronation is somehow, if splendid, a tragic splendour.

TO MRS. JOHNSON: *On the hardness and tenderness of the Christian life; on the consolation of Jesus' human fearfulness in Gethsemane; on anxiety about future evils; on living and receiving one day and grace at a time; on when we become our real selves; on believing in God when God doesn't feel real; on ignoring visions (the saints Lewis refers to are likely to be Teresa of Avila and John of the Cross); and on faith healing.*[28]

17 JULY 1953

There are many interesting points in your letter of June 8. I'm very glad you've seen that Christianity is as hard as nails: i.e., hard

---

[27] *Letters III,* 343.
[28] *Letters III,* 347–349.

and tender at the same time. It's the *blend* that does it: neither quality would be any good without the other. You needn't worry about
not feeling brave. Our Lord didn't—see the scene in Gethsemane.

How thankful I am that when God became Man He did not
choose to become a man of iron nerves: that would not have
helped weaklings like you and me nearly so much. Especially
don't *worry* (you may of course *pray*) about being brave over merely
possible evils in the future. In the old battles it was usually the
reserve, who had to *watch* the carnage, not the troops who were in
it, whose nerve broke first. Similarly I think you in America feel
much more anxiety about atomic bombs than we do: because you
are further from the danger. If and when a horror turns up, you
will *then* be given Grace to help you. I don't think one is usually
given it in advance. 'Give us our *daily* bread'[29] (not an annuity
for life) applies to spiritual gifts too: the little *daily* support for the
daily trial. Life has to be taken day by day and hour by hour.

The writer you quote ('in all those turning lights') *was* very
good at the stage at which you met him: now, as is plain, you've
got beyond him. Poor boob!—he thought his mind was his own!
Never his own until he makes it Christ's: up till then merely a
result of heredity, environment, and the state of his digestion. I
become my own only when I gave myself to Another.

'Does God seem real to me?' It varies: just as lots of other
things I firmly believe in (my own death, the solar system) *feel*
more or less real at different times. I have dreamed dreams but
not seen visions: but don't think all that matters a hoot. And the
saints say that visions are unimportant. If Our Lord *did* seem to
appear to you at your prayer (bodily) what, after all, could you
do but go on with your prayers? How could you know that it was
not an hallucination?

You've got the Coronation right too: especially a sacrificial,
even a tragic rite. And a symbol: for we (Man) have had laid on
us the heavy crown of being lords of this planet, and the same
contract between the frail, tiny person—the huge ritual goes for
us all. . . .

. . . Of course I believe that people are still healed by faith:
whether this has happened in any particular case, one can't of

---

[29] Matthew 6:11; Luke 11:3.

course say without getting a real-Doctor-who-is-also-a-real-Christian to go through the whole case-history.

TO MARY VAN DEUSEN: *On the resolution to her question about joining a religious order; on the impermanence of feelings, good and bad; and on the need for the natural love in marriage to die into divine love.*[30]

23 JULY 1953

I think your decision 'a rule of life, without membership' is a good one. It is a great joy to be able to 'feel' God's love as a reality, and one must give thanks for it and use it. But you must be prepared for the feeling dying away again, for feelings are by nature impermanent. The great thing is to continue to believe when the feeling is absent: and these periods do quite as much for one as those when the feeling is present.

It sounds to me as if Genia had a pretty good husband on the whole. So much matrimonial misery comes to me in my mail that I feel those whose partner has no worse fault than being stupider than themselves may be said to have drawn a prize! It hardly amounts to a Problem. I take it that in every marriage natural love sooner or later, in a high or a low degree, comes up against difficulties (if only the difficulty that the original state of 'being in love' dies a natural death) which force it either to turn into dislike or else to turn into Christian charity. For all our natural feelings are, not resting places, but *points d'appui*, springboards. One has to *go on from* there, or *fall back from* there. The merely human pleasure in being loved must either go bad or become the divine joy of loving. But no doubt Genia knows all this. It's all quite in the ordinary run of Christian life. See I Peter iv, 12 'Think it not strange *et cetera*.'

TO MARY WILLIS SHELBURNE: *On the attractiveness of real holiness (Lewis mentions his spiritual director, Father Adams); and on the follies, miseries, and temptations of being a young, single adult.*[31]

---

[30] *Letters III*, 351–352.
[31] *Letters III*, 351–352.

I am so glad you gave me an account of the lovely priest. How little people know who think that holiness is dull. When one meets the real thing (and perhaps, like you, I have met it only once) it is irresistible. If even 10% of the world's population had it, would not the whole world be converted and happy before a year's end?

Yes, I too think there is lots to be said for being no longer young: and I do most heartily agree that it is just as well to be past the age when one expects or desires to attract the other sex. It's natural enough in our species, as in others, that the young birds should show off their plumage—in the mating season. But the trouble in the modern world is that there's a tendency to rush all the birds on to that age as soon as possible and then keep them there as late as possible, thus losing all the real value of the *other* parts of life in a senseless, pitiful attempt to prolong what, after all, is neither its wisest, its happiest, or most innocent period. I suspect merely commercial motives are behind it all: for it is at the showing-off age that birds of both sexes have least sales-resistance!

TO LAURENCE HARWOOD, *Lewis's twenty-year-old godson, who has just failed his qualifying examinations: On the need to move through and beyond great setbacks; on the poison of indulged resentment; on how hopeless the future may look and yet not be; and on how much of "life is rather like a lumpy bed in a bad hotel."*[32]

2 AUGUST 1953

I was sorry to hear from Owen Barfield that you have taken a nasty knock over History Prelim. Sorry, because I know it can't be much fun for you: not because I think the thing is necessarily a major disaster. We are now so used to the examination system that we hardly remember how very recent it is and how hotly it was opposed by some quite sincere people. Trollope (no fool) was utterly sceptical about its value: and I myself, though a don, sometimes wonder how many of the useful, or even the great,

---

[32] *Letters III*, 352–354.

men of the past would have survived it. It doesn't test all qualities by any means: not even all qualities needed in an academic life. And anyway, what a small part of life that is. And if you are not suited for that, it is well to have been pushed forcibly out of it at an earlier rather than a later stage. It is much worse to waste three or more years getting a Fourth or a Pass. You can now cut your losses and start on something else.

At the moment, I can well imagine, everything seems in ruins. That is an illusion. The world is full of capable and useful people who began life by ploughing in exams. You will laugh at this *contre temps* some day. Of course it would be disastrous to go to the other extreme and conclude that one was a genius because one had failed in a prelim—as if a horse imagined it must be a Derby winner because it couldn't be taught to pull a four-wheeler!—but I don't expect that is the extreme to which you are temperamentally inclined.

Are you in any danger of seeking consolation in *Resentment*? I have no reason to suppose you are, but it is a favourite desire of the human mind (certainly of my mind!) and one wants to be on one's guard against it. And that is about the only way in which an early failure like this can become a real permanent injury. A belief that one has been misused, a tendency ever after to snap and snarl at 'the system'—that, I think, makes a man always a bore, usually an ass, sometimes a villain. So don't think *either* that you are no good *or* that you are a Victim. Write the whole thing off and get on.

You may reply 'It's easy talking'. I shan't blame you if you do. I remember only too well what a hopeless oyster to be opened the world seemed at your age. I would have given a good deal to anyone who could have assured me that I ever would be able to persuade anyone to pay me a living wage for anything I could do. Life consisted of applying for jobs which other people got, writing books that no one would publish, and giving lectures which no one attended. It all *looks* perfectly hopeless. Yet the vast majority of us manage to get in somewhere and shake down somehow in the end.

You are now going through what most people (at any rate most of the people I know) find in retrospect to have been the most unpleasant period of their lives. But it won't last: the road usually improves later. I think life is rather like a lumpy bed in a bad hotel. At first you can't imagine how you can lie on it, much less sleep in it. But presently one finds the right position and finally one is snoring away. By the time one is called it seems a very good bed and one is loth to leave it.

This is a devilish stodgy letter. There's no need to bother answering it.

TO MRS. EMILY MCLAY, *who had asked Lewis about the doctrine of predestination: On the first rule of biblical interpretation; on avoiding generalizations based on one's own experience; and on anxiety about one's own salvation.*[33]

8 AUGUST 1953

I take it as a first principle that we must not interpret any one part of Scripture so that it contradicts other parts: and specially we must not use an Apostle's teaching to contradict that of Our Lord. Whatever St. Paul may have meant, we must not reject the parable of the sheep and the goats (Matt. XXV. 30–46). There, you see there is nothing about Predestination or even about Faith—all depends on works. But how this is to be reconciled with St. Paul's teaching, or with other sayings of Our Lord, I frankly confess I don't know. Even St. Peter you know admits that he was stumped by the Pauline epistles (II Peter III. 16–17).

What I *think* is this. Everyone looking back on *his own* conversion must feel—and I am sure the feeling is in some sense true—'It is not *I* who have done this. I did not choose Christ: He chose me. It is all free grace, which I have done nothing to earn.' That is the Pauline account: and I am sure it is the only true account of every conversion *from the inside.* Very well. It then seems to us logical and natural to turn this personal experience into a general rule 'All conversions depend on God's choice'.

But this I believe is exactly what we must not do: for generalisations are legitimate only when we are dealing with matters to which our faculties are adequate. Here, we are not. *How* our individual experiences are *in reality* consistent with (a) our idea of divine justice, (b) the parable I've just quoted and lots of other

[33] *Letters III,* 354–355.

214 • YOURS, JACK

passages, we don't and can't know: what is clear is that *we* can't find a consistent formula. I think we must take a leaf out of the scientists' book. They are quite familiar with the fact that, for example, light has to be regarded *both* as a wave in the ether and as a stream of particles. No one can make these two views consistent. Of course reality must be self-consistent: but till (if ever) we can *see* the consistency it is better to hold two inconsistent views than to ignore one side of the evidence.

The real interrelation between God's omnipotence and Man's freedom is something we can't find out. Looking at the Sheep and the Goats every man can be quite sure that every kind act he does will be accepted by Christ. Yet, equally, we all do feel sure that all the good in us comes from Grace. We have to leave it at that. I find the best plan is to take the Calvinist view of my own virtues and other people's vices: and the other view of my own vices and other people's virtues. But though there is much to be *puzzled* about, there is nothing to be *worried* about. It is plain from Scripture that, in whatever sense the Pauline doctrine is true, it is not true in any sense which *excludes* its (apparent) opposite.

You know what Luther said: 'Do you doubt if you are chosen? Then say your prayers and you may conclude that you are.'

TO MRS. EMILY MCLAY: *More on biblical interpretation; and on why the meaning of the Bible is not obvious.*[34]

8 AUGUST 1953

Your experience in listening to those philosophers gives you the technique one needs for dealing with the dark places in the Bible. When one of the philosophers, one whom you know on other grounds to be a sane and decent man, said something you didn't understand, you did not at once conclude that he had gone off his head. You assumed you'd missed the point.

Same here. The two things one must *not* do are (a) to believe, on the strength of Scripture or on any other evidence, that God is in any way evil. (In Him is no *darkness* at all.)[35] (b) to wipe off the slate any passage which seems to show that He is. Behind that

---

[34] *Letters III*, 356–357.
[35] I John 1:5.

apparently shocking passage, be sure, there lurks some great truth which you don't understand. If one ever *does* come to understand it, one will see that [He] is good and just and gracious in ways we never dreamed of. Till then, it must be just left on one side.

But why are baffling passages left in at all? Oh, because God speaks not only for us little ones but for the great sages and mystics who *experience* what we only *read about,* and to whom all the words have therefore different (richer) contents. Would not a revelation which contained nothing that you and I did not understand, be for that very reason rather suspect? To a child it would seem a contradiction to say both that his parents made him and that God made him, yet we see both can be true.

TO DON GIOVANNI CALABRIA: *A lament over religious hatred in Northern Ireland; and on the danger of confusing religion and politics.*[36]

10 AUGUST 1953

I have received your letter dated the 5th August. I await with gratitude the pamphlets—a specimen of your people's printing skill: which however I shall not see for 5 weeks because tomorrow I am crossing over (if God so have pleased) to Ireland: my birthplace and dearest refuge so far as charm of landscape goes, and temperate climate, although most dreadful because of the strife, hatred and often civil war between dissenting faiths.

There indeed both yours and ours 'know not by what Spirit they are led'.[37] They take lack of charity for zeal and mutual ignorance for orthodoxy.

I think almost all the crimes which Christians have perpetrated against each other arise from this, that religion is confused with politics. For, above all other spheres of human life, the Devil claims politics for his own, as almost the citadel of his power. Let us, however, with mutual prayers pray with all our power for that charity which 'covers a multitude of sins'.[38]

---

[36] *Letters III,* 357–358.
[37] Luke 9:55.
[38] I Peter 4:8.

TO MARY WILLIS SHELBURNE: *On offering her joblessness and insecurity as voluntary suffering for Christ's sake (Colossians 1:24); on the illusion of independence; and on his own confession of anxiety about poverty, in violation of Matthew 6:25–34.*[39]

10 AUGUST 1953

I have just got your letter of the 6th. Oh I *do* so sympathise with you: job-hunting, even in youth, is a heartbreaking affair and to have to go back to it now must be simply _____ I was going to say 'simply Hell', but no one who is engaged in prayer and humility, as you are, can be there, so I'd better say 'Purgatory'. (We have as a matter of fact good authorities for calling it something other than Purgatory. We are told that even those tribulations which fall upon us by necessity, if embraced for Christ's sake, become as meritorious as *voluntary* sufferings and every missed meal can be converted into a fast if taken in the right way.)

I suppose—though the person who is *not* suffering feels shy about saying it to the person who *is*—that it is good for us to be cured of the illusion of 'independence'. For of course independence, the state of being indebted to no one, is eternally impossible. Who, after all, is more totally dependent than what we call the man 'of independent means'. Every shirt he wears is made by other people out of other organisms and the only difference between him and us is that even the money whereby he pays for it was earned by other people. Of course you *ought* to be dependent on your daughter and son-in-law. Support of parents is a most ancient and universally acknowledged duty. And if you come to find yourself dependent on anyone else you mustn't mind. But I am very, very sorry. I'm a panic-y person about money myself (which is a most shameful confession and a thing dead against Our Lord's words)[40] and poverty frightens me more than anything else except large spiders and the tops of cliffs: one is sometimes even tempted to say that if God wanted us to live like the lilies of the field He might have given us an organism more like theirs! But of course He is right. And when you meet anyone who *does* live like the lilies, one *sees* that He is.

---

[39] *Letters III*, 358–359.
[40] Matthew 6:25–34.

God keep you and encourage you. I am just about to go off to Ireland where I shall be moving about, so I shan't hear from you for several weeks. All blessings and deepest sympathy.

TO MARY VAN DEUSEN: *A letter of correction: On spouses marrying to improve or manage one another; and on mothers-in-law interfering in the marriages of their children.*[41]

14 SEPTEMBER 1953

I am just back from Donegal (which was heavenly) and find as usual a ghastly pile of unanswered letters, so I must be brief. The important idea of a Christian sanatorium is worth a whole letter, but I want to use *this* one for another subject. I hope you won't be angry at what I'm going to say—

I think that idea of Genia's job being to concentrate on 'bringing out the best of Eddie' is really rather dangerous. Wouldn't you yourself think it sounded—well, to put it bluntly, a bit *priggish,* if applied to any other couple? It sounds as if the poor chap were somehow infinitely inferior.

Are you giving full weight to the very raw deal he has had in marrying a girl who has nearly always been ill? Men haven't got your maternal instinct, you know. To find a patient where one hoped for a helpmeet is much more frustrating for the husband than for the wife. And by all I hear he has come through the test very well. But if just as she is ceasing to be a patient she were to become the self-appointed Governess or Improver—well, would any camel's back stand that last straw? I don't think Genia is at present inclined (or not much) to start 'educating' her husband. I am sure you will take care not to influence her in that direction. Because, really, you know, it would be so easy, without in the least intending it, to glide into the rôle (I shudder to write it) of the traditional home-breaking mother-in-law. All those old jokes have *something* behind them.

I do hope I haven't made you an enemy for life. If I have taken too great a liberty, you have rather led me into it. And I did feel signs of danger. And don't you think in general that a girl who has a faithful, kind, sober husband (there are so many of the other

---

[41] *Letters III,* 360–361.

kind) whom she has promised to love, honour, and obey, had better just get on with the job? Do forgive me if I misunderstand and put the point too crudely. At any rate, my prayers will not cease.

TO RHONA BODLE: *On not forcing books on others; and on the providence of reading.*[42]

14 SEPTEMBER 1953

I have had 'Miss Bodle's colleague' in my daily prayers for a long time now: is that the same young man you mention in your letter of July 3rd, or do I now say 'colleagues'? Yes: don't bother him with *my* books if an aunt (it somehow *would* be an aunt—though I must add that most of my aunts were delightful) has been ramming them down his throat.

You know, *The Pilgrim's Progress* is not, I find (to my surprise) everyone's book. I know several people who are both Christians and lovers of literature who can't bear it. I doubt if they were made to read it as children. Indeed, I rather wonder whether that 'being made to read it' has spoiled so many books as is supposed. I suspect that all the people who tell me they were 'put off' Scott by having *Ivanhoe* as a holiday task are people who would never have liked Scott anyway.

I don't believe anything will keep the right reader and the right book apart. But our literary loves are as diverse as our human! You couldn't make me like Henry James or dislike Jane Austen whatever you did. By the bye did Chesterton's *Everlasting Man* (I'm sure I advised you to read it) succeed or fail with you?

TO DON GIOVANNI CALABRIA: *On remedies for the apostasy of Europe, especially a new preparation for the Gospel in the form of teaching on the law of nature.*[43]

15 SEPTEMBER 1953

Regarding the moral condition of our times (since you bid me prattle on) I think this. Older people, as we both are, are always

---

[42] *Letters III*, 362–363.
[43] *Letters III*, 363–366.

'praisers of times past'. They always think the world is worse than it was in their young days. Therefore we ought to take care lest we go wrong. But, with this proviso, certainly I feel that very grave dangers hang over us. This results from the apostasy of the great part of Europe from the Christian faith. Hence a worse state than the one we were in before we received the Faith. For no one returns from Christianity to the same state he was in before Christianity but into a worse state: the difference between a pagan and an apostate is the difference between an unmarried woman and an adulteress. For faith perfects nature but faith lost corrupts nature. Therefore many men of our time have lost not only the supernatural light but also the natural light which pagans possessed.

But God, who is the God of mercies,[44] even now has not altogether cast off the human race. In younger people, although we may see much cruelty and lust, yet at the same time do we not see very many sparks of virtues which perhaps our own generation lacked? How much courage, how much concern for the poor do we see! We must not despair. And (among us) a not inconsiderable number are now returning to the Faith.

So much for the present situation. About remedies the question is more difficult. For my part I believe we ought to work not only at spreading the Gospel (that certainly) but also at a certain preparation for the Gospel. It is necessary to recall many to the law of nature *before* we talk about God. For Christ promises forgiveness of sins: but what is that to those who, since they do not know the law of nature, do not know that they have sinned? Who will take medicine unless he knows he is in the grip of disease? Moral relativity is the enemy we have to overcome before we tackle Atheism. I would almost dare to say 'First let us make the younger generation good pagans and afterwards let us make them Christians.'

---

[44] II Corinthians 1:3.

TO MARY VAN DEUSEN: *On finding helpers for a ministry; and on interpreting the meaning of difficulties in ministry.*[45]

3 OCTOBER 1953

I was extremely glad to get your letter. I was beginning to feel that my own had been presumptuous and intolerable and had been praying not that it might do good but that it might not do harm. Whether I was right or wrong, you came out of it with flying colours: if few can give good advice, fewer still can hear with patience advice either good or bad.

About your Project (it was, wasn't it, for the founding of a sort of rest-home where people in psychological difficulties could get Christian advice, sympathy, and, if necessary, treatment?), the whole thing—as with most conceptions either practical or literary—turns on the execution. All depends on the quality of the individual helpers. I suspect you will find them only by what seems chance but is really an answer to prayer. No 'machinery' of committees and selection and references, however well devised, will do it, I imagine. And perhaps it is just by your discovering, or failing to discover, the right people, that God will show you whether He wishes you to do this or not (Beware here of *my* unsanguine temper, more tempted to sloth than to precipitance, and ready to despond: take my advice always with a grain of salt).

It is hard, when difficulties arise to know whether one is meant to overcome them or whether they are signs that one is on the wrong tract. I suppose the deeper one's own life of prayer and sacraments the more trustworthy one's judgement will be.

You 'get me where I live' about Van's Aunt. I have been in very close contact with a case like that. It is harrowing. My doctor (a very serious Christian) kept on reminding me that *so much* of an old person's speech and behaviour must really be treated as a medical not a spiritual fact: that, as the organism decays, the true state of the soul can less and less express itself through it. So that things may be neither so miserable (nor so wicked, we must sometimes add) as they seem. I sometimes wonder whether the

---

[45] *Letters III*, 369–370.

incarnation of the soul is not gradual at both ends?—i.e., not *fully* there yet in infancy and no longer fully there in old age.

Yours (most relieved)
C. S. Lewis

TO MARY WILLIS SHELBURNE: *On rejoicing over answered prayer; and on our prayers being God's prayers.*[46]

6 NOVEMBER 1953

Oh I *am* glad, I *am* glad. And here's a thing worth recording. Of course I have been praying for you daily, as always, but latterly have found myself doing so with much more concern and especially about 2 nights ago, with such a strong feeling how very nice it would be, if God willed, to get a letter from you with good news. And then, as if by magic (indeed it is the whitest magic in the world) the letter comes to-day. Not (lest I should indulge in folly) that your relief had not in fact occurred *before* my prayer, but as if, in tenderness for my puny faith, God moved me to pray with especial earnestness just before He was going to give me the thing. How true that our prayers are really His prayers: He speaks to Himself through us.

I am also most moved at hearing how you were supported through the period of anxiety. For one *is* sometimes tempted to think that if He wanted us to be as un-anxious as the lilies of the field He really might have given us a constitution more like theirs! But then when the need comes *He* carries out in us His otherwise impossible instructions. In fact He always has to do all the things—all the prayers, all the virtues. No new doctrine, but newly come home to me.

TO MARY WILLIS SHELBURNE: *On sleep; and on anxiety as an affliction and as a moral weakness.*[47]

27 NOVEMBER 1953

About sleep: do you find that the great secret (if one can do it) is not to *care* whether you sleep? Sleep is a jade who scorns her suitors but woos her scorners. . . .

---

[46] *Letters III*, 375–376.
[47] *Letters III*, 377–378.

It is fun to see you agreeing with what you believe to be *my* views on prayer: well you may, for they are not mine but scriptural. 'Our prayers are God talking to Himself' is only Romans, VIII, 26–27.[48] And 'praying to the end' is of course our old acquaintance, the parable of the Unjust Judge.[49]

I am sure you will be glad to hear that your recent adventures have been a great support and 'corroboration' to me. I am also very conscious (and was especially so while praying for you during your workless time) that anxiety is not only a pain which we must ask God to assuage but also a weakness we must ask Him to pardon—for He's told us take no care for the morrow.[50] The news that you had been almost miraculously guarded from that sin and spared that pain and hence the good hope that we shall all find the like mercy when our bad times come, has strengthened me much. God bless you.

TO MARY VAN DEUSEN: *On Lewis's problem with petitionary prayer as described in the New Testament; on the sense in which God wills suffering; on not being too ready to think oneself personally addressed/condemned in a sermon; and on finding peace amidst parish turmoil.*[51]

28 NOVEMBER 1953

Your letter links onto something I've been thinking of lately. There *are* two patterns of prayer in the New Testament (a) That in Gethsemane, 'Not my will but thine'[52] (b) That in Mark xi, 24.[53]

In the one the pray-er sees that what is asked may not be God's will: in the other he has complete faith not only 'in God' but in God's giving him the particular thing asked for. If both are taken as universal rules we get a contradiction, for no one (so far as I can see) could follow both in the same prayer.

I can only suppose that neither is a universal rule, that each has its place, and that when-and-if-God demands faith of the B type,

---

[48] Romans 8:26–27.
[49] Luke 18:2.
[50] Matthew 6:34.
[51] *Letters III*, 378–380. See Lewis's letter to his brother, above, 3 March 1940.
[52] Luke 22:42.
[53] Mark 11:24.

He also gives it, and we shall know that we have to pray in the B manner, and that this is what happens to miracle workers.

If your Rector is such a person then he is right in praying that way himself, though presumably wrong in demanding that everyone should do the same. If he is a presumptuous person who *thinks* he is in the A class and isn't—well, that is not for us to judge.

As to whether God ever wills suffering, I think he is confused. We must distinguish in God, and even in ourselves, absolute will from relative will. No one absolutely wills to have a tooth out, but many will to have a tooth out *rather than* to go on with toothache. Surely in the same way God never absolutely wills the least suffering for any creature, but may will it *rather than* some alternative: e.g., He willed the crucifixion rather than that Man should go unredeemed (and so it was *not,* in all senses, His will that the cup should pass from His Son).

That's how I see the theoretical side of the thing. As for the practical—oh dear, oh dear! I certainly can't conceive any less suitable preparation for Holy Communion than a discussion or any grosser abuse of language than to call a discussion a 'meditation'. I think you and you only can decide whether it's *your* job to 'lead' a study group or not.

As for the 'blasting' sermon no doubt the *type* blasted is an evil one. Is there good evidence that the preacher meant you to be included in that type? It does sometimes happen that utterances intended to be general are given particular application by the hearers. If it really was addressed to you, then no doubt you must just try to forgive it (as you have done) and otherwise do nothing about it.

The Bishop sounds a good one and I don't see how you can go wrong in following his orders. He will know much better than I could at what point the frustrations and the risk of loss of charity (in oneself or others) occasioned by your parochial activities begin to outweigh the probabilities of usefulness. What a coil it all is: so much so that (as the graver matters) only by putting the will of God first and other considerations nowhere can one have peace.

TO MRS. D. JESSUP: *On the meanings of the "world" in Lewis's writings and in the writings of Charles Williams, Evelyn Underhill, and George MacDonald; on the two basic vocations of Christians; and on the proper use of amusements.*[54]

1 DECEMBER 1953

I am so glad to hear that certain mountains have shrunk to molehills. As to the problem of Thomas Merton *versus* C.W., E.U., G.M., and C.S.L.:

A. There are two meanings of *World* in New Testament (i) In 'God so loved the World'[55] it means the Creation—stars, trees, beasts, men, and angels. (ii) In 'Love not the World'[56] it means the 'worldly' life, i.e., the life built up by men in disregard of God, the life of money-making, ambition, snobbery, social success and 'greatness'.

B. Most spiritual writers distinguish two vocations for Christians (i.) The monastic or contemplative life. (ii) The secular or active life. *All* Christians are called to abandon the 'World' (sense ii) in spirit, i.e., to reject as strongly as they possibly can its standards, motives, and prizes. But some are called to 'come out of it'[57] as far as possible by renouncing private property, marriage, their professions, *et cetera;* others have to remain 'in it' but not 'of it'.

I of course am in the second class and write for those who are also in it. This isn't to say that I may not be (you may be sure I am) far too much 'of it'. You, and your friend, must help me against that with your prayers. In so far as she accuses me of 'worldliness' she is right: but if by 'earthiness' she means my tendency to 'come down to brass tacks' and try to deal with the ordinary petty sins and virtues of secular and domestic life, she is wrong. That is a thing that ought to be done and has not yet been done enough.

About avoiding amusements and noise, it depends a bit who one is. Is the temptation to be absorbed by them? Then avoid. Is the temptation to avoid them through distaste when charity bids one to participate? Then participate. At least that's how I see it.

---

[54] *Letters III,* 380–381.
[55] John 3:16.
[56] I John 2:15.
[57] Revelation 18:4.

TO PHYLLIS ELINOR SANDEMAN: *A letter of condolence—on the pain of bereavement, its uses and misuses; on continuing to pray for her husband; on the need to love God first and foremost; on the way all human loves must die in order to rise; and on ignoring religious doubts in seasons of grief.*[58]

22 DECEMBER 1953

First, you may be quite sure that I realise (I'd be a fool if I didn't) that there is something in a loss like yours which no un-married person can understand. Secondly, that nothing I or an-yone can say will remove the *pain*. There are no anaesthetics. About the bewilderment and about the right and wrong ways of using the pain, something may perhaps be done; but one can't stop it hurting. The *worst* way of using the pain, you have already avoided: i.e., resentment.

Now about not wanting to pray, surely there is one person you very much want to pray for: your husband himself. You ask, can he help you, but isn't this probably the time for you to help him? In one way, you see, you are further on than he: you had begun to know God. He couldn't help you in *that* way: it seems to me quite possible that you can now help more than while he was alive. So get on with that right away. Our Lord said that man and wife were one flesh and forbade any man to put them asunder;[59] and we may be sure He doesn't do Himself what He forbade us to do. Your present prayers for your husband are still part of the married life.

Then as for your own shock in discovering that you hadn't got nearly as far as you thought towards loving the God who made your husband and gave him to you more than the gift. Well, no. One keeps on thinking one has crossed that bridge before one has. And God knows that it has to be crossed sooner or later, in this life or in another. And the first step is to discover that one has *not* crossed it yet. I wonder could He have really shown you this in any other way? Or even if we can't answer that, can't we trust Him to know *when* and *how* best the terrible operation can be done? Of course it is easy (I know) for the person who

---

[58] *Letters III*, 392–393.
[59] Matthew 19:5–6; Mark 10:8–9.

isn't feeling the pain to say all these things. You yourself would have been able to say them of anyone else's loss. Whatever *rational* grounds there are for doubt, you knew them all before: can it be rational (of course, it is *natural*) to weight them so differently simply because, this time, oneself is the sufferer? Doesn't that make it obvious that the doubts come not from the reason but from the shrinking nerves? Any any rate, don't try to argue with them: not now, while you are crippled. Ignore them; go on. Be regular in all your religious duties. Remember it is not being loved but loving which is the high and holy thing. You are now practising the second without the full comfort of the first. It was certain from the beginning that you would some day have to do this, for no human love passes onto the eternal level in any other way. God knows, many wives have had to learn it by a path harder than even bereavement: having to love unfaithful, drunken, or childish husbands. And have succeeded too; as God succeeds in loving us. May He help you.

TO MARY VAN DEUSEN: *On one advantage and one disadvantage of being a sickly child; on Christian life under a bad pastor; on the obedience due even a bad pastor; and on the beauty of obedience. Lewis's own parish priest had switched the time for morning prayer and holy communion.*[60]

28 DECEMBER 1953

Thanks for your letter of the 20th; my congratulations to your husband on his interesting work. About Paul, I believe (having been a sickly child myself) that there are compensations. I think that from many minor illnesses in the first 12 years one develops sometimes a certain amount of *immunity* later on; one's system has had so much practice in dealing with bacilli. It also probably helps to make one a reader: not that there isn't a danger of falling or sinking too far into the life of the imagination, but a habit of reading is a great source of happiness.

I think someone ought to write a book on 'Christian life for Laymen under a bad Parish Priest' for the problem is bound to occur in the best churches. The motto would be of course Herbert's

---

[60] *Letters III*, 397–398.

lines about the sermon, 'If all lack sense, God takes a text and preaches patience'.

Like you, we suffer (but under a very good priest) from the virtual extinction of Morning Prayer in favour of an 11 o'clock Celebration. But I suppose there is something to be said for it. This is the only ritual act Our Lord commanded Himself. It is the one we can have *only* through a priest, whereas we can all read Matins to ourselves or our families at home whenever we please. So here I have no difficulty in submission.

Is there not something especially good (and even, in the end, joyful) about mere obedience (in lawful things) to him who bears our Master's authority, however unworthy he be—perhaps all the more, if he *is* unworthy? Perhaps we are put under tiresome priests chiefly to give us the opportunity of learning this beautiful and happy virtue: so that if we use the situation well we can profit more, perhaps, than we should have done under a better man. I have seen lovely children under not very nice parents, and good troops under bad officers: and a good dog with a bad master is a lesson to us all. I mean, of course, as long as the bad orders are not in themselves wrong: and attendance at Holy Communion can't be that!

Yes, we must both go on thinking about the two kinds of prayer. I think the one in Mark xi is for very advanced people: and you point out it was said to the disciples, not to the crowds. All blessings.

TO PHYLLIS ELINOR SANDEMAN: *More on the feelings attendant on bereavement and on the unprotectedness and hopelessness of grieving; and on being "promoted" to a higher grade with harder homework in the school of Christianity. The four heroines Lewis mentions are characters in Shakespeare's* Cymbeline, The Merchant of Venice, The Tempest, *and* The Winter's Tale, *respectively.*[61]

31 DECEMBER 1953

You have of course been much in my prayers since your first letter and to-day's seems like an answer to them. I was afraid of

---

[61] *Letters III,* 398–399.

some real crack in the structure! Now it is clear that you have to deal only with what we may call a 'clean pain'.

I can well understand how in addition to, and mingling with, the void and loneliness, there is a great feeling of unprotectedness and a horror of coping with all the things—the harsh, outer world—from which you have hitherto been shielded. I first met this 'cold blast on the naked heath' at about 9, when my mother died, and there has never really been any sense of security and snugness since. That is, I've not quite succeeded in growing up on that point: there is still too much of 'Mammy's little lost boy' about me. Your position is of course very different, both because dependence on a husband is more legitimate than dependence (after a certain age) on one's mother, and also because, at your age, though it will feel just as bad, it is not so likely to go down into the unconscious and produce a *trauma*. And one sees too (though it sounds brutal to say it) how this miserable necessity of fending for oneself might be an essential part of your spiritual education. I suppose God wants a bit of Imogen and Portia in you, having worked in Miranda and Perdita part enough (it is sometimes helpful to think of oneself as a picture which He is painting).

By the way, I share to the full—no words can say how strongly I share—that distaste for everything communal and collective which you describe in your husband. I really believe I would have come to Christianity much less reluctantly if it had not involved the Church. And I don't wonder you failed to convince him that *that* community is perfectly right. It is holy and commanded: not at present (I think) perfect! No doubt he is learning 'togetherness' now as you, alas, are learning 'aloneness'. Both painful lessons: it can so seldom happen that what we need is what we like (for if we liked it we'd have helped ourselves to it already and wouldn't need it—aren't children made to eat fat which they hate?). You will be all right, Mrs. Sandeman. All will be well in the end, though by hard ways. All earthly loves go through some fire before they can inherit the Kingdom. If it weren't this, it would be some other fire. God bless you. Let us pray for one another.

P. S. *Of course,* I'm not obeying your request, 'Help me to find some comfort in faith again.' We shan't find faith by looking for comfort. That's why, even brutally, I can't help talking in terms of a work to be done. You are, on my view, being moved into a higher form of the great school and set harder work to do. Comfort will come as you master that work, as you learn more and more to be a channel of God's grace to your husband (and perhaps to others): not for trying to get back the conditions you had in the lower form.

Keep clear of Psychical Researchers.

1954

5 JANUARY 1954

Oh I am sorry. How dreadful. I don't know to which of you my sympathy goes out most. Your share is, however, easier to imagine, for I know what it's like to have to be the comforter when one most needs comforting, and the competent arranger at the very moment when one feels most disabled.

I don't know whether anything an outsider can say is much use; and you know already the things we have been taught—that suffering *can* (but oh!, with what difficulty) be offered to God as our part in the whole redemptive suffering of the world beginning with Christ's own suffering: that suffering by itself does not fester or poison, but resentment does; that sufferings which (heaven knows) fell on us without and against our will can be so taken that they are as saving and purifying as the voluntary sufferings of martyrs and ascetics.

And it *is* all true, and it is so hard to go on believing it. Especially as the dark time in which you are now entering (I've tried it; my own life really begins with my mother's illness and death from cancer when I was about 9) is split up into so many minor horrors and fears and upsets, some of them trivial and prosaic.

May God support you. Keep a firm hold of the Cross. And try to keep clear of the modern fancy that all this is abnormal and that you have been singled out for something outrageous. For no one escapes. We are all driven into the front line to be sorted sooner or later. With all blessings and with deep sorrow.

---

[1] *Letters III,* 404–405.

TO MARY VAN DEUSEN: *Expanding on the line from George Herbert mentioned above (28 December 1953), Lewis counseled even greater patience with the behavior of a priest than with his preaching; on a tentative solution to the problem of petitionary prayer; and on the strength of those who are obedient.*[2]

26 JANUARY 1954

I quite agree that God 'takes a text' much more forcibly in the general behaviour of a bad priest than in a bad sermon, which is, in comparison, a trifle. You seem, if I may say so, to be taking the treatment well! Finding (as Shakespeare ought to have said) 'sermons in prigs, books in the cross-grained toughs,' *et cetera*.

I suppose I thought in B type of prayer higher because of the portentous promises attached to it and because it seems the type used by Elijah when he calls down fire on the altar[3] or the Apostles when they heal the sick and raise the dead. But I think we are both coming to the right practical conclusion: not struggling, but always saying, as the disciples did, 'Lord, teach us how to pray.'[4]

That's all modern pseudo-democratic nonsense, isn't it, about obedience being 'weak'. One doesn't think nurses, sailors, and soldiers weak; and when we believe spiritual things to be as important as operations, storms at sea, and 'last stands,' we shall see obedience as a strong thing there too. Surely one of the marks of the disobedient child is that it is *feebler* than the obedient, and can't do dozens of things that the other can?

TO MRS. D. JESSUP: *On the difference between intellectual assent to and integrated realization of doctrines; more on the question of Christian vocation to be in the world and not of the world; and on God's individual care for each of us.*[5]

5 FEBRUARY 1954

I fully agree with you about the difference between a doctrine merely accepted by the intellect and one (as Keats says) 'proved

---

[2] *Letters III*, 418–419.
[3] I Kings 18:36–38.
[4] Luke 11:1.
[5] *Letters III*, 425–426.

in the pulses' so that [it] is solid and palpable. You have clearly progressed from the one stage to the other as regards those sins by which (there again you're right) we daily fashion the Nails. About 2 years ago I made a similar progress from mere intellectual acceptance of, to realisation of, the doctrine that our sins are forgiven. That is perhaps the most blessed thing that ever happened to me. How little they know of Christianity who think that the story *ends* with conversion: novelties we never dreamed of may await us at every turn of the road.

About the question of abandoning the 'World' or fighting right inside it, don't you think that both may be right for different people? Some are called to the one and some to the other. Hence Our Lord, after pointing the contrast between the hermit and ascetic John the Baptist, and Himself who drank wine and went to dinner parties and jostled with every kind of man, concluded 'But Wisdom is justified of *all* her children':[6] meaning, I take it, both these kinds. I fancy we are all too ready, once we are converted ourselves, to assume that God will deal with everyone exactly as He does with us. But He is no mass-producer and treats no two quite alike.

TO MRS. JOHNSON: *On the four kinds of love; on the various forms of charity; on pride as the pleasure of self-approval; and on self-forgetfulness.*[7]

18 FEBRUARY 1954

Of course taking in the poor illegitimate child is 'charity'. *Charity* means *love*. It is called *Agape* in the New Testament[8] to distinguish it from *Eros* (sexual love), *Storgë* (family affection) and *Philia* (friendship). So there are 4 kinds of 'love', all good in their proper place, but *Agape* is the best because it is the kind God has for us and is good in all circumstances. (There are people I *mustn't* feel Eros towards, and people I can't feel Storge or Philia for; but I can practise Agape to God, Angels, Man and Beast, to the good and the bad, the old and the young, the far and the near.

You see Agape is all giving, not getting. Read what St. Paul says about it in First Corinthians Chap. 13. Then look at a picture

---

[6] Luke 7:31–35.
[7] *Letters III,* 428–429.
[8] E.g., I John 4:9.

of Charity (or Agape) in action in St. Luke, chap 10 v. 30–35. And then, better still, look at Matthew chap 25 v. 31–46: from which you see that Christ counts all that you do for *this* baby exactly as if you had done it for Him when He was a baby in the manger at Bethlehem: you are in a sense sharing in the things His mother did for Him. Giving money is only *one* way of showing charity: to give time and toil is far better and (for most of us) harder. And notice, though it is all giving—you needn't expect any reward—how you *do* gets rewarded almost at once.

Yes, I know one doesn't even *want* to be cured of one's pride because it gives pleasure. But the pleasure of pride is like the pleasure of scratching. If there is an itch one does want to scratch: but it is much nicer to have *neither* the itch *nor* the scratch. As long as we have the itch of self-regard we shall want the pleasure of self-approval; but the happiest moments are those when we forget our precious selves and have neither, but have everything else (God, our fellow-humans, animals, the garden and the sky) instead.

Yes, I do believe people are still healed by miracles by faith: but of course whether this has happened in any one particular case, is not so easy to find out.

TO MARY VAN DEUSEN: *On hypochondria; and on courage as the first and most necessary virtue.*[9]

22 FEBRUARY 1954

Thanks for your letter of Jan 13th. I don't think one gains anything from calling Genia's fears 'Hypochondria' and regarding them as something pathological. They are, like the fears of a soldier under fire, rational and natural fears of a real evil, so that her problem, like the soldier's, is moral, not medical. They must be faced on the conscious level and overcome by the Grace of God.

If only people (including myself: I also have fears) were still brought up with the idea that life is a battle where death and wounds await us at every moment, so that courage is the first and most necessary of virtues, things would be easier. As it is, fears are all the harder to combat because they disappoint expectations bred on modern poppycock in which unbroken security is regarded as

---

[9] *Letters III,* 431–432.

somehow 'normal' and the touch of reality as anomalous. Notice, too, how our bad habit of lying to those who are really ill renders vain our true assurances to those who are not!

I've had an exchange of letters with Genia on this very subject. I hope she won't go to a psychiatrist. How could a psychiatrist help her except by saying 'It is perfectly certain that you will *never* get any painful or dangerous disease'—and do you want her to be fool enough to believe *that*?

TO MARY WILLIS SHELBURNE: *On the need to cry; on the need to remember God's past mercies; on the suitability of his Ransom trilogy, especially* That Hideous Strength, *for children; and on the kinds of snobbery. Lewis asks if he may dedicate* The Magician's Nephew *to her friends.*[10]

22 FEBRUARY 1954

I am very sorry indeed to hear that anxieties again assail you. (By the way, don't 'weep inwardly' and get a sore throat. If you must weep, weep: a good honest howl! I suspect we—and especially, my sex—don't cry enough nowadays. Aeneas and Hector and Beowulf and Roland and Lancelot blubbered like school-girls, so why shouldn't we?) You were wonderfully supported in your worries last time: I shall indeed pray that it may be so again.

Would the Kilmer family like to have the next story but one dedicated to them? Let me know: the site is still vacant.

I didn't object to the family reading the trilogy on the ground that it would be too difficult—that would do no harm—but because in the last one there is so much evil, in a form not, I think, suitable for their age, and many specifically sexual problems which it would do them no good to think of at present. I daresay the *Silent Planet* is alright: *Perelandra,* little less so: *T. H. S.* most unsuitable.

I don't think that an *appreciation* of ancient and noble blood is 'snobbery' at all. What is snobbery is a greedy desire to know those who have it, or a mean desire to flatter them, or a conceited desire to boast of their acquaintance. I think it quite legitimate to feel that such things give an added interest to a person who is nice on other grounds, just as a hotel which was nice on other grounds would have an added charm for me if it was also a building with 'historic interest'.

I write in great haste—I can't, like you, do it in working hours! But you're nothing to [Charles] Lamb: as far as I can make out all his letters, which now fill two volumes, were written in the office. Happy days those.

Well I hope I shall have better news in your next. God bless you.

TO MARY WILLIS SHELBURNE: *On disagreeable, nasty people; and on avoiding obsessing about their bullying.*[11]

10 MARCH 1954

I am sorry things are not better. I am very puzzled by people like your Committee Secretary, people who are just nasty. I find it easier to understand the great crimes, for the raw material of them exists in us all; the mere disagreeableness which seems to spring from no recognisable passion is mysterious. (Like the total stranger in a train of whom I once asked 'Do you know when we get to Liverpool' and who replied 'I'm not paid to answer your questions: ask the guard'). I have found it more among boys than anyone else. That makes me think it really comes from inner insecurity—a dim sense that one is Nobody, a strong determination to be Somebody, and a belief that this can be achieved by arrogance. Probably *you*, who can't hit back, come in for a good deal of *resentful* arrogance aroused by others on whom she doesn't vent it, because they *can*. (A bully in an Elizabethan play, having been sat on by a man he dare not fight, says 'I'll go home and beat all my servants'). But I mustn't encourage you to go on thinking about her: that, after all, is almost the greatest evil nasty people can do us—to become an obsession, to haunt our minds. A brief prayer for them, and then away to other subjects, is the thing, if one can only stick to it. I hope the other job will materialise....

I too had mumps after I was grown up. I didn't mind it as long as I had the temperature: but when one came to convalescence and a convalescent appetite and even *thinking* of food started the

---

[11] *Letters III*, 438–439.

salivation and the pain—ugh! I never realised 'the disobedience in our members'[12] so clearly before. Verily 'He that but looketh on a plate of ham and eggs to lust after it, hath already committed breakfast with it in his heart' (or in his glands).[13]

I shall wait anxiously for all your news, always praying not only for a happy issue but that you may be supported in all interim anxieties.

TO RHONA BODLE, *who had written Lewis about difficulties with her father: On his most serious sin; on not expecting to feel affection for a difficult parent; on ways to work on loving such a one; and on Hans Christian Andersen.*[14]

24 MARCH 1954

Oh how you touch my conscience! I treated my own father abominably and no sin in my whole life now seems to be so serious. It is not likely you are equally guilty.

Feelings of affection are not at the command of the will and perhaps the very attempt to produce them has the opposite effect. I have been astonished at the ease (and even the affection) with which I have been able to treat in *other* old men the very same characteristics I was so impatient with in my Father. I wonder can something be done along these lines?—by remembering how merely funny, how endearing in a whimsical way, the things that divide you from your Father would seem if he were a casual acquaintance. By voluntarily standing further off might one in effect come closer? Part of the difficulty, I fancy, is heredity—a deep awareness that what one likes least in our parents has been bequeathed to oneself and, in oneself, needs to be resisted. While my Father was alive I was shocked when I caught myself acting or speaking like him; now I am amused, and not hostilely. At any rate, work now for the night cometh.[15]

I am delighted to hear how well your Sunday School goes on. I have come to like Hans Andersen better since I grew up than I

---

[12] Romans 7:23.
[13] Matthew 5:28.
[14] *Letters III*, 445–446.
[15] John 9:4.

did in childhood. I think both the pathos and the satire—both very delicate, penetrating and ever-present in his work—disquieted me then. I agree about *The Little Mermaid:* I'd add *The Storks, The Seven Swans* and (best of all satires) *The Emperor's New Clothes.*

He was, you know, a friend of Kierkegaard's and a very disappointed novelist, for it was by his novels, not his fairy tales that he wished to be known. I wonder if the story of the *Shadow* is connected with that—the shadow outgrowing the man as a fairy-tale-writer outgrew the novelist. But I'm glad he did! All blessings.

TO MARY VAN DEUSEN: *On God wanting us and not what we can do for God; and on our job to become more and more God's.*[16]

25 MARCH 1954

I must be short for I have had a run of absolutely full days and there are endless things waiting to be done. You ask 'for what' God wants you. Isn't the primary answer that He wants *you.* We're not told that the lost sheep was sought out for anything except itself.[17] Of course, He may have a special job for you: and the *certain* job is that of becoming more and more His. Yes, isn't [William] Law good?

TO MRS. D. JESSUP: *On getting rid of fear; and on the real meaning of faith (the only instance in this collection of a deliberately last letter).*[18]

26 MARCH 1954

I quite understand about closing your correspondence (with me; not with God, I trust). All congratulations on your good news and sympathy on your bad, and thanks for the merry photo. One last word, about getting rid of fear.

Two men had to cross a dangerous bridge. The first convinced himself that it would bear them, and called this conviction faith. The second said 'Whether it breaks or holds, whether I die here

---

[16] *Letters III,* 446.
[17] Matthew 18:12–14; Luke 15:3–7.
[18] *Letters III,* 447–448.

or somewhere else, I am equally in God's good hands.' And the bridge did break and they were both killed: and the second man's faith was not disappointed and the first man's was.

God bless you.

TO MARY WILLIS SHELBURNE *(who had continued to be bullied at work; see the letter to her above, 10 March 1954): On offering one's humiliations; on avoiding both contentment with and anger against oneself; and on the three patiences.*[19]

31 MARCH 1954

(I return the compliment by telling you that my friends call me Jack). I am sorry the persecution still goes on. I had that sort of thing at school, and in the army, and here too when I was a junior fellow, and it does very much darken life. I suppose (though it seems a hard saying) we should mind humiliation less if [we] were humbler. It is, at any rate, a form of suffering which we can try to offer,[20] in our small way, along with the supreme humiliation of Christ Himself. There is, if you notice it, a very great deal in the New Testament about His humiliations as distinct from His sufferings in general. And it is the humble and meek who have all the blessings in the *Magnificat*.[21] So your position is, spiritually, far safer than the opposite one. But don't think I don't know how much easier it is to preach than practice. . . .

How right you are to see that anger (even when directed against oneself) 'worketh not the righteousness of God'.[22] One must never be *either* content with, *or* impatient with, oneself. My old confessor (now dead) used to impress on me the need for the three Patiences: patience with God, with my neighbour, with oneself.

---

[19] *Letters III,* 448–449.
[20] Colossians 1:24.
[21] Luke 1:46–55.
[22] James 1:20.

TO ARTHUR GREEVES: *On setting a time limit in making decisions about matters that do not involve duty or necessity.*[23]

13 APRIL 1954

For one's own peace of mind I think it is best to set a time limit for one's decisions (I mean, decisions of mere pleasure where duty and necessity don't come in).

TO MARY VAN DEUSEN, *whose pastor marred her Easter experience: On the ways in which the devil works to mar liturgical celebrations; on involuntary uncharitable thoughts; on the need to take spiritual holidays; "Act as if everything depended on you. Pray as if everything depended on God" (Saint Ignatius of Loyola); and on the mutual respect parents and children own one another.*[24]

22 APRIL 1954

It *is* a pity, isn't it, that the great feasts which should be times of joy are so often marred in one way or another. (We have a *very* trying curate in our parish.) Some say 'the devil lives very near the altar', anxious to cut us off from grace by instilling sinful thoughts, or, if that fails, at least to deprive us of the sensible comforts of grace by instilling worry, fears, and inconveniences.

I take it your Rector is just an instance of the brother one has to forgive unto seventy times seven.[25] I don't think the *recurrence* of uncharitable thoughts is very serious provided one knocks them on the head each time, though of course it is an unhappiness and a proper ground for self-humiliation. But the real serious sin would lie in yielding to them. And I think you are free to take a spiritual holiday: i.e., when it is very hard to think kindly of someone, one may take a spell of not thinking about him at all. Of course it is hard to be closely connected with something and remain 'detached'. But does not God want us to reach, is He not helping us to reach, a sort of detachment from things (after all) a good deal *closer* than a parish: from our very selves, from all our hopes and fears? If they have a bad priest they need good laity all the more. And when

---

[23] *Letters III*, 453.
[24] *Letters III*, 460–461.
[25] Matthew 18:21–22.

one comes to think of it, the place where one is most wanted can hardly ever be the place where one would have chosen for one's own comfort. (The part of the line which needs troops is not the part where troops will have the best time.) But don't omit those 'holidays'. One has to *act* as if everything depended on one's own exertions and then, as soon as the moment of action is over, 'cast all your care'[26] upon God and realise that in some deeper sense, you don't matter in the least and it is only for *your* sake He uses you to do what He could do very much more easily Himself.

All parents are apt to treat their grown up sons and daughters at times as if they were still children: and perhaps all children are apt to think that this is happening even when it is not. I'm sure myself that *respect*—or let us say frankly *reverence*—is the disinfectant without which no affection will work properly.

TO SHELDON VANAUKEN, *who had asked Lewis how to counsel some Christian homosexuals he and his wife were trying to help: On what is not permitted homosexuals and what might be for their "glorious gain" (Wordsworth, "Character of the Happy Warrior," line 14); on prayer, particularly petitionary prayer; and on the worthiness and unworthiness of the petitioner. Lewis called this letter "an interim report"; he wrote a further letter, loaned to a homosexual and lost.*[27]

14 MAY 1954

I have seen less than you but more than I wanted of this terrible problem. I will discuss your letter with those whom I think wise in Christ. This is only an *interim* report.

First, to map out the boundaries within which all discussion must go on, I take it for certain that the *physical* satisfaction of homosexual desires is sin. This leaves the homosexual no worse off than any normal person who is, for whatever reason, prevented from marrying. Second, our speculations on the cause of the abnormality are not what matters and we must be content with ignorance. The disciples were not told *why* (in terms of efficient cause) the man was born blind (Jn. IX 1–3): only the final cause, that the works of God should be made manifest in him.

---

[26] I Peter 5:7.
[27] *Letters III,* 471–473.

This suggests that in homosexuality, as in every other tribulation, those works can be made manifest: i.e., that every disability conceals a vocation, if only we can find it, which will 'turn the necessity to glorious gain.' Of course, the first step must be to accept any privations which, if so disabled, we can't lawfully get. The homosexual has to accept sexual abstinence just as the poor man has to forego otherwise lawful pleasures because he would be unjust to his wife and children if he took them. That is merely a negative condition.

What should the positive life of the homosexual be? I wish I had a letter which a pious male homosexual, now dead, once wrote to me—but of course it was the sort of letter one takes care to destroy. He believed that his necessity *could* be turned to spiritual gain: that there were certain kinds of sympathy and understanding, a certain social rôle which mere *men* and mere *women* could not give. But it is all horribly vague—too long ago. Perhaps any homosexual who humbly accepts his cross and puts himself under divine guidance will, however, be shown the way. I am sure that any attempt to evade it (e.g., by mock- or quasi-marriage with a member of one's own sex *even* if this does not lead to any carnal act) is the wrong way. Jealousy (this another homosexual admitted to me) is far more rampant and deadly among them than among us. And I don't think little concessions like wearing the clothes of the other sex in private is the right line either. It is the duties, the burdens, the characteristic virtues of the other sex, I expect, which the patient must try to cultivate.

I have mentioned humility because *male* homosexuals (I don't know about women) are rather apt, the moment they find you don't treat them with horror and contempt, to rush to the opposite pole and start implying that they are somehow superior to the normal type. I wish I could be more definite. All I have really said is that, like all other tribulations, it must be offered to God and His guidance how to use it must be sought.

I heard you had been troubled with the old spine again. I hope the silence on this topic in your letter does not merely result from selflessness but means that you are now well. Remember me to your very nice wife. You both keep your place in my daily prayers. It is a sweet duty, praying for our friends. I always feel as if I had had a brief meeting with you when I do so: perhaps it *is* a meeting, and the best kind. Pray for me to be made more charitable: we're in the middle of a faculty crisis which tempts me to hatred many times a day.

P.S. I'd nearly forgotten your other point. I presume God grants prayers when granting would be good for the petitioner and others and denies them when it would not. Might there be cases where

a. The worthiness of the petitioner made it *bad* for him to have his prayers granted: i.e., might lead him to think there was an element of *bargain* about it.

b. The unworthiness made it *bad:* i.e., might lead him to think that God did not demand righteousness.

c. The worthiness made it *good:* i.e., might free him from scruples, show him that his conduct had been right after all.

d. The unworthiness made it *good:* i.e., produced humbled compunction—*unde hoc mihi?* (St. Elizabeth to the Blessed Virgin Mary: "*Whence is this to me,* that the mother of my Lord should come to me?" Luke 1:43.)

All very crude. The point is that worthiness might easily be taken into account though not in the way of direct *earning* and *reward.*

TO MARY VAN DEUSEN, *whose difficult pastor had been promoted: On detachment for the sake of attachment, the* via negativa *for the sake of the* via positiva; *and on gestures and postures of reverence.*[28]

20 MAY 1954

Well, well—so *that* struggle is over. Perhaps God used this reverend man—all as a hair shirt for the faithful and thinks you have worn (or borne) him long enough ('Deliver me from the ungodly who is a sword of thine').[29] It doesn't surprise me in the least that one who can't do a job himself should be set to teach others. Failed schoolmasters become inspectors of schools and failed authors become critics. It's the normal thing.

---

[28] *Letters III,* 477–478.
[29] Psalm 17:13.

When we speak of detachment (from worldly interests) we mean it of course only as a preliminary for *attachment* to spiritual things: as St. Paul wishes to be rid of the earthly body *only* in order to put on the heavenly (2 Cor. V. 1–4). All the Christian demands are in the end positive—to receive, take, embrace something ('Open thy mouth wide and I will fill it')[30]—and negative ('Love not the World')[31] only as means to that. As one might say to a slum-child, 'Stop making that mud pie and come for a holiday to the sea'.

About Reverence, you know, I believe all people all us, all who come from a Western, decayed-Protestant, liberal, commercial background, have a lot of lee-way to make up. We have our own advantages over those who come from a Latin, Catholic, decayed-feudal background: our veracity, manliness, energy. But we are *spiritually ill-bred*: raw and harsh and crude like yokels in a drawing room. How much even of what we take for democratic feeling is really *gaucherie*? I.e., we disapprove of 'bowings and scraping' partly because, not having had good dancing-masters, we don't know how to bow gracefully. What a pity that the progress of democracy in this country has meant that certain people who used to call me *Sir* now don't: it ought to have meant that *I* began calling *them* Sir. And we carry the same boorishness into spiritual matters.

TO DR. F. MORGAN ROBERTS: *On Lewis's own rules about prayer.*[32]

31 JULY 1954

I am certainly unfit to advise anyone else on the devotional life. My own rules are (1) To make sure that, wherever else they may be placed, the main prayers should *not* be put 'last thing at night'. (2) To avoid introspection in prayer—I mean not to watch one's own mind to see if it is in the right frame, but always to turn the attention outwards to God. (3) Never, never to try to generate an emotion by will power. (4) To pray without words when I am able, but to fall back on words when tired or

---

[30] Psalm 81:10.
[31] I John 2:15.
[32] *Letters III,* 500.

otherwise below par. With renewed thanks. Perhaps *you* will sometimes pray for *me*?

TO MARY MARGARET MCCASLIN: *On how, after weathering a bereave-ment, one feels abandoned by God; on how God works on our behalf even when we feel He is inactive; and on the necessity of continuing to use the ordinary means of the spiritual life during times of extraordinary need.*[33]

2 AUGUST 1954

Thank you for your letter of the July 25th. I will certainly put you in my prayers. I can well believe that you were divinely sup-ported at the time of your terrible calamity. People often are. It is afterwards, when the new and bleaker life is beginning to be a routine, that one often feels one has been left rather unaided. I am sure one is not really so. God's presence is not the same as the feeling of God's presence and He may be doing most for us when we think He is doing least.

Loneliness, I am pretty sure, is one of the ways by which we can grow spiritually. Until we are lonely we may easily think we have got further than we really have in Christian love; our (natural and innocent, but merely natural, not heavenly) pleasure in *being loved*—in being, as you say, an object of interest to some-one—can be mistaken for progress in love itself, the outgoing ac-tive love which is concerned with giving, not receiving. It is this latter which is the beginning of sanctity.

But of course you know all this: alas, so much easier to know in theory than to submit to day by day in practice! Be very regular in your prayers and communions: and don't value special 'guid-ances' any more than what comes through ordinary Christian teaching, conscience, and prudence.

I am shocked to hear that your friends think of following *me*. I wanted them to follow Christ. But they'll get over this confusion soon, I trust.

Please accept my deepest sympathy.

---

[33] *Letters III*, 500–501.

TO CYNTHIA DONNELLY, *who had asked Lewis about being a Christian writer: On good work rather than good works.*[34]

14 AUGUST 1954

Thank you for your most kind and encouraging letter. I think you have a mistaken idea of a Christian writer's duty. We must use the talent we have, not the talents we haven't. We must *not* of course write anything that will flatter lust, pride or ambition. But we needn't all write patently moral or theological work. Indeed, work whose Christianity is latent may do quite as much good and may reach some whom the more obvious religious work would scare away.

The first business of a story is to be a *good story*. When Our Lord made a wheel in the carpenter shop, depend upon it: It was first and foremost a *good wheel*. Don't try to 'bring in' specifically Christian bits: if God wants you to serve him in that way (He may not: there are different vocations), you will find it coming in of its own accord. If not, well—a good story which will give innocent pleasure is a good thing, just like cooking a good nourishing meal. (You don't put little texts in your family soup, I'll be bound.)

By the way, none of my stories *began* with a Christian message. I always start from a mental picture—the floating islands, a faun with an umbrella in a snowy wood, an 'injured' human head. Of course my non-fiction works are different. But they succeed because I'm a professional teacher and explanation happens to be one of the things I've learned to do.

But the great thing is to cultivate one's own garden, to do well the job which one's own natural capacities point out (after first doing well whatever the 'duties of one's station' impose). *Any* honest workmanship (whether making stories, shoes, or rabbit hutches) can be done to the glory of God. . . .

TO MAUDE M. MCCASLIN: *Further on the matter of Christian love being more divine for its outgoing and giving qualities.*[35]

---

[34] *Letters III,* 502–503.
[35] *Letters III,* 506.

19 SEPTEMBER 1954

I must have expressed myself badly if you thought I denied that purely human love could be outgoing and giving as well as in-drawing and receptive. I only meant that the former was more es-sentially love and more divine, especially when expended (as it can be by saints) on an unlovable object. All this is much better said by George MacDonald. Look at him in my *George MacDonald: An Anthology.*

TO MARY WILLIS SHELBURNE: *On how God provides for children raised in atheistic and in devout homes; and on the fear of aging.*[36]

19 SEPTEMBER 1954

About the lack of religious education: of course you must be grieved, but remember how much religious education has exactly the opposite effect to that which was intended, how many hard atheists from pious homes. May we not hope, with God's mercy, that a similarly opposite effect may be produced in her case? Par-ents are not Providence: their bad intentions may be frustrated as their good ones. Perhaps prayers as a secret indulgence which [the] father disapproves may have a charm they lacked in houses where they were commanded.

...I can well understand your fears about old age. And of course you are doing the very best thing in meditating on the sufferings of Our Lord.

TO "MRS. JONES" *(identity withheld): On sexual temptation as not only the most recognizable and least disguisable of our temptations but also as the most pleasurable; and on the consequences of the Fall for women and for men.*[37]

27 SEPTEMBER 1954

'Why has sex become man's chief stumbling block?' But has it? Or is it only the most *recognisable* of the stumbling blocks? I mean, we can mistake pride for a good conscience, and cruelty for

[36] *Letters III*, 506–507.
[37] *Letters III*, 510–511.

zeal, and idleness for the peace of God *et cetera*. But when lust is upon us, then, owing to the obvious physical symptoms, we can't pretend it is anything else. Is it perhaps only the least *disguisable* of our dangers. At the same time I think there is something in what you say. If marriage is an image of the mystical marriage between Christ and the Church, then adultery is an image of apostasy. Also, all the sexual vices have this unfair advantage that the very temptation is itself pleasurable: whereas the temptations, say, to anger or cowardice, are in themselves *un*pleasant.

I don't think I can solve your question about the pains of childbirth. I can only say that *vicarious* suffering seems to be deeply embedded in the post-fall world so that the Atonement is simply the supreme instance of a universal law. Would the inequality between man's and woman's share of the cause be less marked if Man (or selected, fortunate men) had not now managed to evade his share? If he still in person tilled the earth and fought the wild beasts? And has civilisation increased the woman's pain? I've heard of savage women who suffer much less. But I am only offering conjecture. I don't know the answer.

TO BELLE ALLEN: *On the power of Satan only to spoil but not to create; on the problem of the suffering of the wicked as well as of the innocent; on the oversimplicity of Christian Science practitioners; and on the essential mystery of suffering, of all of creation and of God so as to turn us into gods.*[38]

1 NOVEMBER 1954

I think it would be dangerous to suppose that Satan had created all the creatures that are disagreeable or dangerous to us for (a) those creatures, if they could think, would have just the same reason for thinking that *we* were created by Satan. (b) I don't think evil, in the strict sense, can *create*. It can spoil something that Another has created. Satan may have corrupted other creatures as well as us. Part of the corruption in us might be the unreasoning horror and disgust we feel at some creatures quite apart from any harm they can do us. (I can't abide a spider myself.) We have scriptural authority for Satan originating diseases—see Luke XIII.16.

---

[38] *Letters III*, 520.

Do you know, the suffering of the innocent is *less* of a problem to me very often than that of the wicked. It sounds absurd: but I've met so many innocent sufferers who seem to be gladly offering their pain to God in Christ as part of the Atonement, so patient, so meek, even so at peace, and so unselfish that we can hardly doubt they are being, as St. Paul says, 'made perfect by suffering'.[39] On the other hand I meet selfish egoists in whom suffering seems to produce only resentment, hate, blasphemy, and more egoism. They are the real problem.

Christian Scientists seem to me to be altogether too simple. Granted that all the evils are illusions, still, the existence of that illusion would be a real evil and presumably a real evil permitted by God. That brings us back to exactly the same point as we began from. We have gained nothing by the theory. We are still faced with the great mystery, not explained, but coloured, transmuted, all through the Cross. Faith, not wild over-simplifications, is what will help, don't you think? It is so very difficult to believe that the travail of all creation[40] which God Himself descended to share, at its most intense, may be necessary in the process of turning finite creatures (with free wills) into—well, into Gods.

TO MARY WILLIS SHELBURNE: *On the need to break open the alabaster jar of one's heart over the feet of Jesus for the contents to become perfume.*[41]

1 NOVEMBER 1954

No, my rheumatism is not really bad. It only produces extreme footsoreness in the left foot, so that after 50 yards, though the right one is fresh as a daisy the left keeps on whimpering 'Stop! Stop! We've been 25 miles already.' The real nuisance is that I am beginning to get horribly fat and this foot comes just when I ought to be slimming by long walks. I have had to give up potatoes, milk, and bread: perhaps having to fast for medical reasons is a just punishment for not having fasted enough on higher grounds!

---

[39] Hebrews 2:10.
[40] Romans 8:22.
[41] *Letters III*, 521–522.

Did I tell you I've been made a professor at Cambridge? I take up my duties on Jan. 1st at Magdalene College, Cambridge (England). Note the difference in spelling. It means rather less work for rather more pay. And I think I shall like Magdalene better than Magdalen. It's a tiny college (a perfect cameo architecturally) and they're so old fashioned, and pious, and gentle and conservative—unlike this leftist, atheist, cynical, hard-boiled, huge Magdalen. Perhaps from being the fogey and 'old woman' here I shall become the *enfant terrible* there.

It is nice to be still under the care of St. Mary Magdalene: she must by now understand my constitution better than a stranger would, don't you think? The allegorical sense of her great action[42] dawned on me the other day. The precious alabaster box which one must *break* over the Holy Feet is one's *heart*. Easier said than done. And the contents become perfume only when it is broken. While they are safe inside they are more like sewage. All very alarming.

TO BEDE GRIFFITHS: *On Lewis's favorite novel by Charles Dickens; on the desire to die; on longing; on joy; on having; and on wanting.*[43]

5 NOVEMBER 1954

The best Dickens always seems to me to be the one I have read last! But in a cool hour I put *Bleak House* top for its sheer prodigality of invention.

About death, I go through different moods, but the times when I can *desire* it are never, I think, those when this world seems harshest. On the contrary, it is just when there seems to be most of Heaven already here that I come nearest to longing for the *patria*. It is the bright frontispiece [which] whets one to read the story itself. All joy (as distinct from mere pleasure, still more amusement) emphasises our pilgrim status: always reminds, beckons, awakes desire. Our best havings are wantings.

---

[42] Luke 7:37–38.
[43] *Letters III*, 522–523.

TO SHELDON VANAUKEN, *whose wife, Jean Palmer "Davy" Davis, was dying: On Lewis's prayers for them by day and by night.*[44]

23 NOVEMBER 1954

It is a long time since you wrote and told me of your wife's grave illness. You asked my prayers and of course have had them: not only daily, for I never wake in the night without remembering you both before God. I have sometimes tried, by sophistical arguments, to persuade myself that your silence might somehow be interpreted as a good omen . . . but how could it?

If you can bear, will you tell me your news. If she has gone where we can feel no anxiety about her, then I must feel anxious about you. I liked you both so well: never two young people more. And to like is to fear. Whatever has happened and in whatever state you are (I have horrid pictures in my mind) all blessings on you.

TO WALTER HOOPER: *On the law of diversion (see* The Screwtape Letters, *VI).* [45]

30 NOVEMBER 1954

Thank you for your kind letter of the 23rd. I am glad if I have been the instrument of Our Lord's help to you: in His hands almost any instrument will do, otherwise none.

We should, I believe, distrust states of mind which turn our attention upon ourselves. Even at our sins we should look no longer than is necessary to know and to repent them: and our virtues or progress (if any) are certainly a dangerous object of contemplation. When the sun is vertically above a man he casts no shadow: similarly when we have come to the Divine meridian our spiritual shadow (that is, our consciousness of self) will vanish. One will thus in a sense be almost nothing: a room to be filled by God and our blessed fellow creatures, who in their turn are rooms we help to fill. But how far one is from this at present!

---

[44] *Letters III*, 531.
[45] *Letters III*, 535.

1955

TO MARY VAN DEUSEN, *who had been reading* Eros and Agape *by the Swedish Lutheran theologian Anders Nygren, at Lewis's recommendation: On an overstrictness in giving the name love to a "need" love and on the final resolution of her problem with her pastor.*[1]

19 JANUARY 1955

Yes: I would certainly agree with 'the disfigured in the best of us, but still an image in the worst'. Nygren is surely wrong if he says that merited love is sinful. It can't be wrong to love the hand that feeds one. How much more wisely Christ put it: 'if you love only them that do good to you, do not the Gentiles [do] as much?'[2] i.e., not that it is sin (indeed not to do it would be sin) but that it is no great matter, is elementary and merely natural. When we say to a boy of 17, 'You ought to be ashamed of yourself, doing simple long division,' we don't mean that there's anything wrong with long division but that he ought by now to have got on to something more advanced. Is it by some such *confusion* Nygren has got where he is? Still his book was well worth reading: we both have the very important idea of Eros and Agape now clearly in our minds, and can keep it after we have let all his exaggerations fade out of our minds.

In a way I am *glad* about your rector's true story. One finds pitiable human weakness where one had expected hard self-righteousness. It is almost a relief.

I am sorry Genia had a bad turn. She is always in my prayers. It makes me feel as if I had a daughter of my own!

TO SHELDON VANAUKEN, *whose wife died on 17 January 1955—he had written to ask Lewis to scatter some of her ashes, conveyed by a friend, at their church near Oxford; Lewis had agreed, but his letter saying so*

---

[1] *Letters III, 555.*
[2] Luke 6:33.

was lost en route: On the feelings of bereavement, the good feelings and the dangerous feelings; on the necessity of bereavement; and on the need to take care of oneself.[3]

10 FEBRUARY 1955

I heard from your friend about 2 days ago, and today I have got your letter of Feb. 5. I am most distressed to find that my answer to your previous letter has never reached you; particularly since its miscarriage has left you in doubt whether I would have accepted the very sacred office of scattering the ashes. I would have liked to do (if you can understand) for the very reason that I would not have liked doing it, since a deep spiritual *gaucherie* makes [me] uneasy in any ceremonial act; and I would have wished in that way to be honoured with a share, however tiny, in this Cross. All you told me in your previous letter and all you tell me in this moves me deeply and it is a high privilege to be admitted to such a beautiful death, an *act* which consummates (not, as so often, an event which merely stops) the earthly life. And how you reassure me when, to describe your own state, you use the simple, obvious, yet now so rare, word *sad*. Neither more nor less nor other than sad. It suggests a clean wound—much here for tears, but 'nothing but good and fair.'

And I am sure it is never sadness—a proper, straight natural response to loss—that does people harm, but all the other things, all the resentment, dismay, doubt and self-pity with which it is usually complicated. I feel (indeed I tried to say something about it in that lost letter) very strongly what you say about the 'curious consolation' that 'nothing now can mar' your joint lives. I sometimes wonder whether bereavement is not, at bottom, the easiest and least perilous of the ways in which men lose the happiness of youthful love. For I believe it must *always* be lost in some way: every merely natural love has to be crucified before it can achieve resurrection and the happy *old* couples have come through a difficult death and rebirth. But far more have missed the rebirth. Your 'Manuscript,' as you well say, has now gone safe to the Printer.

It is remarkable (I have experienced it), that sense that the dead person *is*. And also, I have felt, is active: can sometimes do more

[3] *Letters III*, 560–561.

for you now than before—as if God gave them, as a kind of birthday present on arrival, some great blessing to the beloved they have left behind.

Be careful of your own bodily health. You must be, physically, very tired, much more tired than you know. Above all, don't yield to the feeling that such things 'don't matter *now*.' You must remain, as she wishes, a good *instrument* for all heavenly impulses to work on, and the body is part of the instrument.

I shall be nervous about all letters now that one (and at such a moment) has gone astray. If this reaches you, a line in answer will reassure me.

You are always in my prayers, even whenever I wake in the night. Keep me in yours.

under the Omnipotence
C.S. Lewis

TO MRS. D. JESSUP, *whose husband has left her for another woman: On granting her husband a civil divorce; and on her inability to remarry while he is still alive.*[4]

13 FEBRUARY 1955

I was deeply shocked by the news in your letter of Feb. 7ᵗʰ and can't tell you how much I sympathise with you. The one bright spot is that you are clearly suffering only from what we may call the 'clean pain' of loss, not complicated, as it would be in many women, with those pains of resentment and anger which are so much more likely to fester.

Now as to your problem. I am not quite clear (though you may well have told me long ago—I can't always remember things now) what 'religion' you are of. You have 'left the Episcopal church' and have been staying with nuns. Does this mean you are a Roman Catholic? If so, you have no need of *my* advice. Your own Church has clear and rigid rules on all these subjects and your confessor will tell you exactly what you are, and are not, allowed to do. But this is so obvious that I don't think you can be an R.C. or you wouldn't have asked me.

---

[4] *Letters III,* 562.

What, then, is your allegiance? I doubt if I can give advice simply to a 'mere Christian' as such, for different bodies have differently interpreted Our Lord's words. My own very tentative idea would be that you must always regard yourself as his wife, and therefore incapable of a second marriage while he lives: but that I'm not at all clear that this forbids you to 'divorce' him, i.e., to give him *legal* freedom to make another marriage, though this other would not (in our eyes) be marriage in the full Christian sense. It might, however, prevent connections which would on *any* view be more sinful.

But I express my view with extreme reluctance. I am only an amateur: you must be guided by the experts (in whatever your own communion is). I feel I am failing you—and also that I am writing in a dry, unfeeling way. Believe me, it doesn't represent my real reactions. You have never been out of my daily prayers, and you will be even more in them now. May God continue to support you and keep your great sorrow as pure (so then it will heal) as it now clearly is.

TO MARY WILLIS SHELBURNE: *On feelings or the lack of them in prayer, especially a sense of the presence of God.*[5]

19 FEBRUARY 1955

Thanks for your letter of 14th. But why on earth didn't you write it a day later and tell me the result of the examination?

I don't think we ought to try to keep up our normal prayers when we are ill and over-tired. I would not say this to a beginner who still has the habit to form. But you are past that stage. One mustn't make the Christian life into a punctilious system of *law*, like the Jewish. Two reasons (1.) It raises scruples when we don't keep the routine (2.) It raises presumption when we do. Nothing gives one a more spuriously good conscience than keeping rules, even if there has been a total absence of all real charity and faith. And people who stay away from Mass with the approval of their director and at the bidding of their doctor are just as obedient as those who go. Check all these points with your confessor: I bet he'll say just the same.

---

[5] *Letters III,* 564.

And of course the presence of God is not the same as the *sense* of the presence of God. The latter may be due to imagination: the former may be attended with no 'sensible consolation'. The Father was not *really* absent from the Son when He said 'Why hast thou forsaken me?'[6] You see God Himself, as man, submitted to man's sense of being abandoned. The real parallel on the natural level is one which seems odd for a bachelor to write to a lady, but too illuminating not to be used. The act which engenders a child ought to be, and usually is, attended by pleasure. But it is not the pleasure that produces the child. Where there is pleasure there may be sterility; where there is no pleasure the act may be fertile. And in the spiritual marriage of God and the soul it is the same. It is the actual presence, not the *sensation* of the presence, of the Holy Ghost which begets Christ in us. The *sense* of the presence is a super-added gift for which we give thanks when it comes, and that's all about it.

TO SHELDON VANAUKEN: *On the consolations that often attend the first period after conversion; and on the way we will be able to reveal ourselves to one another in heaven.*[7]

20 FEBRUARY 1955

I was very glad to get your letter of Feb. 14. And here 'luck' worked the other way. It had come unstuck and the envelope was open, but the letter inside, intact.

Your real or supposed change of luck since your conversion (whatever it may really mean) is an old story: read Jeremiah XLIV 15–18. And I have seen it laid down by a modern spiritual author (whose name I forget) that the experience is to be expected. You remember the vision of Our Lord that said to St. Theresa on some frightful occasion, 'This is how I always treat my friends.' (I must not conceal her answer, 'Then, Lord, it is not surprising that You have so few.')

What you say about the total Jean being apprehensible since the moment-by-moment Jean has been withdrawn (backed by the very good analogy of the novel page-by-page and the novel after

---

[6] Psalm 22:1; Matthew 27:46; Mark 15:34.
[7] *Letters III*, 565–566.

you've read it) is most true and important. I see no reason why we should not regard it as what St. Paul calls an *arrabon* or earnest of the mode in which all can reveal themselves to all in heaven.[8] . . .

Do you know Coventry Patmore's *Angel in the House* and (still more, but the first is to be read as a prelude) *Love's Victory*. They deal superbly with some of the experiences you are having.

TO MRS. D. JESSUP: *On no such thing as chance; on the need to make up one's mind about the innocent party's freedom to remarry* before *it becomes a question of the heart.*[9]

2 MARCH 1955

Thank you for your letter of March 25th. It has done me good. You are so clearly being supported and guided through this tribulation by the Holy Spirit: and, as so often is the case, unexpected helps spring up.

Oh what a rare blessing to have a Christian psychotherapist! I don't think your question whether these ones were brought into your life by 'a whimsical fate' or by God, need detain you long. Once one believes in God at all, surely the question is meaningless? Suppose that in a novel a character gets killed in a railway accident. Is his death due to chance (e.g., the signals being wrong) or to the novelist? Well of course, both. The chance *is the way* the novelist removes the character at the exact moment his story requires. There's a good line in Spenser to quote to oneself: 'It chanced (almighty God that chance did guide)'.

I don't think it my business to [speak further] about the remarriage of the innocent party after a divorce. My own opinion carries no authority. All I would say is that the matter should be decided once and for all *now* while the question of re-marriage is purely academic, so as to save you from painful indecisions later on, and also because your whole future attitude to your thoughts and feelings and indeed much of your social behaviour must be governed by it.

I will indeed pray for the other two: especially Kim. And thank you very much for *your* prayers.

---

[8] II Corinthians 1:21–22.
[9] *Letters III*, 574–575.

TO MRS. JOHNSON: *On God's unique way with each soul, even in the pattern of conversion; and on various Christian nonessentials.*[10]

2 MARCH 1955

It is right and inevitable that we should be much concerned about the salvation of those we love. But we must be careful not to expect or demand that their salvation should conform to some ready-made pattern of our own. Some Protestant sects have gone very wrong about this. They have a whole programme of 'conviction', 'conversion,' *et cetera,* marked out, the same for everyone, and will not believe that anyone can be saved who doesn't go through it 'just so'. But (see the last chapter of *Problem of Pain*) God has His own unique way with each soul.

There is no evidence that St. John even underwent the same kind of 'conversion' as St. Paul. It's not essential to believe in the devil; and I'm sure a man can get to Heaven without being accurate about Methuselah's age. Also, as MacDonald says, 'the time for *saying* comes seldom, the time for *being* is always there.' What we practice, not (save at rare intervals) what we preach, is usually our great contribution to the conversion of others.

TO MRS. JOHNSON: *On teetotalism; and on the high calling of being a homemaker.*[11]

16 MARCH 1955

I am afraid I am not going to be much help about all the religious bodies mentioned in your letter of March 2nd. I have always in my books been concerned simply to put forward 'mere' Christianity, and am no guide on these (most regrettable) 'interdenominational' questions. I do however strongly object to the tyrannic and unscriptural insolence of anything that calls itself a Church and makes teetotalism a condition of membership. Apart from the more serious objection (that Our Lord Himself turned water into wine and made wine the medium of the only rite He imposed on all His followers), it is so provincial (what I believe you people call 'small town'). Don't they realise that Christianity

---

[10] *Letters III,* 575–576.
[11] *Letters III,* 581–582.

arose in the Mediterranean world where, then as now, wine was as much part of the normal diet as bread? . . .

I think I can understand that feeling about a housewife's work being like that of Sisyphus (who was the stone rolling gentleman). But it is surely, in reality, the most important work in the world. What do ships, railways, mines, cars, government *et cetera* exist for except that people may be fed, warmed, and safe in their own homes? As Dr. Johnson said, 'To be happy at home is the end of all human endeavour'. (1st to be happy to prepare for being happy in our own real Home hereafter: 2nd, in the meantime, to be happy in our houses.) We wage war in order to have peace, we work in order to have leisure, we produce food in order to eat it. So your job is the one for which all others exist.

TO MARY VAN DEUSEN, *who had sent Lewis printed stationery: On the physical pleasures of youth and of old age; on the sacramentality of eating; on how life expands; and on the human Jesus of the real Gospels.*[12]

19 MARCH 1955

I hope you admire the lovely paper! It almost makes letter writing a pleasure: only I feel that I can't write well enough to live up to it. And the beautiful amplitude of the address! It reminds me of the address I used to put after my name in the fly-leaf of a new book when I was a very small boy, which ended up 'Ireland, the British Isles, Europe, Earth, the Universe'. Thank you very much. You well divined that nice paper would be one of those things which in a bachelor household is always desired and never got.

I feel strongly, with you, that there was something more than a physical pleasure in those youthful activities. Even now, at my age, do we often have a *purely* physical pleasure? Well, perhaps, a few of the more hopelessly prosaic ones: say, scratching or getting one's shoes off when one's feet are tired. I'm sure my meals are too a purely physical pleasure. All the associations of every other time one has had the same food (every rasher of bacon is now 56 years thick with me) come in: and with things like Bread, Wine, Honey, Apples, there are all the echoes of myth, fairy-tale, poetry,

---

[12] *Letters III,* 583–584.

and scripture. So that the physical pleasure is also imaginative and even spiritual. Every meal can be a kind of lower sacrament. 'Devastating gratitude' is a good phrase: but my own experience is rather 'devastating desire'—desire for that-of-which-the-present-joy-is-a-reminder. All my life nature and art have been *reminding* me of something I've never seen: saying 'Look! What does this—and this—remind you of?'

I am so glad that you are finding (as I do too) that life, far from getting dull and empty as one grows older, opens out. It is like being in a house where one keeps on discovering new rooms.

Yes, Jesus Himself, of course: the heart. Not only the God in Him but the historical Man. I don't know that I ever got much from reading things *about* Him. Perhaps, in a queer way, I got most from reading the Apocryphal Gospels.... For there you find things attributed to Him that couldn't be true. You even find wise and beautiful sayings which nevertheless just don't ring true. And have you noticed—reading the true saying in the real Gospels—how hardly one of them could have been guessed in advance?

Genia's theory about the physical cause of depression is probably right nine times out of ten. But the drugs are a matter for the doctor, I presume. She mustn't believe all the disguised-advertisement poppycock in the press! Blessing on you all, from both of us.

TO MARY WILLIS SHELBURNE: *New "light" on Luke 18:9–14, the Pharisee and the publican.*[13]

21 MARCH 1955

We were talking about cats and dogs the other day and decided that both have consciences but the dog, being an honest, humble person, always has a bad one, but the cat is a Pharisee and always has a good one. When he sits and stares you out of countenance he is thanking God that he is not as these dogs, or these humans, or even as these other cats!

---

[13] *Letters III*, 586–587.

TO MARY WILLIS SHELBURNE: *On the danger of misinterpreting facial expressions and tones of voice.*[14]

24 MARCH 1955

Just a line of sympathy and encouragement on the impending operation. Extra faith has been given to meet crises before, and I pray that it will be now. Be very much on your guard against the growth of a feeling that Fr. A. or anyone else 'does not sound interested'. When we are in trouble we easily think this, don't we? And at all times, we very easily misinterpret expressions of face and tones of voice. Often, too, the person we speak to is at that moment full of troubles we know nothing about.

TO MARY WILLIS SHELBURNE: *On the very comforting fact that Jesus was afraid.*[15]

2 APRIL 1955

In great haste. I hope your next letter will bring me news that the operation has gone swimmingly. Fear is horrid, but there's no reason to be ashamed of it. Our Lord was afraid (dreadfully so) in Gethsemane. I always cling to that as a very comforting fact. All blessings.

TO JILL FREUD: *On the effect the reading of* The Passion of Our Lord Jesus Christ *by Pierre Barbet had on Lewis's understanding of the sufferings of Christ.*[16]

6 APRIL 1955

At present I'm on Barbet's book on the Holy Shroud. Do you know it? There are things which I have felt, in previous Holy Weeks, that I was not thinking about enough: after an evening of Barber the difficulty is to think of anything else. In fact one gets, not more than one needs, but a good deal more than one bargained for.

---

[14] *Letters III*, 588–589.
[15] *Letters III*, 590.
[16] *Letters III*, 591.

TO SHELDON VANAUKEN: *On how God's total creation meets us in every event at every moment, thus blurring the distinction between the significant and the fortuitous; on the danger of trying to preserve the past; and on the duty to be as happy as one can.*[17]

6 APRIL 1955

It was a strange experience to get a letter from Jean this morning. I return it. You will see that it deals with a problem on which you also wrote to me, probably at about the same time. Indeed her reason for not sending it might be the discovery that you had done, or were about to do, the same.

I can't now remember what I said in my lost letter [see the letter above, 10 February 1955] about the 'Signs'. My general view is that, once we have accepted an omniscient and providential God, the distinction we used to draw between the significant and the fortuitous must either break down or be restated in some very much subtler form. If an event coming about in the ordinary course of nature becomes to me the occasion of hope and faith and love or increased efforts after virtue, do we suppose that this result was unforeseen by, or is indifferent to, God? Obviously not. What we should have called its fortuitous effects must have been present to Him for all eternity. And indeed, we can't suppose God saying (as a human artist might) 'That effect, though it has turned out rather well, was, I must admit, no part of my original design.' Then the total act of creation, including *our own* creation (which is going on all the time) meets us, doesn't it? in every event at every moment: the act of a Person dealing with persons and knowing what He does. Thus I wouldn't now be bothered by a man who said to me 'This, which you mistake for grace, is really the good functioning of your digestion.' Does my digestion fall outside God's act? He made and allowed to me my colon as much as my guardian angel. . . .

I give no advice about the thesis, and I think you ought to be guided by ordinary academic considerations. Forgive me for suggesting that the form 'What Jean would have liked' could come to have its dangers. The real question is what she wills *now*; and you may be sure her will is now one with God's. A 'sovereignty

---

[17] *Letters III,* 592–593.

in the pluperfect subjective' is often a snare. The danger is that of confusing your love for her (gradually—as the years pass) with your love for a period in your own past; and of trying to preserve the past in a way in which it can't be preserved. Death-corruption-resurrection is the true rhythm: not the pathetic, horrible practice of mummification. Sad you must be at present. You can't develop a false sense of a duty to cling to sadness if—and when, for *nature* will not preserve any psychological state forever—sadness begins to vanish? There is great good in bearing sorrow patiently: I don't know that there is any virtue in sorrow just as such. It is a Christian duty, as you know, for everyone to be as happy as he can. But you know all this already.

All love.

TO RHONA BODLE, *who had written Lewis to complain that New Zealand teachers were now expected to educate against premarital sex without any reference to religion: On the impossibility of chastity without a supernatural and sacramental view; and on the duty those who are spared suffering have to share the suffering of others.*[18]

28 APRIL 1955

Thanks for your letter of March 14th. Yes, here I am (though still, you see, under the same celestial patroness) translated into all the dignity and—what's very much more important—leisure of a professor.

I am liking Cambridge very much. For one thing, it is still, substantially, a country town, nor ruined like poor Oxford by industrialisation. In the university I am pleasantly surprised to find much more Christianity than at Oxford—at least so it seems, but of course it may be just I have fallen across more here by chance. This is a nice college: after the old Magdalen it is so small that I feel I'd like to take it to bed with me or have it swimming in my bath! But very beautiful and gentle and unobtrusive.

It certainly seems very hard that you should be told to arm the young against Venus without calling in Christ. What do they want? I suppose the usual twaddle about bees and orchids (as if approaching a subject by that devious route would make any pos-

18 *Letters III,* 599–600.

sible difference either good or bad). And indeed now that contraceptives have removed the most disastrous consequence for girls, and medicine has largely defeated the worst horrors of syphilis, what argument against promiscuity is there left which will influence the young unless one brings in the whole supernatural and sacramental view of man?

I quite agree that one can't help wondering why one is (so far) spared many temporal tribulations (better than wondering why one has *some!*). I think your answer is the safest if one is to attempt an answer at all: i.e., we're only third line troops. One is sometimes afraid when one reads the beatitudes—I suppose, at any rate, we must try to enter into other's sufferings more deeply than the less fortunate do. I don't know. We must believe that whatever our lot is it has been given us for the best. All blessings.

TO PHILINDA KRIEG, *who had been reading the* Chronicles of Narnia *to her son Laurence, who was now worried that he loved Aslan more than Jesus: A letter meant to be shared with a nine-year-old boy with a prayer he might say, and its codicil of intercession for Lewis.*[19]

6 MAY 1955

Dear Mrs. Krieg

Tell Laurence from me, with my love:

1/ Even if he was loving Aslan more than Jesus (I'll explain in a moment why he can't really be doing this) he would not be an idol-worshipper. If he was an idol-worshipper he'd be doing it on purpose, whereas he's now doing it because he can't help doing it, and trying hard not to do it. But God knows quite well how hard we find it to love Him more than anyone or anything else, and He won't be angry with us as long as we are trying. And He will help us.

2/ But Laurence can't *really* love Aslan more than Jesus, even if he feels that's what he is doing. For the things he loves Aslan for doing or saying are simply the things Jesus really did and said. So that when Laurence thinks he is loving Aslan, he is really loving Jesus: and perhaps loving Him more than he ever did before. Of

---

[19] *Letters III*, 602–603. The entire correspondence is published online at http://home.comcast.net/~krieg5208/Lewis/index.htm.

course there is one thing Aslan has that Jesus has not—I mean, the body of a lion. (But remember, if there are other worlds and they need to be saved and Christ were to save them as He would—He may really have taken all sorts of bodies in them which we don't know about.)

Now if Laurence is bothered because he finds the lion-body seems nicer to him than the man-body, I don't think he *need* be bothered at all. God knows all about the way a little boy's imagination works (He made it, after all) and knows that at a certain age the idea of talking and friendly animals is very attractive. So I don't think He minds if Laurence likes the Lion-body. And anyway, Laurence will find as he grows older, that feeling (liking the lion-body better) will die away of itself, without his taking any trouble about it. So he needn't bother.

3/ If I were Laurence I'd just say in my prayers something like this: 'Dear God, if the things I've been thinking and feeling about those books are things You don't like and are bad for me, please take away those feelings and thoughts. But if they are not bad, then please stop me from worrying about them. And help me every day to love you more in the way that really matters far more than any feelings or imaginations, by doing what you want and growing more like you.' That is the sort of thing I think Laurence should say for himself; but it would be kind and Christian-like if he then added, 'And if Mr. Lewis has worried any other children by his books or done them any harm, then please forgive him and help him never to do it again.'

Will this help? I am terribly sorry to have caused such trouble, and would take it as a great favour if you would write again and tell me how Laurence goes on. I shall of course have him daily in my prayers. He must be a corker of a boy: I hope you are prepared for the possibility he might turn out a saint. I dare say the saints' mothers have, in some ways, a rough time!

TO SHELDON VANAUKEN, *who had written Lewis about the agreement he and his late wife had made not to have children lest the children come between them and to die together, and who now asked Lewis whether suicide for love and not despair might be allowed: The justly famous "severe mercy" letter of correction: On the need to reread one's own story*

as someone else's and to interpret it with the rest of humanity looking on,
with their various ethical sensitivities, from Pagan to Christian; and on
joyfully suffering the birth of the real self.[20]

8 MAY 1955

Your letter is a wonderfully clear and beautiful expression of
an experience often desired but not often achieved to the degree
you and Jean achieved it. My reason for sending it back is my
belief that if you reread it often, till you can look at it as if it were
someone else's story, you will in the end think as I do (but of
course far more deeply and fruitfully than I can, because it will
cost you so much more) about a life so wholly (at first) devoted to
US. Not only as I do, but as the whole 'sense' of the human family
would on their various levels.

Begin at the bottom. What would the grosser Pagans think?
They'd say there was excess in it, that it would provoke the neme-
sis of the gods; they would 'see the red light.' Go up one: the finer
Pagans would blame each withdrawal from the claims of common
humanity as unmanly, uncitizenly, uxorious. If Stoics they would
say that to try to wrest part of the Whole (US) into a self-sufficing
Whole on its own was 'contrary to nature'.

Then come to Christians. They would of course agree that
man and wife are 'one flesh';[21] they would perhaps admit that
this was most admirably realised by Jean and you. But surely they
would add that this One Flesh must not (and in the long run cannot) 'live to itself'[22] any more than the single individual. It was
not made, any more than he, to be its own End. It was made for
God and (in Him) for its neighbours—first and foremost among
them the children it ought to have produced. (The idea behind
your voluntary sterility, that an experience, e.g., maternity, which
cannot be shared should on that account be avoided, is surely
very unsound. For *a*. (forgive me) the conjugal act itself depends
on opposite and reciprocal and therefore unshareable experiences.
Did you want her to feel she had a *woman* in bed with her? *b*. The

---

[20] *Letters III*, 605–606.
[21] Genesis 2:24.
[22] Romans 14:8.

experience of a woman denied maternity is one you *did not* and *could not* share with her. To be denied paternity is different and trivial in comparison.)

One way or another the thing had to die. Perpetual springtime is not allowed. You were not cutting the wood of life according to the grain. There are various possible ways in which it could have died though both the parties went on living. You have been treated with a severe mercy. You have been brought to see (how true and how very frequent this is!) that you were jealous of God. And from US you have been led back to US AND GOD: it remains to go on to GOD AND US.

She was further on than you, and she can help you more where she now is than she could have done on earth. You must go on. That is one of the many reasons why suicide is out of the question. (Another is the absence of any ground for believing that death *by that route* would reunite you with her. Why should it? You might be digging an eternally unbridgeable chasm. Disobedience is not the way to get nearer to the obedient.)

There's no other man, in such affliction as yours, to whom I'd dare write so plainly. And that, if you can believe me, is the strongest proof of my belief in you and love for you. To fools and weaklings one writes soft things. You spared her (very wrongly) the pains of childbirth; do not evade your own, the travail you must undergo while Christ is being born in you.[23] Do you imagine she herself can now have any greater care about you than that this spiritual maternity of yours should be patiently suffered and joyfully delivered?

God bless you. Pray for me.

TO MRS. JOHNSON: *On various passages in the Bible and how to interpret them, not just individually, but to see the gradual unfolding and purification of the revelation of God's character.*[24]

---

[23] Cf. Galatians 4:19.
[24] *Letters III*, 607–609.

Clearly, from a passage in *Hebrews,*[25] there is something very special about Melchisedech, but I don't know what it is. There's lots to find out, here and hereafter, isn't there?

My own view about Elisha and the bears[26] (not that I haven't known small boys who'd be much improved by the same treatment!) and other episodes is something like this. If you take the Bible as a whole, you see a process in which something which, in its earliest levels (those aren't necessarily the ones that come first in the Book as now arranged) was hardly moral at all, and was in some ways not unlike the Pagan religions, is gradually purged and enlightened till it becomes the religion of the great prophets and Our Lord Himself. That whole process is the greatest revelation of God's true nature. At first hardly anything comes through but mere power. Then (very important) the truth that He is One and there is no other God. Then justice, then mercy, love, wisdom.

Of course Our Lord never drank *spirits* (they had no distilled liquors) but of course the wine of the Bible was real fermented wine and alcoholic. The repeated references to the sin of drunkenness in the Bible, from Noah's first discovery of wine[27] down to the warnings in St. Paul's epistles,[28] make this perfectly plain. The other theory could be (honestly) held only by a very ignorant person. One can understand the bitterness of some 'temperance' fanatics if one has ever lived with a drunkard: what one finds it harder to excuse is any educated person telling such lies about history.

I think myself that the point of the shocking reply to the Syrophenician woman[29] (it came alright in the end) is to remind all us Gentile Christians—who forget it easily enough and even flirt with anti-Semitism—that the Jews are spiritually *senior* to us, that God *did* entrust the descendants of Abraham with the first revelation of Himself. To 'put us in our place.'

---

[25] Hebrews 6:20; 7:1–28.
[26] II Kings 2:23–24.
[27] Genesis 9:20–21.
[28] Romans 13:13; Ephesians 5:18; I Timothy 3:3.
[29] Mark 7:24–30.

TO SHELDON VANAUKEN: *On the experience of the replacement for time in eternity; on the relationship between spouses in heaven; and on the need to follow Dante's advice and to allow God to turn us from any rivulet to the fountain. Lewis loans him the five sonnets later published in* Poems, *125–127, and* Collected Poems, *139–141.*[30]

5 JUNE 1955

What you say about time is what I've long thought. It is inadequate to, and partially transcended by, very simple experiences. E.g., *when* do we hear a musical air? Until the last note is sounded it is incomplete; as soon as that sounds it's already over. And I'm pretty sure eternal life doesn't mean this width-less line of moments endlessly prolonged (as if by prolongation it could 'catch up with' that which it so obviously could never hold) but getting off that line onto its plane or even the solid. Read von Hügel's *Eternal Life* and Boethius *Consolation. . . .*

About the nature of the relation between spouses in eternity, I base my idea on St. Paul's dictum that 'he that is joined with a harlot is one flesh'.[31] If the lowest and most corrupt form of sexual union has some mystical 'oneness' involved in it (and by the way what an argument *against* 'casual practice'!) *a fortiori* the blessed and lawful form must have it *par excellence.* That is, I think the union between the risen spouses will be as close as that between the soul and its own risen body. But (and this, as you see, is the snag) the risen body is the body that has died. ('*If* we share this death, we shall also share this resurrection.')[32] And so—as you say in one of your postscripts—your love for Jean must, in one sense, be 'killed' and 'God must do it.' You'd better read the *Paradiso,* hadn't you? Note the moment at which Beatrice turns her eyes away from Dante 'to the eternal Fountain', and Dante is quite content. But of course it's all in the text 'Seek ye first the Kingdom . . . and all these other things shall be added unto you.'[33] Infinite comfort in the second part: inexorable demand in the first. Hopeless if it were

---

[30] *Letters III,* 616–617.
[31] I Corinthians 6:16.
[32] Romans 6:5.
[33] Matthew 6:33.

to be done by your own endeavours at some particular moment. But 'God must do it.'

Your part is what you are already doing: 'Take me—no conditions.' After that, through the daily duty, through the increasing effort after holiness—well, like the seed growing secretly.[34] What you say about the *she* in you and the *he* in her certainly does *not* seem to me the plains of Gomorrah and *is* in some sense (*what* I don't well know) probably true. There might be an element of delusion in the form it took: I don't know.... Possibly all those fine points which distinguish your loss from all the other losses suffered by other lovers are less important than they (very naturally) seem to you.

These sonnets, written about 10 years ago, are not in every way addressed to your condition, but they put some things perhaps a little better than I could put them here. I am in great trouble about my dear brother's dipsomania: pray for him and me. God bless you.

P. S. Let me have the sonnets back sometime: but no hurry.

TO MARY WILLIS SHELBURNE: *On learning to work with jealous colleagues; and on meekness toward oneself when one fails to control uncharitable thoughts.*[35]

21 JUNE 1955

I'm sorry about your two jealous colleagues. I suppose the only way with thorns in the flesh[36] (until one can get them out) is not to press on the place where they are embedded: i.e., to stop one's thoughts (firmly but gently: no good snapping at oneself, it only increases the fuss—read St. François de Sales' chapter on meekness towards oneself)[37] whenever one finds them moving towards the unpleasant people.

---

[34] Mark 4:28.
[35] *Letters III*, 621–622.
[36] II Corinthians 12:7–10.
[37] *Introduction to the Devout Life* (New York: Random House, 2002), III, 9.

TO MARY WILLIS SHELBURNE: *On understanding and dealing with difficult people and oneself.*[38]

30 JUNE 1955

About prides, superiorities, and affronts there's no book better than Law's *Serious Call to a Devout and Holy Life* where you'll find all of us pinned like butterflies on cards—the cards being little stories of typical characters in the most sober, astringent 18th century prose.

TO MARY VAN DEUSEN: *On fasting; and on the depths within the self.*[39]

7 JULY 1955

It has seemed odd to me that we should make such a point of fasting [before] Communion. The Roman Catholics, you know, have now so far modified their rule as to allow liquid food—coffee, cocoa *et cetera*. I practice the fast myself and habit has made it easy as regards food: not as regards water for I'm a thirsty creature. But I never thought it important: nor do I understand on what authority some priests impose it.

Yes, I think I understand the bit in which you describe that 'variety of religious experience'. I never had it—I mean in that sudden way: but I think all of us find that one result of the Faith is an increasing awareness that what we once called 'ourselves' is only like the skin on the saucepan of boiled milk or the earth-crust on the fiery earth-depths. I fancy that all the things the Freudians say are true, but that many things they don't say are equally true about that depth.

TO WARFIELD M. FIROR, *who had written about Martin Buber's book,* I and Thou: *On the untrustworthiness of self-consciousness.*[40]

11 JULY 1955

I read Buber's book and have talked to Gabriel Marcel who came (independently) to much the same position. I thought Buber

---

[38] *Letters III,* 626.
[39] *Letters III,* 629–630.
[40] *Letters III,* 631–632.

had grasped one most important truth: the immense depth of the *Thou* experience (firstly, of God, and secondly, of my neighbour) and the danger of letting it get submerged by the shallower *He* or, still shallower, *They* experiences. But I thought that he ignored (1.) The Incarnation. He is a Jew. Our Lord, besides being the divine *Thou* is also a historical character, who must be considered also as *He*. Indeed this is the essence of our faith. 'Crucified *under Pontius Pilate*'—date, and signature of a civil servant and all, crude, historical event.

(2.) The *Ye* or *You* (Plural) experience. One's two best friends, or one's parents, or one's wife and daughter, at times are very distinctly neither *Thou* nor *They* but 'You two'.

What I had not yet thought about was your objection, that he ignores the *Me*. You are probably right. He might even have said that just as the *Thou* is deeper than *Me*, so the *I* is deeper than the *Me*. For I believe self consciousness to be full of deception and that the object I call *me* and think about (both in my moments of pride and in my moments of humility) is very different from the *I* who think about it.

TO JANET WISE, *who had asked Lewis for a list of modern books on theology to help her understand the various positions on the authority of the Bible: On the kinds of inspired writings in the Bible; on canonicity; and on how we owe the very Bible itself to the "agreed affirmation of all Christendom."*[41]

5 OCTOBER 1955

I am very ill acquainted with modern theological literature, having seldom found it helpful. One book did a great deal for me: G. K. Chesterton's *The Everlasting Man*. But I can't give you such a list as you want. A pious and sensible man, who is necessarily knowing about books . . . would probably be able to advise.

My own position is not Fundamentalist, if Fundamentalism means accepting as a point of faith at the outset the proposition 'Every statement in the Bible is completely true in the literal, historical sense.' That would break down at once on the parables. All the same commonsense and general understanding of literary

---

[41] *Letters III*, 652–653.

kinds would forbid anyone to take the parables as historical statements, carried a very little further, would force us to distinguish
between (1.) Books like *Acts* or the account of David's reign,[42]
which are everywhere dovetailed into a known history, geogra-
phy, and genealogies (2.) Books like *Esther*, or *Jonah* or *Job* which
deal with otherwise unknown characters living in unspecified
period, and pretty well *proclaim* themselves to be sacred fiction.

Such distinctions are not new. Calvin left the historicity of
Job an open question and, from earlier, St. Jerome said that the
whole Mosaic account of creation was done 'after the method of a
popular poet'. Of course I believe the composition, presentation,
and selection for inclusion in the Bible, of all the books to have
been guided by the Holy Ghost. But I think He meant us to have
sacred myth and sacred fiction as well as sacred history.

Mind you, I never think a story unhistorical *because* it is miraculous. I accept miracles. It's almost the manner that distinguishes
the fictions from the histories. Compare the 'Once upon a time'
opening of *Job* with the accounts of David, St. Paul, or Our Lord
Himself. The basis of our Faith is not the Bible taken by itself but
the agreed affirmation of all Christendom: to which we owe the
Bible itself.

TO MARY WILLIS SHELBURNE: *On domestic difficulties as the ordinary
experience of home life.*[43]

5 OCTOBER 1955

I am sorry you tell me so little about yourself in your letter, for even when I don't write I pray. Your oppressed daughter
and granddaughter are much in my mind. You have no idea how
many instances of domestic nastiness come before me in my mail:
how deceptive the smooth surface of life is! The only 'ordinary'
homes seem to be the ones we don't know much about, just as the
only blue mountains are those 10 miles away. And now, I really
must tackle the remaining letters. With all good wishes.

---

[42] In I Samuel 16 to I Kings 2; I Chronicles 2–29.
[43] *Letters III*, 655–656.

TO MARY VAN DEUSEN, *who had written him of her diagnosis of cancer: On his empathy for her and even more for those in her situation who do not have faith; on the right to happiness; and on how fear of cancer may be worse than the reality of cancer.*[44]

9 OCTOBER 1955

I have just got your letter of the 3rd. The news which it contained came like a thunderbolt—especially as the letter began (and it was rather wonderful that it did begin) on such a trivial subject as my book. And if that first sentence flattered my egoism, imagine how I was rebuked when I came to the next, and was suddenly brought up against the real great issues.

It is difficult to write because you must know by now what I do not yet know. I can't tell whether I am writing to one who is giving thanks for an escape (oh how I hope you are in that position) or to one who is right up against the Cross. Thank heaven it is *His* Cross and not merely ours. I was most struck by your saying 'It doesn't seem too bad: for *me*, that is.' So I am sure you are being supported. (What must such a situation be to those who are the majority, who have no faith, who have never thought of death, and to whom all affliction is a mere meaningless, monstrous interruption of a worldly happiness to which they feel they have a *right?*)

God bless and keep you: and your husband too. You will indeed, indeed, be in my prayers. I once had a bad scare about cancer myself, so *that* part I can, I think, imagine. But of course it is now, for you, either better or worse than a scare. If the reality is worse. At any rate it must be different. (The Litany [in the *Book of Common Prayer*] distinguishes 'thine agony and blood sweat' from 'Thy cross and passion', the fear from the reality). You know how I shall await your next letter.

---

[44] *Letters III*, 655–656.

TO MARY WILLIS SHELBURNE: *On anxiety about the future; on mutual support of faith; on how hard it is not to feel indignant about problem relatives; and on the uselessness of reading the newspaper.*[45]

26 OCTOBER 1955

The anxiety about the future is, however, a thing we can all understand, and *very* hard to bear. You were almost miraculously supported in such anxiety before and I pray you may be now. And I think it is happening. Your faith is a support to me as well as to yourself. But how one even *ought* to feel—let alone, how one can succeed in feeling—about your unspeakable son-in-law, is a problem. It is very hard to believe that all one's indignation is simply bad: but I suppose one must stick to the text 'The wrath of *man* worketh not the righteousness of *God*'.[46] I suppose one must keep on remembering that there is always something deeply wrong inside with a man so bad as this. For yourself I can only hope—and passages in your letter confirm my hope—that through all this you are being brought closer to God than you would have been otherwise. And it is not forever (wouldn't it be ghastly to be *immortal* on earth, like the Wandering Jew?). It will all one day go away like a dream.

TO MARY VAN DEUSEN: *On the necessity to pray with thanksgiving; and on the ordinary and the extraordinary means of discernment.*[47]

9 NOVEMBER 1955

It was a great relief to get your letter telling me the happy results of the medical examination. My prayers for you have been accompanied by thanks.[48] (By the way, it is important to *keep* on giving thanks. Otherwise, as one continues to pray for the others who have not yet been relieved, one simply fails to notice how many of one's intercessory prayers have been granted—never notices how the list of *Thank-you's* grows and perhaps outstrips the list of mere *Please's*.) . . .

---

[45] *Letters III*, 667.
[46] James 1:20.
[47] *Letters III*, 670.
[48] Philippians 4:6.

I don't know anything about syndromes. Presumably the suspicion of cancer arose from pain which has now turned out to be rheumatism or indigestion?... Try to tell me it all in words of one syllable: remembering that I am both ignorant and sceptical about psychology, especially the amateur psychology of the patient's family. The ordinary hum-drum rules of spiritual and corporal health—or else the professional doctor and the professional *directeur*—seem to me the thing to rely on; and, of course, the recognition that as we grow older we shall have more ailments. But as you know I'm 'of the earth, earthy'.[49]

Meanwhile, you are surely rejoicing, 'Turn again to thy rest, oh my soul.'[50]

TO MARY WILLIS SHELBURNE: *On keeping to a regular pattern of religious life during the storms of life.*[51]

9 NOVEMBER 1955

I agree: the only thing one can usually change in one's situation is oneself. And yet one can't change that either—only ask Our Lord to do so, keeping on meanwhile with one's sacraments, prayers, and ordinary rule of life. One mustn't fuss too much about one's state. Do you read St. Francis de Sales? He has good things to say on this subject.[52] All good wishes.

TO MARY WILLIS SHELBURNE: *On the hard task of learning to depend only on God and on nothing and no one else.*[53]

6 DECEMBER 1955

I was most distressed by the news in your letter of Dec. 2nd.... And I can't help you, because under the modern laws I'm not allowed to send money to America. (What a barbarous system we live under. I knew a man who had to risk *prison* in order to smuggle a little money to his own sister, widowed in the U.S.A.)

---

[49] I Corinthians 15:47.
[50] Psalm 116:7.
[51] *Letters III*, 672.
[52] *Introduction to Devout Life*, III, 10.
[53] *Letters III*, 679.

By the way, we mustn't be too sure there was any irony about your just having refused that other job. There may have been a snag about it which God knew and you didn't.

I feel it almost impossible to say anything (in my comfort and security—apparent security, for real security is in Heaven and thus earth affords only imitations) which would not sound horribly false and facile. Also, you know it all better than I do. I should in your place be (I *have* in similar places *been*) far more panic-stricken and even perhaps rebellious. For it is a dreadful truth that the state of (as you say) 'having to depend solely on God' is what we all dread most. And of course that just shows how very much, how almost exclusively, we have been depending on things. That trouble goes so far back in our lives and is now so deeply ingrained, we *will* not turn to Him as long as He leaves us anything else to turn to. I suppose all one can say is that it was bound to come. In the hour of death and the day of judgement, what else shall we have? Perhaps when those moments come, they will feel happiest who have been forced (however unwillingly) to begin practising it here on earth. It is good of Him to *force* us: but dear me, how hard to *feel* that it is good at the time. . . .

All's well—I'm half ashamed it should be—with me. God bless and keep you. You shall be constantly in my prayers by day and night.

TO MARY VAN DEUSEN: *On how liking to do something is another instance of love replacing law, with an extended meditation on Psalm 36.*[54]

16 DECEMBER 1955

About the psychological causes of illness I think I'm probably a bit more sceptical than you, but as we're both mere laymen I daresay this only means we're following different fashions. . . .

Well, I think I do know that any work for the prisoner of war, which is all (as the parable tells us)[55] done really to Him, and especially if it is undertaken in the teeth of one's natural inclination, is a good thing. So the Gift Shop is a good thing. Whether it will cure headaches I've no idea: but I'm sure it's grand for the soul.

---

[54] *Letters III*, 684–686.
[55] Matthew 25:34–46.

But don't be sorry if you grow to like it. Surely that is what ought to happen? Isn't duty only a second-best to keep one going until one learns to *like* the thing, and then it is a duty no more. When love fulfils the Law,[56] sin (as such) flies out of the window. Isn't that part of what St. Paul meant by being free from the Law?[57] And of what St. Augustine meant by 'Have charity and do what you like'? Re-read Psalms 36, taking oneself as the wicked man in verses 1–4, and oneself under Grace as speaking for the rest of the Psalm except that the 'foot of pride' and 'the ungodly' in 11, 12 and one's old self again, trying to come back. Aren't 5 and 6 absolute corkers? And what unabashed hedonism in 8!

TO FATHER PETER MILWARD, SJ: *On how the salutary practice of transferring names from the list of those to be prayed for to those to thank God about provides some "proof" of the efficacy of petitionary prayer. Lewis had thought that his brother's resolution to give up drinking alcohol altogether would stick—alas it did not.*[58]

17 DECEMBER 1955

Give thanks for me, for a great family anxiety has been lifted and perhaps forever removed. No doubt you have found, like me, that if one regularly transfers people from one's urgent-petition-list to one's thanksgiving list, the mere statistics of the two lists are some corroboration of faith. (Not of course that the efficacy of prayer could strictly be either proved or disproved by empirical evidence.)

TO MARY WILLIS SHELBURNE: *On the reason for Lewis's "allergy" to Christmas; and on trusting that God's arms are supporting one even if one doesn't feel them.*[59]

19 DECEMBER 1955

I do hope you will get the nicer of those two jobs, which is certainly the one I also would prefer in your place. Not of

---

[56] Matthew 5:17.
[57] Romans 8:2.
[58] *Letters III,* 686–687.
[59] *Letters III,* 688–689.

course that one can be sure what either is like till one has got inside. Things turn out both so much [better] and so much worse than they look, don't they? Be sure you remain very much in my thoughts and prayers.

I seem to have been writing Christmas letters most of this day! I'm afraid I hate the weeks just before Christmas, and so much of the (very commercialised and vulgarised) fuss has nothing to do with the Nativity at all. I wish we didn't live in a world where buying and selling things (especially selling) seems to have become almost more important than either producing or using them.

All blessings. 'Beneath are the everlasting arms'[60] even when it doesn't feel at all like it.

---

[60] Deuteronomy 33:27.

1956

TO PHILINDA KRIEG: *On the necessity to work through dullness, even in religious matters.*[1]

28 JANUARY 1956

About an hour after posting my last letter to Laurence I realised that I had attributed to *The Silver Chair* what really comes in *The Horse and His Boy*. I thought Laurence would enjoy catching me out on my own books and should have been much disappointed if he had not!

One is sorry the Sunday Schools should be so dull. Yet I wonder. In this all important subject, as in every other, the youngsters must meet, if not exactly the dull, at any rate the hard and the dry, sooner or later. The modern attempt is to keep it as late as possible: but does that do any good? They've got to cut their teeth. Aren't many parts of the Bible itself, read at home, quite simple enough and interesting enough to be a counterpoise to the dull teaching?

Anyway, there is no use trying to keep the first thrill. It will come to life again and again only on *one* condition: that we turn our backs on it and get to work and go through all the dullness. . . .

I don't think any book I could write would help. *You* can help: but in the main there is something at this stage which Laurence can (and need we doubt, he will) do for himself.

Love to both.

Of course he must pray to God to keep his interest alive. He *knows* God is not really dull. He must still remember that and trust in Him even when God doesn't show him any of the interestingnesses. He is there alright behind the dull work.

---

[1] *Letters III*, 698–699.

TO MARY VAN DEUSEN: *On joy (in Lewis's sense of "longing" or "yearning") as incapable of examination; and on the glories of Psalm 19.*[2]

5 FEBRUARY 1956

Thank you for your letter of Jan. 31st. I agree with you about the early Church and find the Acts one of the most exciting parts of the Bible. I don't know whether your 'harmony' is my 'joy' or not, though I suspect they have in common at any rate one thing: that both are already 'shattered' when one first observes them. I suppose this is partly due to the name of time—there being no real *present*, every moment already past however quickly you try to grab it. How rich we shall be when we get off this single railway-line into the rich green country left and right. . . .

I am so glad you took to Psalm xxxvi. My other great favourite is xix. First, the mere glory of nature (between the Psalms and Wordsworth—a long gap in history—you get nothing equal to either on this theme). Then the disinfectant, inexorable sun beating down on the desert and 'nothing hid from the heat thereof'.[3] There—implicit, not stated—the imaginative identification of that heat and light with the 'undefiled' law, the 'clean' fear of the Lord, searching every cranny. Then the characteristically Jewish feeling that the Law is not only obligatory but beautiful, ravishing: delighting the heart, better than gold, sweeter than honey. Only after that, the (more Christian like) self examination and humble petition. Nearly all that could be said before the Incarnation is said in this Psalm. It is so much *better Paganism* than the real Pagans ever did! And in one way more glorious, more soaring and triumphant, than Christian poetry. For as God humbled Himself to become Man, so religion humbled itself to become Christianity.

TO BEDE GRIFFITHS, *to whom Lewis had dedicated* Surprised by Joy, *in response to Griffiths's having dedicated his autobiography,* The Golden String, *to Lewis: On the insights provided by writing autobiography; and on the necessity and danger of engaging in interreligious dialogue.*[4]

---

[2] *Letters III*, 701–702.
[3] Psalm 19:6.
[4] *Letters III*, 703–704.

8 FEBRUARY 1956

I have just got your letter of Jan. 1ˢᵗ, which is full of interest. I am having a copy of the book sent you and would have done so long ago, but I had lost your address.

Yes, I do feel the old Magdalen years to have been a very important period in both our lives. More generally, I feel the whole of one's youth to be immensely important and even of immense length. The gradual *reading* of one's own life, seeing the pattern emerge, is a great illumination at our age. And partly, I hope, getting *freed from* the past as past by apprehending it as structure. If ever I write a story about someone like *She*[5] or the Wandering Jew who lived for millennia, I should make a great point of this: he would, after 10,000 years, still feel his first 50 years to be the biggest part of his life. I am glad you found a Chestertonian quality in the book. Actually, it seems to me that one can hardly say anything either bad enough or good enough about life.

The one picture that is utterly false is the supposedly realistic fiction of the XIX century where all the real horrors and heavens are excluded. The reality is a queer mixture of idyll, tragedy, farce, hymn, melodrama: and the characters (even the same characters) far better *and* worse than one ever imagined. . . .

You are (as you well know) on dangerous ground about Hinduism, but someone must go to dangerous places. One often wonders how different the content of our faith will look when we see it in the total context. Might it be as if one were living on an infinite earth? Further knowledge would leave our map of, say, the Atlantic quite *correct,* but if it turned out to be the estuary of a great river—and the continent through which that river flowed turned out to be itself an island—off the shores of a still greater continent—and so on! You see what I mean? Not one jot of Revelation will be proved false: but so many new truths might be added.

By the way, that business of having to look up the same word ten times in one evening is no proof of failing powers. You have simply forgotten that it was exactly like that when we began Latin or even French.

---

[5] The two-thousand-year-old sorceress of Rider Haggard's novel.

Your Hindus certainly sound delightful. But what do they *deny*? That's always been my trouble with Indians—to find any proposition they would pronounce false. But truth must surely involve exclusions?

I'm reading [Steven] Runciman's *History of the Crusades:* a terrible revelation—the old civilisation of the Eastern Mediterranean destroyed by Turkish barbarians from the East and Frankish barbarians from the West.

Oremus pro invicem.

TO PHILINDA KRIEG: *On how to raise an adolescent.*[6]

16 FEBRUARY 1956

What to do about adolescence, I've no idea: except a recurrent bachelor's wonder how any one has the nerve to produce and bring up a child at all—yet quite ordinary people seem to do it quite well. Perhaps the uneducated do it best very often. I suppose they don't attempt to replace Providence as to the Destiny, but just carry on from day to day on ordinary principles of affection, justice, veracity, and humour.

By the way, my *Christian Behaviour,* if suited for anyone (of which I'm no judge) is quite as suitable for 16 year-olds as for anyone else. Of course one does at that age believe anyone rather than one's parents. The hard thing is that (after childhood) parents seem usually to be most appreciated when they're dead. I find so many terms of expression *et cetera* of my father's coming out in me and *like* it now—I'd have fought against it as long as he was alive.

Give my love to Laurence.

TO MRS. JOHNSON: *On drinking alcoholic beverages, on smoking, and on birthcontrol; on differences in doctrine and in religious taste; and on minding one's own (religious) business.*[7]

---

[6] *Letters III,* 709–710.
[7] *Letters III,* 719–720.

13 MARCH 1956

You'll find my views about drinks in *Christian Behaviour*.[8] Our Lord would not have made miraculous wine at Cana[9] if the Lord meant us to be teetotallers. See also Matt xi.19.[10] Smoking is much harder to justify. I'd like to give it up but I'd find this very hard, i.e., I *can* abstain, but I can't concentrate on anything else while abstaining—not-smoking is a whole time job.

Birth control I won't give a view on: I'm certainly not prepared to say that it is always wrong. The doctrines about the Blessed Virgin which you mention are Roman Catholic doctrines aren't they? And as I'm not an Roman Catholic I don't see that I need bother about them. But the habit (of various Protestant sects) of plastering the landscape with religious slogans about the Blood of the Lamb *et cetera* is a different matter. There is no question here of doctrinal difference: we agree with the doctrines they are advertising. What we disagree with is their *taste*. Well, let's go on disagreeing but don't let's *judge*. What doesn't suit us may suit possible converts of a different type.

My model here is the behaviour of the congregation at a 'Russian Orthodox' service, where some sit, some stand, some kneel, some lie on their faces, some walk about, and *no one takes the slightest notice of what anyone else is doing.* That is good sense, good manners, and good Christianity. 'Mind one's own business' is a good rule in religion as in other things.

. . . All your news is very good and I give thanks for you many times a day. Keep on, keep on: 'To him that overcometh I will give the Morning Star.'[11] All blessings.

---

[8] *Mere Christianity* (London: 1952; HarperCollins, Signature Classics, 2002), III, 2.
[9] John 2:1–11.
[10] Matthew 11:19.
[11] Revelation 2:26–28.

TO MARY WILLIS SHELBURNE: *On intemperance in work.*[12]

19 MARCH 1956

A line in haste about the bits underlined in your letter (which I enclose for reference). Don't be too easily convinced that God really wants you to do all sorts of work you needn't do. Each must do his duty 'in that state of life to which God has called him'.[13] Remember that a belief in the virtues of doing for doing's sake is characteristically feminine, characteristically American, and characteristically modern: so that *three* veils may divide you from the correct view!

There can be intemperance in work just as in drink. What feels like zeal may be only fidgets or even the flattering of one's self-importance. As MacDonald says, 'In holy things may be unholy greed.' And by doing what 'one's station and its duties' does not demand, one can make oneself less fit for the duties it *does* demand and so commit some injustice. Just you give Mary a little chance as well as Martha![14]

TO MRS. R. E. HALVORSON: *On church music as a preparation for or even a medium for meeting God but also a distraction and impediment; on feelings; and on the general rules for discernment.*[15]

MARCH 1956

I am glad to hear that you are still numbered among my enthusiastic readers. Concerning hymn singing and organ playing: if they have been helpful and edified anyone, then the fact that they set my teeth on edge is infinitely unimportant.

One must first distinguish the effect which music has on people like me who are musically illiterate and get only the emotional effect, and that which it has on real musical scholars who perceive the structure and get an intellectual satisfaction as well.

Either of these effects is, I think, ambivalent from the religious point of view: i.e., *each* can be a preparation for or even a medium

---

[12] *Letters III*, 720.
[13] From the Catechism of the Book of Common Prayer.
[14] Luke 10:38–42.
[15] *Letters III*, 731–732.

for meeting God but can also be a distraction and impediment. In that respect music is not different from a good many other things, human relations, landscape, poetry, philosophy. The most relevant one is wine which can be used sacramentally or for getting drunk or neutrally.

I think every *natural* thing which is not in itself sinful can become the servant of the spiritual life, but none is automatically so. When it is not, it becomes either just trivial (as music is to millions of people) or a dangerous idol. The emotional effect of music may be not only a distraction (to some people at some times) but a delusion: i.e., feeling certain emotions in church they mistake them for religious emotions when they may be wholly natural. That means that even genuinely religious emotion is only a servant. No soul is saved by having it or damned by lacking it. The love we are commanded to have for God and our neighbour is a state of the *will*, not of the affections (though if they ever also play their part so much the better). So that the test of music or religion or even visions if one has them is always the same—do they make one more obedient, more God-centred, and neighbour-centred and *less self-centred*? 'Though I speak with the tongues of Bach and Palestrina and have not charity *et cetera*![16]

TO JULIE HALVORSON, *possibly the daughter of the foregoing woman.*[17]

MARCH 1956

Thank you for the most charming letter I have received in a long time. It made me very happy.

I am also glad that your class has been enjoying the Narnian stories. But especially am I happy that you know who Aslan is. Never forget Him.

---

[16] Cf. I Corinthians 13:1.
[17] *Letters III,* 732.

TO MARY VAN DEUSEN: *On seeking Jesus or seeking oneself; and on first and second things—later developed into the essay "First and Second Things."*[18]

2 APRIL 1956

Yes, certainly the thing is always to be seeking God's way—and I wish I lived up to this. As the author of the *Imitation* says 'If you seek Jesus in all things you will find Him in all things: and if you seek yourself in all things you will find yourself, to your undoing.' . . .

I'm a little, not unamusedly, surprised that my *Surprised by Joy* causes you envy. I doubt if you would really have enjoyed my life much more than your own. And the whole modern world ludicrously over-values books and learning and what (I loathe the word) they call 'culture'. And of course 'culture' itself is the greatest sufferer by this error: for second things are always corrupted when they are put first. Never forget this: souls are immortal, and your children and grandchildren will still be alive when my books have, like the galaxy and Nature herself, passed away.

TO MARY WILLIS SHELBURNE: *On ways to deal with suffering.*[19]

26 APRIL 1956

I am most sorry to hear about your recent experiences. Though I am not doctor enough nor psychologist enough to understand them, I can see that they must have been very unpleasant indeed. You may be very sure of my continued, and increased, prayers. One of the many reasons for wishing to be a better Christian is that, if one were, one's prayers for others might be more effectual. Things do come all together and so quickly in life, don't they?

Of course we have all been taught what to do with suffering—offer it in Christ to God as our little, little share of Christ's sufferings[20]—but it is so hard to do. I am afraid I can better imagine, than *really* enter into, this. I suppose that if one loves a person enough one would actually wish to share every part of his life: and I suppose the great saints thus really *want* to share the divine

---

[18] *Letters III,* 732–733.
[19] *Letters III,* 743.
[20] Colossians 1:24.

sufferings and that is how they can actually desire pain. But this is far beyond me. To grin and bear it and (in some feeble, desperate way) to *trust* is the utmost most of us can manage. One tries to take a lesson not only from the saints but from the beasts: how well a sick dog trusts one if one has to do things that hurt it! And this, I know, in some measure you will be able to do.

Well, I hope your next news will be better. Meanwhile, may Our Lord support you as only He can.

TO LAURENCE KRIEG, *a ten-year-old, who had asked if the human children in* The Last Battle *knew the Apostles' Creed and had confided in Lewis that he, Laurence, had "only believed the part about life after death for a short time. But since I read* The Last Battle *I believe it all the time": On how hard it is to feel belief or unbelief in anything for any length of time.*[21]

27 APRIL 1956

Thanks for your nice letter and the photograph. I am so glad you like *The Last Battle*. As to whether they knew their Creed, I suppose Professor Kirke and the Lady Polly and the Pevensies did, but probably Eustace and Pole, who had been brought up at that rotten school, did *not*.

Your mother tells me you have all been having chicken pox. I had it long after I was grown up and it's much worse if you are a man for of course you can't shave with the spots on your face. So I grew a beard and though my hair is black the beard was half yellow and half red! You should have seen me.

Yes, people do find it hard to keep on feeling as if you believed in the next life: but then it is just as hard to keep on feeling as if you believed you were going to be nothing after death. I know this because in the old days before I was a Christian I used to try.

Last night a young thrush flew into my sitting room and spent the whole night there. I didn't know what to do, but in the morning one of the college servants very cleverly caught it and put it out without hurting it. Its mother was waiting for it outside and was very glad to meet it again. (By the way, I always forget which

---

[21] *Letters III,* 744–745. See http://home.comcast.net/~krieg5208/Lewis/index. htm.

birds you have in America. Have you thrushes? They have lovely songs and speckled chests.)

Good-bye for the present and love to you all.

TO MARY VAN DEUSEN: *More on his experience of the reality of the forgiveness of sins; further reflections on the palpability of believing in anything; and on envy as sadness over another's good.*[22]

15 MAY 1956

Almost exactly the same thing that happened to you about the Incarnation happened to me a few years ago about the Forgiveness of Sins. Like you, I had *assented* to the doctrine years earlier and would have said I believed it. Then, one blessed day, it suddenly became real to me and made what I had previously called 'belief' look absolutely unreal. It is a wonderful thing. But not, on inferior matters, so very uncommon. We all in one sense 'believe' we are mortal: but until one's forties does one *really* believe one is going to die? On the edge of a cliff can't one believe, and yet not really believe, that there's no danger? But certainly this real belief in the truths of our religion is a great gift from God. When in Hebrews 'faith' is defined as 'the substance of things hoped for',[23] I would translate 'substance' as 'substantialness' or 'solidity' or (almost) 'palpableness'. . . .

Envy (*invidia*) certainly did mean 'grief at another's good' but as the word is now used I don't think it means anything at all wrong. If I say I envy you those lobsters I hardly mean more than 'congratulations'.

TO VALERIE PITT: *On how God's will always involves submission, sometimes even for God; and on the invocation of the saints.*[24]

17 MAY 1956

A great deal of what you say is very helpful. I fully agree that 'Thy will be done'[25] should *principally* be taken in the sense 'God's

---

[22] *Letters III,* 750–751.
[23] Hebrews 11:1.
[24] *Letters III,* 752.
[25] Matthew 6:10.

will has blank well got to be done even if I have to go and do it myself': I doubt if the submissive aspect of it can be entirely extruded. It sometimes *is* 'nasty', and may in a sense be so to God Himself—i.e., what He wills in the situations sin has created is not what He would will *simpliciter* [simply, unconditionally] ('I *would have* gathered you as a hen gathers her chicks— but now').[26]

Whether the invocation of saints helps one's devotions or not (it wouldn't, I believe, help mine) I don't see how it helps the theoretical problem.

TO MARY WILLIS SHELBURNE: *On the varied reactions to unrestrained anger; and on how feeling hurt is seldom unmixed with lower feelings.*[27]

21 MAY 1956

What a horrid adventure. To meet unrestrained anger in any human being is in itself always very shocking. I think the effect may be partly physical. Have you noticed how *one* angry man bursts out (say, in a crowded 'bus) and a tension comes over everyone? Indeed one nearly becomes equally angry oneself. When one gets this shock along with injustice, of course there is a compound reaction.

It is at first sight so easy to forgive (especially when one knows that the anger was pathological) but then one sort of wakes up five minutes later and finds one hasn't really forgiven at all—the resentment is still tingling through one's veins. And how one has to watch that 'feeling hurt'—so seldom (as one would like to believe) mere sorrow, so nearly always mixed with wounded pride, self-justification, fright, even (hiding in the corners) desire for retaliation. But obviously you know all this and have fought your best.

But there remains the quite separate trouble of having lost your job. Oh dear. I *am* sorry. Surely all these Church people will find some way to provide for you. I will indeed pray—oh, what a business life is. Well, both you and I have most of it behind, not ahead. There will come a moment that will change all this. Nightmares don't last.

---

[26] Matthew 23:37.
[27] *Letters III*, 755–756.

TO KEITH MASSON: *On different approaches to moral principles, especially those governing the essential evils of masturbation—the damage it does to one's ability to love and to one's imagination; on the holy uses of the imagination and the unholy; "the main work of life is to come out of our selves."*[28]

3 JUNE 1956

There is, first, a difference of approach. You rather take the line that a traditional moral principle must produce a proof of its validity before it is accepted: I rather, that it must be accepted until someone produces a conclusive refutation of it.

But apart from that:—I agree that the stuff about 'wastage of vital fluids' is rubbish. For me the real evil of masturbation would be that it takes an appetite which, in lawful use, leads the individual out of himself to complete (and correct) his own personality in that of another (and finally in children and even grandchildren) and turns it back: sends the man back into the prison of himself, there to keep a harem of imaginary brides. And this harem, once admitted, works against his *ever* getting out and really uniting with a real woman. For the harem is always accessible, always subservient, calls for no sacrifices or adjustments, and can be endowed with erotic and psychological attractions which no real woman can rival. Among those shadowy brides he is always adored, always the perfect lover: no demand is made on his unselfishness, no mortification ever imposed on his vanity. In the end, they become merely the medium through which he increasingly adores himself. Do read Charles Williams' *Descent into Hell* and study the character of Mr. Wentworth. And it is not only the faculty of love which is thus sterilized, forced back on itself, but also the faculty of imagination.

The true exercise of imagination, in my view, is (a) To help us to understand other people (b) To respond to, and, some of us, to produce, art. But it has also a bad use: to provide for us, in shadowy form, a substitute for virtues, successes, distinctions *et cetera* which ought to be sought *outside* in the real world—e.g., picturing all I'd do if I were rich instead of earning and saving.

---

[28] *Letters III,* 758–759.

Masturbation involves this abuse of imagination in erotic matters (which I think bad in itself) and thereby encourages a similar
abuse of it in all spheres. After all, almost the *main* work of life
is to *come out* of our selves, out of the little, dark prison we are
all born in. Masturbation is to be avoided as *all* things are to be
avoided which retard this process. The danger is that of coming
to *love* the prison.

TO MARY WILLIS SHELBURNE: *On learning to receive; on the illusion of
independence; on taking difficult times bit by bit; and on the tolerability
of the present moment.*[29]

14 JUNE 1956

I have your letter of the 11th—along with a letter from another
lady in almost exactly the same position. Oh dear, what a hard,
frightening world it is! And yet not wholly: I am rejoiced to hear
that you have some true friends who will not let you sink. And
why should there be any (let alone 'too much') 'cringing inside'?
We are all members of one another and must all learn to receive as
well as to give. I am only sorry that [U.S.] laws prevent me from
giving you any lessons in the art. Isn't the spiritual value of having
to accept money just this, that it makes palpable the total dependence in which we always live anyway? For if you were what is
called 'independent' (i.e., living on inherited wealth), every bit
you put into your mouth and every stitch on your back would still
be coming from the sweat and skill of others while you (as a person) would not really be doing anything in return. It took me a
long time to see this—tho', heaven knows, with the Cross before
our eyes we have little excuse to forget our insolvency.

The great thing with unhappy times is to take them bit by bit,
hour by hour, like an illness. It is seldom the *present,* the exact
present, that is unbearable.

I shall pray for you whenever I wake in the night, and hope
for better news.

---

[29] *Letters III,* 761–762.

TO MARY VAN DEUSEN: *On how hard it is to be a defender and explainer of Christian teachings.*[30]

18 JUNE 1956

I envy you not having to think any more about Christian apologetics. My correspondents force the subject on me again and again. It is very wearing, and not very good for one's faith. A Christian doctrine never seems less real to me than when I have just (even if successfully) been defending it. It is particularly tormenting when those who were converted by my books begin to relapse and raise new difficulties. I know you pray for me: bear all these hammerings in mind.

TO MARY WILLIS SHELBURNE: *On avoiding having a special standard for oneself.*[31]

5 JULY 1956

Thank you for your letter of June 30th. Yes, what your Franciscan author says is very true. As someone says, 'The Devil used to try to prevent people from doing good works, but he has now learned a trick worth two of that: he *organises* 'em instead.'

I am very, very glad that God has sent you good friends who won't let you sink, and that you have turned the corner about that bad feeling that one must not take help even when one needs it. If it were really true that to receive money or money's worth degraded the recipient, then every act of alms we have done in our lives would be wicked! Dives was quite right to leave Lazarus lying at his gate![32] Or else (which might be even worse) we should have to hold that to receive was good enough for those we call 'the poor' but not for our precious selves however poor we become!

How difficult it is to avoid having a special standard for oneself! De Quincey says somewhere that probably no murderer mentally describes his own act by the word *murder:* and how many people

---

[30] *Letters III,* 762.
[31] *Letters III,* 767–769.
[32] Luke 16:19–22.

in the whole world believe themselves to be snobs, prigs, bores, bullies or tale-bearers? . . .

. . . We have no resources but our prayers.

TO MARY WILLIS SHELBURNE, *whose married daughter, Lorraine, had hurt her in some way: On hurting and being hurt; on how Christian spirituality does not despise but rather embraces matter; on bearing one's actual distress rather than imagined distress; and on the only fear that God teaches.*[33]

3 AUGUST 1956

I have your letter of July 30th and am very sorry to hear that you are still in difficulties. Your 'pleasures' (i.e., social engagements) seem to be almost as much of an affliction as anything else!—but I can understand that. About Lorraine, I think what one has to remember when people 'hurt' one is that in 99 cases out of 100 they intended to hurt very much less, or not at all, and are often quite unconscious of the whole thing. I've learned this from the cases in which I was the 'hurter'. When I have been really wicked and angry, and meant to be nasty, the other party never cared or even didn't notice. On the other hand, when I have found out afterwards that I had deeply hurt someone, it had nearly always been quite unconscious on my part. (I *loathe* 'sensitive' people who are 'easily hurt' by the way, don't you? They are a social pest. Vanity is usually the real trouble). . . .

I have known nice (and nasty) Hindus. I should have thought the nice ones were precisely 'Pagans', if one uses *Pagan* not in the popular modern sense—which means pretty nearly 'irreligious',—but strictly. I.e., I think that all extreme refinement and that spirituality which takes the form of despising matter, is very like Pythagoras and Plato and Marcus Aurelius. Poor dears: they don't know about the sacraments nor the resurrection of the body.

Yes, I know how terrible that doubt is 'Perhaps He will not.' But it is so seldom the present and the actual that is intolerable. Remember one is given strength to bear what happens to one, but

---

[33] *Letters III,* 775–776.

not the 100 and 1 different things that *might* happen. And don't say God has proved that *He* can *make you fear* poverty, illness, *et cetera*. I am sure God never teaches us the fear of anything but Himself. As the only two good lines in one of our bad hymns says 'Fear Him ye saints and you will then have nothing else to fear.' . . . Not all the things you fear can happen to you: the one (if any) that does will perhaps turn out very different from what you think. Of course I know this is easier to say to another than to realise oneself. And always remember that poverty and every other ill, lovingly accepted, has all the spiritual value of voluntary poverty or penance. God bless you; you are always in my prayers.

TO MRS. JOHNSON: *On the good the dead do by dying well and by comforting us (in the Holy Spirit) afterward; and on how heaven and earth are better than we can imagine.*[34]

7 AUGUST 1956

Would you believe it!—I had recently felt anxious as to how you were getting on and in praying for you (as of course I do for all who correspond with me on religious matters) I had added a prayer that I might soon hear some good news of you. And also at once your letter . . . arrived.

All you tell me is good and very good. Your mother-in-law has done good to the whole circle by the way she died. And where she has gone I don't doubt she will do you more still. For I believe that what was true of Our Lord Himself ('It is expedient for you that I go, for then the Comforter will come to you')[35] is true in its degree (of course, an infinitesimal degree in comparison, but still true) of all His followers. I think they do something for us by dying and shortly after they have died which they couldn't do before—and sometimes one can almost *feel* it happening. (You are right by the way: there *is* a lot to be said for dying—and being born—at home.)

No, I don't wish I knew Heaven was like the picture in my *Great Divorce*, because, if we knew that, we should know it was no better. The good things even of this world are far too good ever

[34] *Letters III*, 778.
[35] John 16:7.

to be reached by imagination. Even the common orange, you know: no one could have imagined it before he tasted it. How much less Heaven.

TO MARY VAN DEUSEN: *On how relatively hard it is to understand one's vocation but how relatively easy it is to know what to do next.*[36]

17 AUGUST 1956

Do you think one's vocation which looks so cryptic as a whole, is usually fairly clear from day to day and moment to moment? One usually has an idea what to do *next*. Need one know any more? If would be a pity if when *He* came He found me thinking about my vocation at a moment when I would have been better employed writing a letter, making a bed, entertaining a bore—or something quite dull and obvious.

TO MARY WILLIS SHELBURNE, *who had euthanized her cat Fanda: On how we love God, and everything God has made, too little.*[37]

18 AUGUST 1956

It's no good giving you an address for I am moving about. Your letter of Aug. 12th reached me today. I am delighted to hear about the job. It sounds exactly the thing, sent by God, at your most need. I will never laugh at anyone for grieving over a loved beast. I think God wants us to love Him *more,* not to love creatures (even animals) *less.* We love everything *in one way* too much (i.e., at the expense of our love for Him) but in another way we love everything too little.

No person, animal, flower, or even pebble, has ever been loved too much—i.e., more than every one of God's works deserves. But you need not feel 'like a murderer'. Rather rejoice that God's law allows you to extend to Fanda that last mercy which (no doubt, quite rightly) we are forbidden to extend to suffering humans. You'll get over this. I will rejoice in the job.

I'm writing on a dressing table in a small, dark hotel bedroom, very sleepy, so I'll close. God bless you—and Fanda!

---

[36] *Letters III,* 781.
[37] *Letters III,* 781–782.

TO SHELDON VANAUKEN, *who had confessed to Lewis that, in his discouragement over the remoteness of God, he had tried to reject Christ: On how it often seems that God is "playing fast and loose" with us but how God is really the adult or the master to the child or the dog.*[38]

27 AUGUST 1956

I am very glad . . . to hear that you are re-visiting England. We must have some good and long talks together and perhaps we shall both get high.

At the moment the really important thing seems to be that you were brought to realise the impossibility (strict sense) of rejecting Christ. Of course He must often seem to us to be playing fast and loose with us. The adult must seem to mislead the child, and the Master the dog. They misread the signs. Their ignorance and their wishes twist everything. You are so sure you know what the promise promised! And the danger is that when what He means by 'win' appears, you will ignore it because it is not what you thought it would be—as He Himself was rejected because He was not like the Messiah the Jews had in mind. But I am, I fancy, repeating things I said before. I look forward very much to our meeting again. God bless you.

TO MARY WILLIS SHELBURNE: *On how God uses our fellow human beings to do good to us and to themselves.*[39]

8 SEPTEMBER 1956

It certainly looks as if God were looking after you financially. I expect that the instruments He uses are kind human beings: and all the better if so, for then it is good for them as well as for you.

TO MARY VAN DEUSEN, *who had reported to Lewis that the pastor who had given her so much trouble had actually been ill: On the theological meaning of envy.*[40]

---

[38] *Letters III,* 783–784.
[39] *Letters III,* 785–786.
[40] *Letters III,* 795.

8 OCTOBER 1956

About Envy, the question (as so often) is one of language. In modern English 'I envy you' is used to mean 'I'd like to be doing what you're doing' or even 'I congratulate you.' What the moral Theologians meant by the 'sin of Envy' (*Invidia*) was *grudging* the other things one hadn't got oneself and hating the others for having them—wanting to scratch another girl's face because she was prettier than you, hoping another man's business would crash because he was richer than you—and so forth.

One is almost relieved to hear that your poor ex-Rector was not (as he seemed) wicked but only desperately ill. We know so little: 'judge not.'[41]

TO MICHAEL EDWARDS: *On the meaning of the Fall and of the Redemption; on the plain rules of ordinary discernment; and on the need to give up our sins and to attend to our daily duties before we add personal sacrificing.*[42]

20 OCTOBER 1956

Most of your questions about unfallen man can't, as you see, be answered. I suppose there are three conditions: unfallen, fallen, and redeemed. The third is not usually thought to be a mere reproduction of the first. In it the whole travail produced by the Fall will be turned to account and many things that would not have been without the Fall will be *redeemed,* become the occasions of good. The Cross itself is the supreme instance.

Our job is not to try to recover the unfallen stage but to go on to the redeemed one. In our use of the various things that have come in since the Fall, hadn't we better be guided by the solitary plain moral rules—namely, kindness, courage, chastity *et cetera*—rather than by speculation? . . .

As for 'giving up' things—well, when we've given up all our *sins* (the things everyone knows to be sins), we can think again! The problem will not be immediate. The devil is fond of distracting us

---

[41] Matthew 7:1.
[42] *Letters III,* 799–800.

from our plain daily duties by suggesting vague and rather faddy ones, you know.

TO MARY NEYLAN: *On his need for prayer for his future wife and for himself.*[43]

14 NOVEMBER 1956

I wish you and Dan would pray hard for a lady called Joy Gresham and me—I am likely very shortly to be both a bridegroom and a widower, for she has cancer. You needn't mention this till the marriage (which will be at a hospital bedside if it occurs) is announced. I'll tell you the whole story someday.... I'm not much in the way of visiting anyone at present.

TO MRS. MARY MARGARET MCCASLIN: *On the meaning of suffering incurred as the result of making a sacrifice.*[44]

15 NOVEMBER 1956

Thank you for your letter of Nov. 9th. I will indeed pray for you: I did so already, but will do so more. You have made a great sacrifice for conscience' sake. Such things, we may be sure, enrich one: but God knows it doesn't *feel* like it at the time. It did not, even for Our Lord Himself, in Gethsemane. I always try to remember what MacDonald said: 'The Son of God died not that we might not suffer but that our sufferings might become like His.'

But of course the real difficulty is not in rising to this point of view but in *staying* there. One does it—and ten minutes later it all has to be done over again. And one gets too *tired,* doesn't one? Well, thousands of others are going through the same....

May God strengthen you, as only He can.

[43] *Letters III,* 805.
[44] *Letters III,* 806.

1957

TO MRS. D. JESSUP, *whose divorce was now final: On Lewis's need for prayer.*[1]

29 JANUARY 1957

But of course I remember your previous letters, for 'John, Kim, and *Mrs.* Jessup' have been in my prayers this long time. Your news is very good and I thank God for it. How little we know what the result of any event is going to be! A diseased limb of your family has been amputated and now that the pain of the operation is over, the whole body feels better.

I want *your* prayers now. I have lately married a very ill, probably a dying, woman. My world is not bleak or meaningless, but it is tragic.

If there is more pity and depth in *[Till We Have Faces]* than in its predecessors, perhaps my own recent life has something to do with it. I am very glad you liked it: It has had a less favourable reception not only from critics but from most friends than any I ever wrote.

TO MARY WILLIS SHELBURNE: *On his experience of the transformation of* philia *into* eros, *aided by* agape; *on the ability to care about others even in one's own difficulties; and on the first hint of approaching death.*[2]

17 FEBRUARY 1957

There is no great mystery about my marriage. I have known the lady a long time: no one can mark the exact moment at which friendship becomes love. You can well understand how illness— the fact that she was facing pain and death and anxiety about the future of her children—would be an *extra* reason for marrying her or a reason for marrying her sooner.

---

[1] *Letters III,* 829.
[2] *Letters III,* 834.

If I write very shortly it is not because I am reticent but because I am tired and busy. My brother is also ill and causes a good deal of anxiety, and of course I lose his secretarial help: so that I have not only much to bear but much to *do*. I can't type: you could hardly conceive what hundreds of hours a year I spend coaxing a rheumatic wrist to drive this pen across paper.

What a divine mercy about the last moment money for the rent! Clearly He who feeds the sparrows has you in His care.[3] Never suppose that the amount 'on my own plate' shuts up my sympathy for the great troubles you are undergoing. I pray for you every day. Ah well, we shall all be out of it in a comparatively few years.

TO MRS. D. JESSUP: *On the blessings experienced in Joy's last illness.*[4]

19 FEBRUARY 1957

Thank you for your most kind letter. For your prayers we shall be most grateful. There is nothing else you can do. The disease, as you have guessed, is cancer, diagnosed too late in its secondary stage. The little primary growth from which all started had been shown to several doctors on both sides of the Atlantic (my wife is an American) and pooh-poohed by them all.

Perhaps you have read my wife's book on the Commandments, published under the name Joy Davidman, *Smoke on the Mountain*?

All you say, and more, is true. She is in no pain, her faith unimpaired, her mind at peace, and her spirits good. You could hardly believe what happiness, even gaiety, there is between us.

The cold reception of [*Till We Have Faces*], far from being the last straw, is hardly even a straw. You need waste no sympathy for me on that score.

---

[3] Matthew 6:26.
[4] *Letters III*, 835.

TO SISTER PENELOPE: *On the beauty, tragedy, happiness, and gaiety that had entered Lewis's life.*[5]

6 MARCH 1957

Yes, it is true. I married (knowingly) a very sick, save by near-miracle a dying, woman. She is the Joy Davidman whose *Smoke on the Mountain* I think you read. She is in the Wingfield Morris Hospital at Headington. When I see her each week end she is, to a layman's eyes (but not to a doctor's knowledge) in full convalescence, better every week. The disease is of course cancer: by which I lost my mother, my father, and my favourite aunt. She knows her own state of course: I would allow no lies to be told to a grown-up and a Christian. As you can imagine new beauty and new tragedy have entered my life. You would be surprised (or perhaps you would not?) to know how much of a strange sort of happiness and even gaiety there is between us. . . .

I don't doubt that Joy and I (and David and Douglas, the two boys) will have your prayers. Douglas is an absolute charmer (11½). David, at first sight less engaging, is at any rate a comically appropriate stepson for me (13), being almost exactly what I was—bookworm, pedant, and a bit of a prig.

TO LAURENCE KRIEG: *On Lewis's confidence in Jesus' knowing best with respect to Joy's health prospects; and on his sadness, shared with a boy Douglas's age.*[6]

21 APRIL 1957

Well, I can't say I have had a happy Easter, for I have lately got married and my wife is very, very ill. I am sure Aslan knows best and whether He leaves her with me or takes her to His own country, He will do what is right. But of course it makes me very sad. I am sure you and your mother will pray for us.

---

[5] *Letters III*, 837–838.
[6] *Letters III*, 847–848.

TO MRS. JOHNSON: *On the real meaning of heaven—enjoying God forever.*[7]

25 MAY 1957

It was nice to hear from you again. I can't remember how up to date you are with my news. Did I tell you that a new element of both beauty and tragedy had entered my life? I am newly married, and to a dying woman (She was the Joy Davidman whose *Smoke on the Mountain*, a lively modern treatment of the Ten Commandments, you may have read. An American). She is, and I try to be, very brave. I acquired two schoolboy stepsons. I myself am, not dangerously, but painfully and disablingly, ill with a slipped disc. So life is rather full. . . .

. . . Of course Heaven is leisure ('there remaineth a *rest* for the people of God'):[8] but I picture it pretty vigorous too as our best leisure really is. Man was created 'to glorify God and *enjoy* Him forever.' Whether that is best pictured as being in love, or like being one of an orchestra who are playing a great work with perfect success, or like surf bathing, or like endlessly exploring a wonderful country or endlessly reading a glorious story—who knows? Dante says Heaven 'grew drunken with its universal laughter.'

Pray for us both.

TO DOROTHY L. SAYERS: *On the deep lessons in love that Lewis was learning.*[9]

25 JUNE 1957

I ought to tell you my own news. On examination it turned out that Joy's previous marriage, made in her pre-Christian days, was no marriage: the man had a wife still living. The Bishop of Oxford said it was not the present policy to approve re-marriage in such cases, but that his view did not bind the conscience of any individual priest. Then dear Father Bide (do you know him?) who had come to lay his hands on Joy—for he has on his record what

---

[7] *Letters III,* 855–856.
[8] Hebrews 4:9.
[9] *Letters III,* 860–862.

looks very like one miracle—without being asked and merely on being told the situation at once said he would marry us. So we had a bedside marriage with a nuptial Mass.

When I last wrote to you I would not have wished this; you will gather (and may say 'guessed as much') that my feelings had changed. They say a rival often turns a friend into a lover. Thanatos [the Greek god of death], certainly (they say) approaching but at an uncertain speed, is a most efficient rival for this purpose. We soon learn to love what we know we must lose.

I hope you give us your blessing: I know you'll give us your prayers. She is home now, not because she is better (though in fact she *seems* amazingly better) but because they can do no more for her at the Wingfield: totally bed-ridden but—you'd be surprised—we have much gaiety and even some happiness. Indeed, the situation is not easy to describe. My heart is breaking and I was never so happy before: at any rate there is more in life than I knew about. My own physical pains lately (which were among the severest I've known) had an odd element of relief in them.

TO MARY WILLIS SHELBURNE: *On living in the present moment.*[10]

20 OCTOBER 1957

We are shocked and distressed at the news in your letter of the 15th. I think I see from what you say that God is already giving you new spiritual strength with which to meet this terrible affliction—just as He did to us in Joy's worst times. But pain is pain. I wish I could relieve any of it for you—one is so ineffective. The great thing, as you have obviously seen, (both as regards pain and financial worries) is to live from day to day and hour to hour not adding the past or future to the present. As one lived in the Front Line: 'They're not shelling us at the moment, and it's not raining, and the rations have come up, so let's enjoy ourselves.' In fact, as Our Lord said, 'Sufficient unto the day'.[11]

You may be sure you will be very much in our prayers. All my news is good, very good up-to-date, though of course we

[10] *Letters III,* 889.
[11] Matthew 6:34.

live always under the sword of Damocles. God bless and keep you, dear friend. It'll be nice when we all wake up from this life which has indeed something like nightmare about it.

TO LAURENCE KRIEG: *Helping a young friend understand what an adult is going through—"Aslan has done great things for us."*[12]

23 DECEMBER 1957

It is lovely to hear that you still enjoy the Narnian stories. I hope you are well. I forget how much of my news you and your mother know. It is wonderful. Last year I married, at her bedside in hospital, a woman who seemed to be dying: so you can imagine it was a sad wedding. But Aslan has done great things for us and she is now walking about again, showing the doctors how wrong they were, and making me very happy. I was also ill myself but am now better. Good wishes to you all.

---

[12] *Letters III,* 908–909.

1958

TO MR. PITMAN, *who, inspired by a scene in* The Great Divorce, *Chapter 11, had written about masturbation: On the lessons Lewis learned from his struggles with the temptation and the sin—it is a sin principally against the imagination; a tribulation like any other; a temptation that does not last forever; one requiring sweetness and not hatred toward oneself or toward sexuality or toward the body; one not to be treated melodramatically; one to be careful of when tired or sad and to be supplanted by real love of any kind, perhaps especially for, toward, and even with the person one loves.*[1]

13 FEBRUARY 1958

I am not quite clear whether you are talking of this problem as it applies to the married or the unmarried. The idea of permanent sexual abstinence within marriage (if that is what you mean at one point in your letter) would seem to be vetoed by St. Paul's advice, or even command, in I Cor vii, 5–6.[2]

The metamorphosis of the lizard into the stallion was meant to symbolise perfect sublimation, after painful struggle and agonising surrender, not by ordinary psychological law but by supernatural Grace. The evidence seems to be that God sometimes works such a complete metamorphosis and sometimes not. We don't know why: God forbid we should presume it went by merit.

He never in my unmarried days did it for me. He gave me— at least and after many ups and downs, the power to resist the temptation so far as the *act* was concerned. He never stopped the recurrent temptations, nor was I guarded from the sin of *mental* consent. I don't mean I wasn't given sufficient Grace. I mean that I sometimes fell into it, Grace or no.

One may, I suppose, regard this as partly penal. One is paying for the physical (and still more the imaginative) sins of one's earlier life. One may also regard it as a tribulation, like any other.

---

[1] *Letters III,* 919–921.
[2] I Corinthians 7:5–6.

The great discovery for me was that the attack does *not* last for-ever. It is the devil's lie that the only escape from the tension is through yielding. After prolonged resistance it will go away: what seemed yesterday impossible to turn one's mind from will to-day be utterly unenchanted, insipid, tedious.

Do you know St. François de Sales' chapter *De la douceur:*[3] meekness to God, to one's neighbour, and (surprisingly and im-portantly) to *oneself*? Disgust, self-contempt, self-hatred—rheto-ric against the sin and (still more) vilification of sexuality or the body in themselves—are emphatically *not* the weapons for this warfare. We must be *relieved,* not horrified, by the fact that the whole thing is humiliating, undignified, ridiculous; the *lofty* vices would be far worse. Nor must we exaggerate our suffering. We talk of 'torture': five minutes of really acute toothache would re-store our sense of proportion! In a word, no melodrama. The sin, if we fall into it, must be repented, like all our others. God will forgive. The temptation is a darn nuisance, to be born with pa-tience as long as God wills.

On the purely physical side (but people no doubt differ) I've always found that *tea* and bodily weariness are the two great dis-posing factors, and therefore the great dangers. Sadness is also a danger: lust in my experience follows disgruntlement nearly al-ways. Love of every sort is a guard against lust, even, by a divine paradox, sexual *love* is a guard against lust. No woman is more easily and painlessly abstained from, if need be, than the woman one loves. And I'm sure purely male society is an enemy to chas-tity. I don't mean a temptation to homosexuality: I mean that the absence of ordinary female society provokes the normal appetite.

TO MARY WILLIS SHELBURNE: *On how sometimes the service God wants is our not being used at all or as we expected or as we perceive.*[4]

22 FEBRUARY 1958

Yes, we must not fret about not doing God those supposed services which He in fact does not allow us to do. Very often I

<hr>

[3] *Introduction to the Devout Life,* III, 9.
[4] *Letters III,* 922–923.

expect, the service He really demands is that of *not* being (apparently) used, or not in the way we expected, or not in a way we can perceive.

TO MARY WILLIS SHELBURNE: *On dryness in prayer; on his wife's experience of being nagged by God until she surrendered to His peace and delight; on keeping our hands empty so that we can receive; and on the things that keep our hands full—sins, earthly cares, attempts to worship God in the way we want, and the tiny distractions of what we are to do next.*[5]

31 MARCH 1958

We all go through periods of dryness in our prayers, don't we? I doubt (but ask your *directeur*) whether they are necessarily a bad symptom. I sometimes suspect that what we *feel* to be our best prayers are really our worst; that what we are enjoying is the satisfaction of apparent success, as in executing a dance or reciting a poem. Do our prayers sometimes go wrong because we insist on trying to talk to God when He wants to talk to us?

Joy tells me that once, years ago, she was haunted one morning by a feeling that God wanted something of her, a persistent pressure like the nag of a neglected duty. And till mid-morning she kept on wondering what it was. But the moment she stopped worrying, the answer came through as plain as a spoken voice. It was 'I don't want you to *do* anything, I want to *give* you something': and immediately her heart was full of peace and delight. St. Augustine says 'God gives where He finds empty hands.' A man whose hands are full of parcels can't receive a gift. Perhaps these parcels are not always sins or earthly cares, but sometimes our own fussy attempts to worship Him in *our* way. Incidentally, what most often interrupts my own prayers is not great distractions but tiny ones—things one will have to do or avoid in the course of the next hour.

---

[5] *Letters III*, 930–931.

TO MARY WILLIS SHELBURNE: *On how difficult it is to feel forgiven of sins, even those long forgiven.*[6]

15 APRIL 1958

About past, long past, sins: I had been a Christian for many years before I *really* believed in the forgiveness of sins, or more strictly, before my theoretical belief became a reality to me. I fancy this may not be so uncommon.

TO SHELDON VANAUKEN: *On the "miracle" of Joy's remission and how it makes Lewis tremble to respond with goodness to God's goodness; and on how not to take providence into one's own hands.*[7]

26 APRIL 1958

A letter from you is always a refreshment. First as to your question. Joy's improvement continues. Indeed except that she is a cripple with a limp (the doctors, rather than the disease, shortened one leg) she is in full health. She had an X-ray examination last week which shows that the bones have re-built themselves 'firm as rock'. The Doctor, doubtless without what a Christian would regard as true seriousness, used the word *miraculous*. I am also, by the way, nearly quite restored myself. I sometimes tremble when I think how good Joy and I ought to be: how good we would have *promised* to be if God had offered us these mercies at that price.

...More and more I see how useless it is to try to play Providence either to oneself or to another. All we can do is to try to follow the plain rules of charity, justice and commonsense and leave the issue to God.

All blessings. I wish we lived nearer.

TO LEE TURNER: *On the biblical foundations for a biblical theology of inspiration and of the incarnation; and on the advantage of reading the Bible in many translations, if one reads Hebrew and Greek.*[8]

---

[6] *Letters III*, 935.
[7] *Letters III*, 940–941.
[8] *Letters III*, 960–961.

19 JULY 1957

The main difficulty seems to me not the question *whether* the Bible is 'inspired', but what exactly we mean by this. Our ancestors, I take it, believed that the Holy Spirit either just replaced the minds of the authors (like the supposed 'control' in automatic writing) or at least dictated to them as to secretaries.

Scripture itself refutes these ideas. St. Paul distinguishes between what 'the Lord' says and what he says 'of himself'[9]—yet *both* are 'Scripture'. Similarly the passages in which the prophets describe theophanies and their own reactions to them would be absurd if they were not writing for themselves. Thus, without any modern scholarship, we are driven a long way from the extreme view of inspiration.

I myself think of it as analogous to the Incarnation—that, as in Christ a human soul-and-body are taken up and made the vehicle of Deity, so in Scripture, a mass of human legend, history, moral teaching, *et cetera,* are taken up and made the vehicle of God's Word. Errors of minor fact are permitted to remain. (Was Our Lord Himself incapable, *qua* [as] Man, of such errors? Would it be a real human incarnation if He was?) One must remember of course that our modern and western attention to dates, numbers, *et cetera,* simply did not exist in the ancient world. No one was looking for *that* sort of truth. (You'd find something of my views about all this in my forthcoming book on the Psalms.) As for translations, even if one doesn't know Greek (and I know no Hebrew myself) we have now so many different translations that by using and comparing them all one can usually see what is happening. The blessed and significant thing is that none of all this has bothered your personal faith in Our Lord. Do you see a clear reason why it need bother anyone else's?

---

[9] I Corinthians 7:8–10.

TO MARY WILLIS SHELBURNE: *More on feeling forgiven of sins, even sins long forgiven; and on ways to heal a troubled conscience.*[10]

21 JULY 1958

(1.) Remember what St. John says: 'If our *heart* condemn us, God is stronger than our heart.'[11] The *feeling* of being, or not being, forgiven and loved, is not what matters. One must come down to brass tacks. If there is a particular sin on your conscience, repent and confess it. If there isn't, tell the despondent devil not to be silly. You can't help *hearing* his voice (the odious inner radio) but you must treat it merely like a buzzing in your ears or any other irrational nuisance.

(2). Remember the story in the *Imitation,* how the Christ on the crucifix suddenly spoke to the monk who was so anxious about his salvation and said, 'If you knew that all was well, what would you, today, do, or stop doing?' When you have found the answer, do it or stop doing it. You see, one must always get back to the practical and definite. What the devil loves is that vague cloud of unspecified guilt feeling or unspecified virtue by which he lures us into despair or presumption. 'Details, please!' is the answer. (3.) The sense of dereliction cannot be a bad symptom for Our Lord Himself experienced it in its depth—'Why hast thou forsaken me?'[12]

TO MARY VAN DEUSEN: *On the providence of books and the providence of being reminded of something one has read in the past; and on how real ecumenism discussions can only happen between people at the centers of their traditions.*[13]

27 OCTOBER 1958

What you say about books turning up at what seems to be just the right moment is well supported from my own experience. So much so that now, if I lose or forget something I've read that seems important, I do not much bother, for I feel a confidence

[10] *Letters III,* 962–963.
[11] I John 3:20.
[12] Matthew 27:46; Psalm 22:1.
[13] *Letters III,* 982–983.

that if I really need it it will be given to me again, and just in time—in a book on some quite different subject I shall find it quoted or a man I didn't much want to talk to will mention it in conversation.

It is hardly possible, at such a distance from the scene of action, to have an opinion as to how you should cope with Dr. Higgins. I think, urgently, that it is false wisdom to have any 'denomination' represented for ecumenical purposes by those who are on its *fringe*. People (perhaps naturally) think this will help re-union, whereas in fact it invalidates the whole discussion. Each body should rather be represented by its *centre*. Only then will any agreements that are achieved be of real value.

TO MARY WILLIS SHELBURNE: *On living one day at a time; and on wrinkles as honorable insignia.*[14]

30 OCTOBER 1958

I suppose living from day to day ('take no thought for the morrow')[15] is precisely what we have to learn—though the Old Adam in me sometimes murmurs that if God wanted me to live like the lilies of the field,[16] I wonder He didn't give me the same lack of nerves and imagination as they enjoy! Or is that just the point, the precise purpose of this Divine paradox and audacity called Man—to do *with* a mind what other organisms do without it?

As for wrinkles—pshaw! Why shouldn't we have wrinkles? Honorable insignia of long service in this warfare. All well with us, in haste, with love.

TO MARY VAN DEUSEN: *On the dangers and evil in spiritualistic practices.*[17]

14 DECEMBER 1958

I don't see anything sinful in *speculating* about the perception of the apostles, though I doubt if we have evidence enough to make

---

[14] *Letters III,* 984–985.
[15] Matthew 6:34.
[16] Ibid., 6:28.
[17] *Letters III,* 996–998.

it very useful. But spiritualistic *practices* are a very different thing. First, the record of proved fraud in such matters is usually very big and black: there's money in mediumship! Second, it very often has extremely bad effects on those who dabble in it: even insanity. And thirdly, most supposed communications through mediums are the silliest, sentimental, or even incoherent, twaddle. Why go to spirits to hear bosh when you can hear sense from quite a lot of your neighbours?

But I *think* the practice is a sin as well as folly. Necromancy (commerce with the dead) is strictly forbidden in the Old Testament, isn't it?[18] The New frowns on any excessive and irregular interest ever in angels.[19] Now the whole tradition of Christendom is dead against it. I would be shocked at any Christians being, or consulting, a medium.

It is Resurrection, not 'survival' that we think of, and the spirit that concerns us is the Holy Spirit!

---

[18] Deuteronomy 18:9–14; I Samuel 28:11–20; Isaiah 8:19–20.
[19] Colossians 2:18.

1959

TO MARY VAN DEUSEN: *On prayer as our best mode of helping others.*[1]

1 JANUARY 1959

I am rejoiced to hear that your grand-daughter's eye trouble is well cleared up. Of course Genia is always in my prayers. And how wise you are to make prayers your mode of helping: for parents and in-laws and neighbours who try to help in other ways so often do harm! I am no unconditional believer in the popular theory that 'to talk things over' invariably mends matters. I have known it do so, and I have known it do the reverse. . . .

We are all well. It is almost as if we had died and were in a new life. A very happy new year to you and yours.

TO EDWARD LOFSTROM: *On what Lewis attempted in the Chronicles of Narnia; on the character of the man Jesus—his tenderness, ferocity, and even humor; and on the need to do one's duty while having patience with God.*[2]

16 JANUARY 1959

1. I am afraid I don't know the answer to your question about books of Christian instruction for children. Most of those I have seen—but I haven't seen many—seem to me namby-pamby and 'sissie' and calculated to nauseate any child worth his salt. Of course I have tried to do what I can for children—in a mythical and fantastic form by my seven 'Narnian' fairy tales. They work well with some children but not with others. Sorry this looks like salesmanship: but honestly if I knew anything else I'd mention it.

2. Of course. 'Gentle Jesus', my elbow! The most striking thing about Our Lord is the union of great ferocity with extreme tenderness. (Remember Pascal? 'I do not admire the extreme of one

---

[1] *Letters III*, 1008.
[2] *Letters III*, 1010–1011.

virtue unless you show me at the same time the extreme of the opposite virtue. One shows one's greatness not by being at an extremity but by being simultaneously at two extremities *and filling all the space between.*')

Add to this that He is also a supreme ironist, dialectician, and (occasionally) humourist. So go on! You are on the right track now: getting to the real Man behind all the plaster dolls that have been substituted for Him. This is the appearance in Human form of the God who made the Tiger *and* the Lamb, the avalanche *and* the rose. He'll frighten and puzzle you: but the real Christ *can* be loved and admired as the doll can't.

3. 'For him who is haunted by the smell of invisible roses the cure is work' (MacDonald). If we feel we have talents that don't find expression in our ordinary duties and recreations, I think we must just go on doing the ordinary things as well as we can. If God wants to use these suspected talents, He will: in His own time and way. At all costs one must keep clear of all the witch-doctors and their patent cures—as you say yourself.

TO DON LUIGI PEDROLLO: *On the secret griefs of his spiritual father, Saint Giovanni (John) Calabria.*[3]

19 JANUARY 1959

It was good of you, reverend Father, to send me this most beautiful book about the life of dearest Father John. I thank you. I hope that from reading this book I shall become better informed about many things which till now have remained obscure; for often this holy man in his letters implied that he laboured under I know not what secret grief, in the hidden counsels of God who chastises everyone whom He receives as a son.[4]

Happily it occurs that I write to you in this Week when all who profess themselves Christians are bound to offer prayers for the reunion of the Church, now, alas, torn and divided.

[3] *Letters III,* 1012–1013.
[4] Hebrews 12:7.

TO DON HOLMES: *On trying to avoid groups of thoroughly bad people but not individuals; and on the disadvantage of approaching the Bible with reverence and the readiness to be edified.*[5]

17 FEBRUARY 1957

Thank you for your kind and encouraging letter. As to your questions:

1. I think one probably *should,* when one decently can, avoid meeting—when they are *en masse,* as a group—*thoroughly* bad people whether they profess Christianity or not. Meeting them *singly* is another matter. And of course one may have particular duties (pastoral, family, pedagogic *et cetera, et cetera*) which oblige one to meet them. But there's no universal rule. One has to decide in each case whether one is more likely to do good or to receive harm.

2. If my books are sometimes permitted by God to deliver to particular readers a more perceptible challenge than Scripture itself, I think this is because, in a sense, they catch people unprepared. We approach the Bible with reverence and with readiness to be edified. But by a curious and unhappy psychological law these attitudes often inhibit the very thing they are intended to facilitate. You see this in other things: many a couple never felt less in love than on their wedding day, many a man never felt less merry than at Christmas dinner, and when at a lecture we say 'I *must* attend', attention instantly vanishes.

3. If you think I can help you about any particular problem, of course write. But general correspondence—what is call 'having a pen-friend'—is quite impossible for me. The daily letter writing is the chief burden of my life. I hope this doesn't sound unpleasant? There are only 24 hours in a day!

TO EDWARD LOFSTROM, *who seemed to be suffering from an exaggerated sense of self-consciousness and guilt: On the need to seek relief from medical professionals.*[6]

---

[5] *Letters III,* 1022–1023.
[6] *Letters III,* 1023.

18 FEBRUARY 1959

I certainly had not realised from your previous letter how distressing the problem was. My allusion to the psychotherapists was a fling at the increasing modern habit of seeing *all* personal difficulties in terms of disease and cure, and so reducing things that are really moral or intellectual or both to the pathological level. In your own case there certainly does seem to be a pathological element. And of course it is 'proper' to make all efforts after relief. I wrote under the false impression that, like a good many people, you were regarding as a peculiar medical condition of your own things which were in fact the common infirmities of us all. Now I know better. I need not say you have my sympathy.

But I dare not advise. Amateur advice in such cases is unlikely to do good and may do harm. You must go to the professionals. All you can get from me is my prayers, and these you shall have.

TO EDWARD LOFSTROM: *On his need to think less and to fulfill his daily duties with charity and justice.*[7]

8 MARCH 1959

I very much doubt if any book, least of all a book by me, would much help anyone in the condition you describe. For a book can offer only thoughts and thoughts are not what such a person, perhaps, needs most. One can argue against egoism, but then egoism is not his trouble. If he were a real egoist he would be either blissfully unconscious of the fact or else fully convinced that egoism was the rational attitude. You, on the other hand, suffer from a more than ordinary horror of egoism which you share with us all. And therefore, as you will see, the thing you need is not to think more or better about it but to think less: to *act* unselfishly—that is, charitably and justly—and leave the state of your feelings for God to deal with in His own way and His own time. And this of course you know better than I do.

But how to do it? For the very effort to forget something is itself a remembering of that something! I think, if I were in your shoes I should try to regard this sense of self-imprisonment not

---

[7] *Letters III*, 1027–1028.

at all as a sin but as a mere tribulation, like rheumatism, to be endured in the same way. It has no doubt its medical side: diet, exercise, and recreations might all be considered. And, though this is a hard saying, your early upbringing may have something to do with it. Great piety in the parents *can* produce in the child a mistaken sense of guilt: may lead him to regard as sin what is really not sin at all but merely the fact that he is a boy and not a mature Christian. At any rate, remember: 'I cannot turn one hair black or white: but I can brush my hair daily and go to the barber at regular intervals.' In other words we must divert our efforts from our general condition or frame of mind (which we can't alter by direct action of the will) to what is in our power—our words and acts. Try to remember that the 'bottomless sea' can't hurt us as long as we keep on *swimming*. You will be in my prayers.

TO MARY VAN DEUSEN: *On the different experience of time as one anticipates something dreadful and as the dreadful thing recedes.*[8]

16 MARCH 1959

Oh, I am sorry. Operations are horrid things. I will indeed have you all in my prayers. May the time seem as short as possible till the blessed time when the event is a day further away each morning instead of a day nearer. 'Time and the hour ride through the roughest day.' God bless and strengthen both of you.

TO DON LUIGI PEDROLLO: *On Lewis's need for prayer as he began* The Four Loves.[9]

28 MARCH 1959

With a grateful heart I salute you and yours on this solemn and serious day on which the Lord preached to the souls in prison.[10] I and mine are well.

Now I am writing a little book on *The Four Loves*, i.e., in Greek: *Storgé, Philia, Eros,* and *Agapé*—I use these words because there are no names for them in Latin.

---

[8] *Letters III*, 1031.
[9] *Letters III*, 1035–1036.
[10] I Peter 3:19.

Pray for me that God grant me to say things helpful to salvation, or at least not harmful. For this is a work 'full of dangerous hazard'.

TO MARY VAN DEUSEN: *On how one responds to the diagnosis of serious illness and on four strategies for coping.*[11]

10 APRIL 1959

I have just had Sister Hildegarde's letter. My heart goes out to you. You are now just where I was a little over two years ago—they wrongly diagnosed Joy's condition as uremia before they discovered cancer of the bone.

I know all the different ways in which it gets one: wild hopes, bitter nostalgia for lost happiness, mere physical terror turning one sick, agonised pity and self-pity. In fact, Gethsemane. I had one (paradoxical) support which you lack—that of being in severe pain myself. Apart from that what helped Joy and me through it was *1.* That she was always told the whole truth about her own state. There was no miserable pretence. That means that both can face it side-by-side, instead of becoming something like adversaries in a battle-of-wits. *2.* Take it day by day and hour by hour (as we took the front line). It is quite astonishing how many happy—even gay—moments we had together when there was no hope. *3.* Don't think of it as something *sent* by God. Death and disease are the work of the Devil. It is *permitted* by God: i.e., our General has put you in a fort exposed to enemy fire. *4.* Remember other sufferers. It's fatal to start thinking 'Why should this happen to *us* when everyone else is so happy.' You are (I was and may be again) one of a huge company. Of course we shall pray for you all we know how. God bless you both.

TO VERA GEBBERT: *On the significances of the cross.*[12]

8 MAY 1959

Well yes of course the Cross *is* a sad thing, but are we not to be reminded that there is in it a sad significance as well as a symbol of a victory?

---

[11] *Letters III*, 1038–1039.
[12] *Letters III*, 1046–1047.

TO RICHARD LADBOROUGH: *On how to cope with a truly boring colleague who deserved to be kept in employment and to have his benefits increased.*[13]

3 JUNE 1959

Remembering that (spoken) words are winged, I thought it might be useful to repeat in writing what I said, or think I said, or would now wish to have said, to you about P.W. this evening.

1. I think well of him. He has given us good service without counting the cost and he seems to me to be a friendly, decent, straightforward sort of person.

2. I have come to feel—I did not feel at first—that he is a very great bore. I am not sure that I know anyone whose conversation fatigues and dejects me more.

3. In view of the services we have already accepted from him, I think it would be ungrateful or even dishonourable—in view of the services he may still do us in the future I think it would be foolish—to allow any decisions we make about him to be at all influenced by his boringness. It would be useful to retain him. If we do, it would be proper to increase his dining rights.

I feel very strongly that to suffer bores patiently—'gladly' may be impossible—is a plain duty, and that it is even plainer when we owe them some gratitude.

Anyway, it really comes under the Golden Rule. Each of us, no doubt, is a bore to some people. I should like those whom I bore to treat me kindly and justly and therefore I must be kind and just to those who bore me.

He is, so far as I am concerned, the only bore at our High Table.* Can one expect to have less than one? We are being let off very lightly.

*I see of course who the other might be and why I should not recognise him if he were!

---

[13] *Letters III,* 1055.

TO MARY WILLIS SHELBURNE: *On how often one's inner state differs from external circumstances; and on the proper attitude toward death and dying.*[14]

7 JUNE 1959

I am sorry to hear that so many troubles crowd upon you but glad to hear that, by God's grace, you are so untroubled. So often, whether for good or ill, one's inner state seems to have so little connection with the circumstances. I can *now* hardly bear to look back on the summer before last when Joy was apparently dying and I was often screaming with the pain of osteoporosis: yet at the time we were in reality far from unhappy. May the peace of God continue to infold you. . . .

What a state we have got into when we can't say 'I'll be happy when God calls me' without being afraid one will be thought 'morbid'. After all, St. Paul said just the same.[15] If we really believe what we say we believe—if we really think that home is elsewhere and that this life is a 'wandering to find home', why should we not look forward to the arrival? There are, aren't there, only three things we can do about death: to desire it, to fear it, or to ignore it. The third alternative, which is the one the modern world calls 'healthy' is surely the most uneasy and precarious of all.

TO MARY WILLIS SHELBURNE: *On whether we dare hope that dying is like having a tooth extracted; on purgatory; and yet more on forgiveness and the feeling of being forgiven.*[16]

7 JULY 1959

... You seem to have had a very nasty experience. I can see why you describe it as 'looking into the face of death': but who knows whether that face, when we really look at it, will be at all like that? Let us hope better things. I had a tooth out the other day, and came away wondering whether we dare hope that the moment of death may be very like that delicious moment when

---

[14] *Letters III*, 1056.
[15] Philippians 1:21.
[16] *Letters III*, 1064.

one realises that the tooth is really out and a voice says 'Rinse your mouth out with this.' 'This' of course will be Purgatory. . . .

You surely don't mean 'feeling that we are not *worthy* to be forgiven'? For of course we aren't. Forgiveness by its nature is for the unworthy. You mean 'Feeling that we *are not* forgiven.' I have known that. I 'believed' theoretically in the divine forgiveness for years before it really came home to me. It is a wonderful moment when it does.

TO MARY VAN DEUSEN: *On living in the present moment; on the difference between hope and hopes; and on one of Lewis's often recommended books,* Symbolism and Belief.[17]

7 JULY 1959

I am glad to hear that the news is at any rate 'so far, so good'. As my wife and I discovered during our terrible time two years ago, the great thing, both for the patient and for the lover of the patient, is to live it day by day, in the *present* endurance and the *present* case, giving as little of one's mind as possible to fears or hopes (hopes beget fears)—as animals live, and soldiers, and, I expect, saints. . . .

I am so glad you liked Edwin Bevan's book. It *does* clear things up, doesn't it?

TO MARY WILLIS SHELBURNE: *On why we are not to know what is coming next.*[18]

3 AUGUST 1959

I have your letter of 30 July. It has puzzled me. I understood that you were going to the doctors for heart trouble. How and why do the psychiatrists come into the picture? But since they have come, I am glad to hear they are nice.

I sympathise most deeply with you on the loss of Fr. Louis. But for good as well as for ill one never knows what is coming next. You remember the *Imitation* says 'Bear your cross, for if you try to get rid of it you will probably find another and worse one.' But

---

[17] *Letters III,* 1065.
[18] *Letters III,* 1072.

there is a brighter side to the same principle. When we lose one blessing, another is often most unexpectedly given in its place.

We are all well here though I am frantically busy: and though I get no more tired now than I did when I was younger, I take much longer to get un-tired afterwards. All blessings and sympathy.

TO MARY VAN DEUSEN. *On what really matters in the education and formation of a schoolboy.*[19]

6 SEPTEMBER 1959

Your italic typewriter is very pleasant to the eye. I have prayed for Paul and his Headmaster. Do not attach too much importance to the latter! I think headmasters' influence on—and even knowledge of—their own schools is greatly exaggerated by a kind of romanticism. What really matters, for learning, is of course the immediate teacher. What matters for happiness and morals is the other boys.

TO MARY VAN DEUSEN: *On the distinction between belief and imagination and the difficulty of imagining the things we believe; and a word of correction about the way she torments herself and her daughter in their religious disputes.*[20]

8 SEPTEMBER 1959

No one, I presume, can imagine life in the glorified Body. On this, and on the distinction (in general) between belief and imagination, I have said all I can in *Miracles* [Chapters 10 and 16]. Lor' bless me, I can picture very few of the things I believe in—I can't picture will, thought, time, atoms, astronomical distances, New York, nor even (at the moment) my mother's face. . . . .

By the way, is it necessary to salvation, to charity, or to affection, that you and Genia should achieve precise verbal agreement on these points? If not, why worry? Live and let live. 'Take life easy as the leaves grow in the tree.' There is, if you will forgive me for saying so, a self-tormenting and a mutually tormenting element in both of you.

---

[19] *Letters III*, 1085.
[20] *Letters III*, 1086–1087.

TO EDWARD LOFSTROM.[21]

20 SEPTEMBER 1959

I think your comparison between the self and the telescope is singularly accurate. The instrument vanishes from consciousness just in so far it is perfected. But *until* then we must attend to it: otherwise we shall be like the man who mistakes a smudge on the glass for a gigantic animal on the Moon. You are still in my prayers.

TO MARY WILLIS SHELBURNE: *On the return of Joy's cancer.*[22]

18 OCTOBER 1959

Will you redouble your prayers for us? Apparently the wonderful recovery Joy made in 1957 was only a reprieve, not a pardon. The last X Ray check reveals cancerous spots returning in many of her bones. There seems to be some hope of a few years life still and there are still things the doctors can do. But they are all in the nature of 'rearguard actions'. We are in retreat. The tide has turned. Of course God can do again what He did before. The sky is not now so dark as it was when I married her in hospital. Her courage is wonderful and she gives me more support than I can give her.

The dreadful thing, as you know, is the waking each morning—the moment at which it all flows back on one.

TO RHONA BODLE: *On the difficulties of godparenting.*[23]

18 OCTOBER 1959

It was nice to hear from you again. Of course you will have my friend's prayers—you always have—in the extremely delicate and important work you are doing. God-children are a terrible problem. One seems to have promised what, if the parents are the wrong sort, one cannot perform.

Will you also pray for me? My wife (I married in 1957) has cancer.

---

[21] *Letters III*, 1089.
[22] *Letters III*, 1092.
[23] *Letters III*, 1098.

TO SIR HENRY WILLINK, *whose wife had just died*: *On bereavement and grieving.*[24]

3 DECEMBER 1959

Dear Master,

I have learned now that while those who speak about one's miseries usually hurt one, those who keep silence hurt more. They help to increase the sense of *general* isolation which makes a sort of fringe to the sorrow itself. You know what cogent reason I have to feel *with* you: but I can feel *for* you too. I know that what you are facing must be worse than what I must shortly face myself, because your happiness has lasted so much longer and is therefore so much more intertwined with your whole life. As Scott said in like case, 'What am I to do with that daily portion of my thoughts which has for so many years been hers?'

People talk as if grief were just a feeling—as if it weren't the continually renewed shock of setting out again and again on familiar roads and being brought up short by the grim frontier post that now blocks them. I, to be sure, believe there is something beyond it: but the moment one tries to use that as a consolation (that is not its function) the belief crumbles. It is quite useless knocking at the door of Heaven for earthly comfort: it's not the sort of comfort they supply there.

You are probably very exhausted physically. Hug that and all the little indulgences to which it entitles you. I think it is tiny little things which (next to the very greatest things) help most at such a time.

I have myself twice known, after a loss, a strange excited (but utterly un-spooky) sense of the person's presence all about me. It may be a pure hallucination. But the fact that it always goes off after a few weeks proves nothing either way.

I wish I had known your wife better. But she has a bright place in my memory. . . . She will be very greatly missed—on her own account, quite apart from any sympathy with you—by every fellow of this College.

---

[24] *Letters III,* 1102–1103.

...I shall not be at the funeral. You can understand and forgive my desire, now, to spend every possible moment at home. Forgive me if I have said anything amiss in this letter. I am too much involved myself to practise any skill.

TO MARY VAN DEUSEN. *On the drawbacks of living inside a tragedy.*[25]

8 DECEMBER 1959

I am very glad to hear all your good—indeed excellent—news. So is my brother, who has read your letter.

My news is very difficult. The last X-ray check-up which Joy had was the first which we approached without dread: she seemed so obviously in complete health. The photographs told a different tale. The disease is returning. Not in one place but in many. It is true that the situation is not (yet) as bad as it was in the spring of '57 when her life was not worth six weeks' purchase. But her recovery then was seemingly miraculous. Dare one hope again? Have we ever heard of a miracle repeated? At present she is to all appearance quite well: we shouldn't know she had cancer if we didn't know. The condemned cell *looks* like an ordinary and comfortable sitting room. I know we shall have your prayers. Forgive me for writing so egotistical a letter. One of the drawbacks about living in a tragedy is that one can't very well see out of the windows. Pray particularly that our faith may grow stronger and stronger.

TO DON LUIGI PEDROLLO: *Almost a prayer for those in declining health.*[26]

15 DECEMBER 1959

I send you my cordial thanks for your kind letter.

Be assured that your House is daily named in my prayers. And do you persevere in prayers for us. For now, after two years' remission, my wife's mortal illness has returned. May it please the Lord that, whatever is His will for the body, the minds of both of

[25] *Letters III,* 1105–1106.
[26] *Letters III,* 1109.

us may remain unharmed; that faith unimpaired may strengthen us, contrition soften us and peace make us joyful.

And that, up till now, has happened; nor would you readily believe what joys we sometimes experience in the midst of troubles. What wonder? For has He not promised comfort to those who mourn?[27]

---

[27] Matthew 5:4.

1960

TO MICHAEL EDWARDS, *who had asked Lewis which denomination he should join: On why Lewis steadfastly resisted defending anything else than mere Christianity; and on the illusion of "stable sentiments," "successful adjustment to life," and "getting and being what one wants."*[1]

11 FEBRUARY 1960

As regards the 'interdenominational' question, I have never said anything in print except that I am *not* offering guidance on it (this comes in the preface to *Mere Christianity*). Whatever utility I have as a defender of 'mere' Christianity would be lost if I did, and I should become only one more participant in the dog-fight. And I have an idea that the more people there are preaching 'mere' Christianity, the more chance there is of some day ending that dog-fight. I should therefore probably be of very little use to you in your own decision. Of course come and see me if, after consideration, you think it worth doing: my own idea is that you would be wasting your time.

As to your other question, I wonder whether you are on the right tract in expecting 'stable sentiments' and 'successful adjustment to life'. This is the language of modern psychology rather than of religion or even of common experience, and I sometimes think that when the psychologists speak of adjustment to life they really mean perfect happiness and unbroken good fortune! Not to get—or, worse still, to *be*—what one wants is not a disease that can be cured, but the normal condition of man. To feel guilty, when one is guilty, and to realise, not without pain, one's moral and intellectual inadequacy, is not a disease, but commonsense. To find that one's emotions do not 'come to heel' and line up as stable sentiments in permanent conformity with one's convictions is simply the facts of being a fallen, and still imperfectly redeemed, man. We may be thankful if, by continual prayer and self-discipline, we can, over years, make some approach to that stability. After all,

---

[1] *Letters III*, 1133–1134.

St. Paul who was a good deal further along the road than you and I, could still write *Romans,* chapter 7, verses 21–23.

TO FATHER PETER MILWARD, SJ: *On the techniques of successful lecturing and preaching.*[2]

7 MARCH 1960

As an old lecturer may I give a bit of advice about preaching? The joints (we have finished point A: now for B *or* Here the digression ends) cannot be made too clear. Unless you seem to yourself to be exaggerating them almost absurdly they will escape 9/10 of your hearers. Also, slow, slow. If you want people to weep by the end, make them laugh in the beginning. I hope your priesthood will be blessed. I really agree with your maxim 'the greater the author the less he understands his own work'. In haste.

TO PETER BIDE, *whose wife, Margaret, also had cancer: On the propriety of praying prayers that question God and challenge God rather than insincere prayers; and on the need to risk the heresy that God the Father suffers (Patripassianism) in order to avoid the greater heresy that God is indifferent when we suffer (see the letter below to Gracia Fay Bouwman, 19 July 1960).*[3]

14 JUNE 1960

I know your faith will stand firm.

Joy says (do you agree?) that we needn't be too afraid of questionings and expostulations: it was the impatience of Job, not the theodicies of Elihu,[4] that was pleasing to God. Does He like us to 'stand up to Him' a bit? Certainly He cannot like mere flattery—resentment masquerading as submission through fear.

How impossible it would be now to face it without rage if God Himself had not shared the horrors of the world He made! I know this is Patripassianism. But the other way of putting it, however

---

[2] *Letters III,* 1138.
[3] *Letters III,* 1161–1162.
[4] Job 32:2.

theologically defensible, lets in (psychologically) perhaps a more serious error.

Joy had her right breast removed about 10 days ago, or—as she characteristically put it—became an Amazon. . . .

Thus we can still play the fool . . . you will not misunderstand it. I wish we could meet. Till we do, be sure of our prayers.

TO PHOEBE HESKETH: *On how sorrow seems to isolate; and on how hard it is to forgive. Lewis reveals that Joy's physician had failed to diagnose her cancer at a stage when it could have been treated successfully.*[5]

14 JUNE 1960

The most mischievous—and painful—by-product of any sorrow is the illusion that it isolates one, that one is kicked out alone for this from an otherwise cheerful, bustling, 'normal' world. How much better to realise that one is just doing one's turn in the line like all the rest of the ragged and tired human regiment! Yours is a very terrible bit of it. But I'd sooner be you . . . than the doctor (one of the closest friends) who could and should have diagnosed Joy's trouble when she went to him about the symptoms years ago before we were married. The real trouble about the duty of forgiveness is that you do it with all your might on Monday and then find on Wednesday that it hasn't stayed put and all has to be done over again.

Yes, we will pray for one another.

TO PETER BIDE: *On bereavement.*[6]

14 JULY 1960

Joy died at 10 o'clock last night in the [hospital]. I was alone with her at the moment, but she was not conscious. I had never seen the moment of *natural* death before. It was far less dreadful than I had expected—indeed there's nothing to it. Pray for her soul. I have prayed twice daily of late for us four together—you and Margy and me and Joy. I shall continue for you two.

---

[5] *Letters III*, 1162.
[6] *Letters III*, 1169.

I can't *understand* my loss yet and hardly (except for brief but terrible moments) feel more than a kind of bewilderment, almost a psychological paralysis. A bit like the first moments after being hit by a shell.

I'd like to meet. Perhaps I could come up to town some day when you are in town and take you to lunch at the Athenaeum. For I am—oh God that I were not—very free now. One doesn't realise in early life that the price of freedom is loneliness. To be happy one must be tied. God bless all three of us.

TO GRACIA FAY BOUWMAN: *On which God to pray to—the God pictured by the scriptures or the God conceptualized by philosophy.*[7]

19 JULY 1960

I haven't a copy of the *The Problem of Pain* to hand and I can't remember the exact words I used. What I would *now* say would be something like this.

We have A. The scriptural representative of God—a god not only of love but of *storgé* whose 'bowels are moved'[8] with compassion and who also can fall into 'fury'.[9]

B. A philosophical concept of the Absolute Being to which (one can hardly say 'to whom') all these human characteristics are inapplicable.

We have a tendency to regard B as the literal truth and A either as poetical decoration or as a concession to the 'primitive' mind of the ancient Jews.

We are right in thinking that A cannot be literally true. But no more can B. B is an abstract construction of our own minds. It represents to us as an abstraction, a mere concept, what must in reality be the most concrete of all Facts. B can make no claim to be a revelation: *we* have made it. A does make this claim.

If we accept A literally we shall remain on the mythological level. But it is no improvement to take B literally. Both are only shadows or hints of the reality. A cannot really imagine, and B cannot really conceptualise, God as He is in Himself. To prefer

---

[7] *Letters III*, 1172–1174.

[8] Jeremiah 31:20.

[9] Isaiah 51:17.

A is to think that the symbol *we* have made is better than the symbol *He* has made. I think we are right to use B as a corrective wherever A, taken literally, threatens to become absurd: but we must instantly plunge back into A. Only God Himself knows in what sense He is 'like' a father or King, capable of love and anger. But since He has given us that picture of Himself we may be sure that it is more importantly 'like' than any concept we might try to substitute for it. You'll find this dealt with more fully in Chapter XI of my *Miracles*.

We can get no further than this in knowledge about (*savoir*) God: but we are vouchsafed some knowledge-by-acquaintance (*connaitre*) *of* Him in our devotional and sacramental life. This, if it clothes itself in words and images at all, always borrows them from the A view. But these are not the real point, are they? It is as the moment of personal contact fades that they press upon the mind. We cry 'Father' without attending to all those implications which would become more mythological the further we pursued them. As Buber might say [in his book *I and Thou*] God is most fully real to us as *Thou*, less so as *He*, least so as *It*. We must worship the *Thou*, not the *He* in our own minds, which is just as much an image (therefore a possible *idol*) as a figure of word or stone.

TO ARTHUR GREEVES: *On Joy's death.*[10]

30 AUGUST 1960

It is nice to hear from you. It might have been worse. Joy got away easier than many who die of cancer. There were a couple of hours of atrocious pain on her last morning, but the rest of the day mostly asleep, though rational whenever she was conscious. Two of her last remarks were 'You have made me happy' and 'I am at peace with God.' She died at 10 that evening. I'd seen violent death but never seen natural death before. There's really nothing to it, is there?

One thing I've been glad about is that in the Easter Vac she realised her life long dream of seeing Greece. We had a wonderful time there. And many happy moments even after that. The night before she died we had a long, quiet, nourishing, and tranquil talk.

[10] *Letters III*, 1181–1182.

W. is away on his Irish holiday and has, as usual, drunk himself into hospital. Douglas—the younger boy—is, as always, an absolute brick, and a very bright spot in my life. I'm quite well myself.

TO MRS. RAY GARRETT: *On the real program of the spiritual life—living in the present moment.*[11]

12 SEPTEMBER 1960

The whole lesson of my life has been that no 'methods of stimulation' are of any lasting use. They are indeed like drugs—a stronger dose is needed each time and soon no possible dose is effective. We must not bother about thrills at all. *Do* the present duty—*bear* the present pain—*enjoy* the present pleasure—and leave emotions and 'experiences' to look after themselves. That's the programme, isn't it?

TO PETER BIDE, *whose wife had died on 17 September: On grief.*[12]

20 SEPTEMBER 1960

My dear Peter

I have just come in from saying my morning prayers in the wood, including as always one for 'Peter and Margy and Joy and me', and found your letter. I hope they are allowed to meet and help one another. You and I at any rate can. I shall be here on Wednesday next. If you could let me have a card mentioning the probable time of your arrival, all the better. If not, I shall just 'stand by'.

Yes—at first one is sort of concussed and 'life has no taste and no direction'. One soon discovers, however, that grief is not a state but a process—like a walk in a winding valley with a new prospect at every bend.

God bless all four of us.

---

[11] *Letters III,* 1183–1184.
[12] *Letters III,* 1185.

TO SHELDON VANAUKEN: *On grieving.*[13]

23 SEPTEMBER 1960

My great recent discovery is that when I mourn Joy least I feel nearest to her. Passionate sorrow *cuts us off* from the dead (there are ballads and folk-tales which hint this). Do you think that much of the traditional ritual of mourning had, unconsciously, that very purpose? For of course the primitive mind is very anxious to *keep them away.*

Like you, I can't imagine real Eros coming twice. I still feel married to Joy.

TO MARY WILLIS SHELBURNE: *On the lessons learned about grieving.*[14]

24 SEPTEMBER 1960

As to *how* I take sorrow, the answer is 'In nearly all the possible ways.' Because, as you probably know, it isn't a state but a process. It keeps on changing—like a winding road with quite a new landscape at each bend. Two curious discoveries I have made. The moments at which you call most desperately and clamorously to God for help are precisely those when you seem to get none. And the moments at which I feel nearest to Joy are precisely those when I mourn her *least.* Very queer. In both cases a clamorous need seems to shut one off from the thing needed. No one ever told me this. It is almost like 'Don't knock and it shall be opened to you.' I must think it over.

My youngest stepson is the greatest comfort to me. My brother is still away in Ireland.

TO VERA GEBBERT: *On the impossibility of imagining the life of the world to come.*[15]

16 OCTOBER 1960

I wasn't at all questioning the life after death, you know: only saying that its character is for us unimaginable. . . .

---

[13] *Letters III,* 1187.
[14] *Letters III,* 1188.
[15] *Letters III,* 1198.

But don't let us trouble one another about it. We shall know when we are dead ourselves. The Bible seems scrupulously to avoid any *descriptions* of the other world, or worlds, except in terms of parable or allegory.

TO MARY WILLIS SHELBURNE: *On how troubling it is to be angry with someone you love; on how to avoid nursing the anger and on how to re-member that we are forgiven to the extent that we forgive; and on the need to avoid injustice and to pray for those who are truly unkind.*[16]

28 OCTOBER 1960

Dear, dear, this is very distressing news. How many things have come upon you at once! . . .

It's the mixture, or alternation, of resentment and affection that is so very uneasy, isn't it? For the indulgence of either imme-diately comes slap up against the other, which then, a few seconds later comes slap up against it, so that the mind does a diabolical 'shuttle-service' to and fro between them. We've all at some time in our lives, I expect, had this experience. Except possibly anxi-ety nothing is more hostile to sleep. One must try, I suppose, to keep on remembering that the love part of the suffering is good and purgatorial while the anger part is bad and infernal. Yet how madly one cherishes that base part as if it were one's dearest pos-session—dwells on everything that can aggravate the offence—and keeps on thinking of things one would like to say to the other party! I suppose all one can do is to keep on meditating on the petition 'Forgive us our trespasses *as we* forgive those that trespass against *us*'.[17]

I find *fear* a great help—the fear that my own unforgivingness will exclude me from all the promises. Fear tames wrath. And *this* fear (we have Our Lord's word for it) is wholly well-grounded. The human heart (mine anyway) is 'desperately wicked'.[18] Joy of-ten quoted this in connection with the great difficulty she found in forgiving a very near and very nasty relative of her own. One has to keep on doing it over again, doesn't one? . . .

---

[16] *Letters III,* 1203–1204.
[17] Matthew 6:9; Luke 11:4.
[18] Jeremiah 17:9.

P. S.—It's also useful to think 'Either X is not so bad as, in my present anger, I think. If not, how unjust I must be. If so, how terribly X needs my prayers.'

TO MARY WILLIS SHELBURNE: *On forgetting; on the fear of nursing homes; and on how to avoid some misunderstandings in family life.*[19]

24 NOVEMBER 1960

Thanks for your letter of the 20th. About forgetting things, Dr. Johnson said 'If, on leaving the company, a young man cannot remember where he has left his hat, it is nothing. But when an old man forgets, everyone says, Ah, his memory is going.' So with ourselves. We have *always* been forgetting things: but now, when we do so, we attribute it to our age. Why, it was years ago that, on finishing my work before lunch, I stopped myself only just in time from putting my cigarette-end into my spectacle case and throwing my spectacles into the fire!

What I was writing about last time was the pain and resentment you were feeling about some thing your daughter had said or done. I wasn't trying to lecture. Rather, to compare notes about temptation we all have to contend with.

There, by the way, is a sentence ending with a preposition. The silly 'rule' against it was invented by Dryden. I think he disliked it only because you can't do it in either French or Latin which he thought more 'polite' languages than English.

As for the bug-bear of Old People's Homes, remember that our ignorance works both ways. Just as some of the things we have longed and hoped for turn out to be dust and ashes when we get them, so the things we have most dreaded sometimes turn out to be quite nice. If you ever do have to go to a Home, Christ will be there just as much as in any other place.

The bit of conversation with your daughter which you quoted sounds as if there were nothing much wrong on either side but nerves. But I admit I don't know the cure. Slowing down the *speed* of the conversation (so far as this depends on oneself) is sometimes helpful. Also sitting down. I think we all talk more excitedly when standing. (Notice how often the actors in a comedy *sit* whereas those in a tragedy usually stand.)

---

[19] *Letters III*, 1212–1213.

1961

TO DON LUIGI PEDROLLO, *who had asked for the letters of Giovanni Calabria, so that they could be conveyed to his biographer: On the reason why Lewis did not keep the letters he received from Saint John Calabria.*[1]

3 JANUARY 1961

I wish I could send you copies of the letters which the Venerable Father Don John Calabria wrote. But I have neither the letters themselves nor copies of them. It is my practice to consign to the flames all letters after two days—not, believe me, because I esteem them of no value, rather because I do not wish to relinquish things often worthy of sacred silence to subsequent reading by posterity.

For nowadays inquisitive researchers dig out all our affairs and besmirch them with the poison of 'publicity' (as a barbarous thing I am giving it a barbarous name).

This is the last thing I would wish to happen to the letters of Father John.

That admirable man, to others most lenient but to himself most severe, not to say savage, out of humility and with a certain holy imprudence wrote many things which I think should be kept quiet. If you would politely convey this explanation of mine to Father Mondrone, I would be grateful.

We greatly rejoice at the recent meeting between the Holy Father [Pope John XXIII] and our Archbishop [of Canterbury, Geoffrey Fisher]. May the Lord confirm this happy omen.

My wife died in the month of July. For her and for me redouble your prayers. You and your House are ever in mine.

---

[1] *Letters III*, 1220–1221.

TO MARY WILLIS SHELBURNE, *whose daughter and son-in-law have asked her to live with them: On how to make a choice between crosses; and on how to live in someone else's home.*[2]

9 JANUARY 1961

I don't feel at all 'wise' and the only bit of advice I can give you with perfect confidence is—*don't* sit up writing long letters either to me or to anyone else when you are tired! It is very bad for you. Now as to the main issue.

Whatever you decide to *do,* get your own attitude right. They are behaving as if they were penitent and wished to make restitution. Their penitence may no doubt be very imperfect and their motives very mixed. But so are all *our* repentances and all *our* motives. Accept theirs as you hope God will accept yours. Remember that He has promised to forgive you *as,* and only *as,* you forgive them.

The decision, however, remains, I agree, a terrible one to make, and only someone who really knew you and Don and Lorraine— I have met none of the three—is really qualified to give you advice. Is it not possible to give their plan a trial run, with the understanding on both sides that after 6 months or a year it can be continued or discontinued and 'no offence'? Of course this would involve giving up a great deal, including your cat. But I'm afraid as we grow older life consists more and more in either giving up things or waiting for them to be taken from us.

As you rightly see, to become a member of their household would involve a severe and continual self-suppression. You would have to be silent about many things when you longed to speak. But the alternative is also bad.

Is it not impossible to predict which way will give you less unhappiness? Isn't one therefore thrown back on asking which will be best for the others? But how to decide that I don't know.

The only certain thing is that your acceptance (if you accept) or your refusal (if you refuse) must be made with perfect charity and courtesy. May God's grace give you the necessary humility. Try not to think—much less, speak—of *their* sins. One's own are a much more profitable theme! And if, on consideration, one can

---

[2] *Letters III,* 1224–1226.

find no faults on one's own side, then cry for mercy: for this *must* be a most dangerous delusion. Incidentally, I can't help feeling that you should take Lorraine's account of Don with a grain of salt. On your own showing she can't be an easy woman to live with and there is usually something to be said on both sides.

Well, I'm afraid all this comes to precious little. But I don't, and can't *know* enough. I can only pray that you may be guided to the right choice. It is (no disguising it) only a choice between Crosses. The more one can accept that fact, the less one can think about happiness on earth, the less, I believe, one suffers. Or at any rate the suffering becomes more purgatorial and less infernal.

TO HUGH KILMER, *the oldest of the Kilmer children to whom Lewis had dedicated* The Magician's Nephew, *at this time a student for the Roman Catholic priesthood, who had asked some questions about* Miracles, *perhaps Chapter 16: On the possible differences between the glorified body of Jesus and our own glorified bodies, including being in one place and not in another simultaneously and being in a kind of glorified time* (aevum) *rather than either in unredeemed time* (tempus) *or in the kind of eternity proper to bodiless spirits* (aeternitas) *or in God's own ability to be everywhere all at once* (totum simul). *Lewis treats him as an equal by addressing him by his surname.*[3]

15 FEBRUARY 1961

Dear Kilmer,

If I had time to re-read my own book (by now a pretty old one) I'd be able to answer you better, meanwhile:

1. Can we assume that whatever is true of the glorified body of our Lord is equally true of the glorified body of each Christian? I doubt it. His natural body did not undergo dissolution.

2. I don't accept the implication of your phrase '*restricted* by external quantity', for restriction suggests imperfection. But to be in one place (or therefore not in another) seems to me possibly part of the perfection of a finite creature—as it belongs to the perfection of a statue to end where it does or of a musical note to be just so loud (neither more or less) or of a metrical verse.

---

[3] *Letters III*, 1239.

3. I am not at all sure that blessed souls have a strictly timeless being (a *totum simul*) like God. Don't some theologians interpose *aevum* as a half-way house between *tempus* and *aeternitas*?

In general, I incline to think that though the blessed will participate in the Divine Nature, they will do so always in a mode which does not simply annihilate their humanity. Otherwise it is difficult to see why the species was created at all.

Of course I'm only guessing.

TO MARY WILLIS SHELBURNE, *who had decided to live with her daughter and son-in-law: On the need for patience and self-sacrifice; on being content to pray for those with whom one lives and refraining from meddling and instructing; and on therapy for pets.*[4]

24 FEBRUARY 1961

I am very glad you have made the decision and I believe it is the right one. I realise that you are taking on a very different life, which will involve much frustration, self-effacement, and patience. There will be every opportunity and necessity of mortifying the 'highly developed pride' diagnosed by the grapho-analyst! There will have to be plenty of 'turning back' and 'change of purpose'—except, to be sure, the constant and prayerful purpose of continual sacrifice. The great thing is that you realise all that; and as the comic beatitude says, 'Blessed are they that expect little for they shall not be disappointed.' I hope and pray you will be able to do them some good, but probably if you do, it will not be by any voluntary and conscious actions. Your prayers for them will be more use. Probably the safe rule will be 'When in doubt what to do or say, do or say nothing.' I feel this very much with my stepsons. I so easily *meddle* and *gas:* when all the time what will really influence them, for good or ill, is not anything I do or say but what I *am*. And this unfortunately one can't know and can't much alter, though God can. Two rules from William Law [*A Serious Call to a Devout and Holy Life*, XVI] must be always in our minds.

1. 'There can be no surer proof of a confirmed pride than a belief that one is sufficiently humble.'

_____

[4] *Letters III*, 1242–1243.

2. 'I earnestly beseech all who conceive they have suffered an affront to believe that it is very much less than they suppose.'

I hope your vet is not a charlatan? Psychological diagnoses even about human patients seem to me pretty phoney. They must be even phonier when applied to animals. You can't put a cat on a couch and make it tell you its dreams or produce words by 'free association'. Also—I have a great respect for cats—they are very shrewd people and would probably see through the analyst a good deal better than he'd see through them.

TO MARY WILLIS SHELBURNE: *More on how to live with difficult human beings.*[5]

28 MARCH 1961

The unexpected crisis which hurried you into that house has all the air of an act of God: It looks as if He meant you to be there. While you were still debating whether the move was to your interest, He suddenly made it your duty. A pretty clear call, I take it. As to the 'sincerity' of Don's behaviour, remember (let us look in *our own* hearts for the truth!) humans are very seldom either totally sincere or totally hypocritical. Their moods change, their motives are mixed, and they are often themselves quite mistaken as to what their motives are. There is probably some real repentance and desire for amendment on Don's part: it won't necessarily be permanent any more than our own countless repentances and good resolutions are. There is also probably a desire, whether conscious or unconscious, to make a party *with* you *against* Lorraine. There is also perhaps a desire to make Lorraine feel, 'If he is so nice to Mother, perhaps it may be my fault that he is not nice to me.' Also, a desire to make you feel, 'Since he really behaves like this, perhaps most of Lorraine's complaints about his treatment are untrue or exaggerated.' But all these mixed up together: the good motives partly poisoned by the bad ones and the bad ones partly modified by the good ones. At any rate, 'charity hopeth all things, believeth all things.'[6] The rule is to give every one 'the benefit of the doubt' about sincerity yet at the same time to be on one's

[5] *Letters III*, 1249–1250.
[6] I Corinthians 13:7.

guard. Above all, be guarded when either complains to you about the other. They may, at that moment, be quite sincere. But when they are next reunited to each other (and of course sex probably insures reconciliation from time to time) they will infallibly repeat to each other all you have said. Here, as usual, the *Imitation* is a good guide: 'I have often repented of speech but hardly ever of silence.' And don't believe ¼ of what they say. Without any intention of lying, people so arrogant as Don and so obviously unstable as Lorraine can hardly tell anything without misrepresentation. Notice this even when they are talking on quite neutral matters.

'My own life as a person seems definitely at an end.' I know it's easy for me to give good advice to others in situations which I probably could not face myself. But that can't be helped: I must say what I think true. Surely the main purpose of our life is to reach the point at which 'one's own life as a person' *is* at an end. One must in this sense 'die', become 'naught', relinquish one's freedom and independence. 'Not I, but Christ that dwelleth in me'[7]—'He must grow greater and I must grow less'[8]—'He that loseth his life shall find it.'[9] But you know all this quite as well as I do. It may well involve eating white bread instead of brown! How many millions at this moment have no bread at all?

P.S. Of course the little addition to your income can continue.

TO HUGH KILMER: *On rejoicing over being good at being what one is, an angel, a human being, or an apple tree.*[10]

5 APRIL 1961

Your definition of gaiety is very much to the point. Perhaps one can carry it further. A creature can never be a perfect *being*, but may be a perfect *creature*—e.g., a good angel or a good apple-tree. Gaiety at its highest may be an (intellectual) creature's delighted recognition that its imperfection as a being may constitute

---

[7] John 14:10.
[8] John 3:30.
[9] Matthew 10:39.
[10] *Letters III*, 1252.

part of its perfection as an element in the whole hierarchical order of creation. I mean, while it is a pity there should be bad men or bad dogs, part of the excellence of a good man is that he is *not* an angel, and of a good dog that it is *not* a man. This is an extension of what St. Paul says about the body and the members. A good toe-nail is not an unsuccessful attempt at a brain: and if it were conscious it would delight in being simply a good toe-nail.

TO MARY WILLIS SHELBURNE: *On how grating one's voice, looks, and mannerisms can be on others. Jeanne is the daughter of Lorraine and Don.*[11]

21 APRIL 1961

I have your letter of the 16th. You were (very naturally) distraught when you wrote it, and you don't even make clear to me *exactly what* Jeanne did! Did she get, as they say, 'into trouble' those two nights? If nothing worse happened than being out and alone in wet weather, I should have thought a girl in reasonable health would get over it alright, and so, I hope, will you all. Don seems to be doing his best now, whatever he did in the past; and with such a wife and such a daughter his home life can't be a bed of roses. It is a pity he 'gets on your nerves' but you are, rightly, controlling your reactions. I know well how a person's very voice, looks, and mannerisms may grate on one! I always try to remember that mine probably do the same to him—and of course I never hear or see myself.

TO MARGARET GRAY, *who had asked Lewis for a reading list and who had mentioned that she had been consoled by a very real experience of her late husband: On the books Lewis most often recommended.*[12]

9 MAY 1961

How right you are when you say 'Christianity is a terrible thing for a lifelong atheist to have to face'! In people like us— adult converts in the 20th century—I take this feeling to be a good symptom. By the way, you have had in most respects a tougher life than I, but there's one thing I envy you. I lost my wife last

---

[11] *Letters III,* 1258–1259.
[12] *Letters III,* 1264–1265.

summer after a very late, very short, and intensely happy married life, but I have not been vouchsafed (and why the deuce should I be?) a visit like yours—or certainly not except for one split second. Now about reading.

For a good ('popular') defence of our position against modern waffle, to fall back on, I know nothing better than G. K. Chesterton's *The Everlasting Man*. Harder reading, but very protective, is Edwyn Bevan's *Symbolism and Belief*. Charles Williams's *He Came Down from Heaven* doesn't suit everyone, but try it.

For meditative and devotional reading (a little bit at a time, more like sucking a lozenge than eating a slice of bread) I suggest the *Imitation of Christ* (astringent) and Traherne's *Centuries of Meditations* (joyous). Also my selection from MacDonald, *George MacDonald: An Anthology*. I can't read Kierkegaard myself, but some people find him helpful.

For Christian morals I suggest my wife's (Joy Davidman) *Smoke on the Mountain,* Gore's *The Sermon on the Mount* and (perhaps) his *Philosophy of the Good Life*. And possibly (but with a grain of salt, for he is too puritanical) William Law's *Serious Call to a Devout and Holy Life*. I know the very title makes me shudder, but we have both got a lot of shuddering to get through before we're done!

You'll want a mouth-wash for the *imagination*. I'm told that Mauriac's novels (all excellently translated, if your French is rusty) are good, though very severe. Dorothy Sayers' *Man Born to Be King* (those broadcast plays) certainly is. So, to me, but not to everyone, are Charles Williams's fantastic novels. *Pilgrim's Progress,* if you ignore some straw-splitting dialogues in Calvinist theology and concentrate on the story, is first class.

St. Augustine's *Confessions* will give you the record of an earlier adult convert, with many very great devotional passages intermixed.

Do you read poetry? George Herbert at his best is extremely nutritious.

I don't mention the Bible because I take that for granted. A modern translation is for most purposes far more useful than Authorised Version.

As regards my own books, you might (or might not) care for *Transposition, The Great Divorce,* or *The Four Loves.*

Yes—'being done good to'—grrr! I never asked ever to be.

TO MARY WILLIS SHELBURNE: *On being overconcerned about the past of others and of our own.*[13]

5 JUNE 1961

We must beware of the Past, mustn't we? I mean that any fixing of the mind on old evils beyond what is absolutely necessary for repenting our own sins and forgiving those of others is certainly useless and usually bad for us. Notice in Dante that the lost souls are entirely concerned with their past. Not so the saved. This is one of the dangers of being, like you and me, old. There's so much past, now, isn't there? And so little else. But we must try very hard not to keep on endlessly chewing the cud. We must look forward more eagerly to sloughing that old skin off forever—metaphors getting a bit mixed here, but you know what I mean.

TO HARVEY KARLSEN, *who seems to have written Lewis about a habit of masturbation: On the remedies for sexual temptation—frequent and regular prayer and communions, monthly confession, avoiding discouragement, not exaggerating nor minimizing one's sins, avoiding either trains of thought or social situations that lead to temptation, and applying the brakes, gently and quietly, while the danger is still a good way off.*[14]

13 OCTOBER 1961

Your letter did not reach me till to-day. Of course I have had and still have plenty of temptations. Frequent and regular prayer, and frequent and regular Communions, are a great help, whether they *feel* at the time as if they were doing you good or whether they don't. I also found great help in monthly confession to a wise old clergyman.

Perhaps, however, the most important thing is to *keep on:* not to be discouraged however often one yields to the temptation, but always to pick yourself up again and ask forgiveness. In reviewing

---

[13] *Letters III,* 1273–1274.
[14] *Letters III,* 1285–1286.

your sins don't either exaggerate them or minimise them. Call them by their ordinary names and try to see them as you would see the same faults in somebody else—no special blackening or whitewashing. Remember the condition on which we are promised forgiveness: we shall always be forgiven provided that we forgive all who sin against us. If we do that we have nothing to fear: if we don't, all else will be in vain. Of course there are other helps which are more commonsense. We must learn by experience to avoid either trains of thought or social situations which *for us* (not necessarily for everyone) lead to temptations. Like motoring—don't wait till the last moment before you put on the brakes but put them on, gently and quietly, while the danger is still a good way off. I would write at more length, but I am ill. God bless you.

TO ARTHUR GREEVES: *On great books for spiritual reading.*[15]

12 NOVEMBER 1961

Yes. The *Imitation* is very severe; useful at times when one is tempted to be too easily satisfied with one's progress, but certainly not at times of discouragement. And of course it is written for monks, not for people living in the world like us.

A good book to balance it is Traherne's *Centuries of Meditations,* which I expect you know. (Not to be confused with his poems, which I don't recommend.) There is all the gold and fragrance!

Midway between the two I'd put the anonymous *Theologia Germanica.* . . . This is curiously like the sort of letters we used to write 45 years ago!

P. S. I never read St. John of the Cross.

TO ARTHUR GREEVES: *On a limitation of* The Imitation of Christ.[16]

24 NOVEMBER 1961

I don't think the author of the *Imitation* was ever aware of the beauty of nature as we understand it.

---

[15] *Letters III,* 1295–1296.
[16] *Letters III,* 1297.

TO MARY VAN DEUSEN: *On prayers for the dead; and on the authority of the Bible over the Church.*[17]

28 DECEMBER 1961

I've found the passage—I Cor. XV, 29. Also I Pet. III 19–20 bears indirectly on the subject. It implies that something can be done for the dead. If so, why should we not pray for them?

Beware of the argument 'the Church gave the Bible (and therefore the Bible can never give us grounds for criticising the Church)'. It is perfectly possible to accept B on the authority of A and yet regard B as a higher authority than A. It happens when I recommend a book to a pupil. I first sent him to the book, but, having gone to it, he knows (for *I've* told him) that the author knows more about that subject than I.

---

[17] *Letters III,* 1307–1308.

1962

TO MARY WILLIS SHELBURNE: *On rejoicing in the present moment or at least refraining from trying to live in the past or the future.*[1]

4 MAY 1962

Thank you all for your kind prayers. You have mine daily. Yes—it is sometimes hard to obey St. Paul's 'Rejoice.'[2] We must try to take life moment by moment. The actual *present* is usually pretty tolerable, I think, if only we refrain from adding to its burden that of the past and the future. How right Our Lord is about 'sufficient to the day'.[3] Do even pious people in their reverence for the more radiantly divine element in His sayings, sometimes attend too little to their sheer practical common-sense?

TO STUART ROBERTSON: *On the various paradoxes of the New Testament, especially of faith and works.*[4]

6 MAY 1962

On this point as on others the New Testament is highly paradoxical. St. Paul at the outset of an epistle sometimes talks as if the converts whom he is addressing were already wholly new creatures, already in the world of light, their old nature completely crucified. Yet by the end of the same epistle he will be warning the same people to avoid the very grossest vices.

Of himself he speaks sometimes as if his reward was perfectly sure: elsewhere he fears lest, having preached to others, he should be himself a castaway.[5]

Our Lord Himself sometimes speaks as if all depended on faith, yet in the parable of the sheep and the goats all seems to depend

---

[1] *Letters III*, 1335–1336.
[2] Philippians 4:4.
[3] Matthew 6:34.
[4] *Letters III*, 1336–1337.
[5] I Corinthians 9:27.

on works: even works done or undone by those who had no idea what they were doing or undoing.[6]

The best I can do about these mysteries is to think that the New Testament gives us a sort of double vision. A. Into our salvation as eternal fact, as it (and all else) is in the timeless vision of God. B. Into the same thing as a process worked out in time. Both must be true in some sense but it is beyond our capacity to envisage both together. Can one get a faint idea of it by thinking of A. A musical score as it is written down with all the notes there at once. B. The same thing *played* as a process in time? For *practical* purposes, however, it seems to me we must usually live by the second vision 'working out our own salvation in fear and trembling'[7] (but it adds 'for'—not 'though'—but 'for'—'it is God who worketh in us').[8]

And in this temporal process surely God saves different souls in different ways? To preach instantaneous conversion and eternal security as if they must be the experiences of all who are saved, seems to me very dangerous: the very way to drive some into presumption and others into despair. How very different were the callings of the disciples.

I don't agree that if anyone were completely a new creature, you and I would necessarily recognise him as such. It takes holiness to detect holiness.

TO MR. GREEN, *who seems to have thought he had committed the unforgivable sin: A model letter of extraordinary care in which Lewis shares his own apostasy, reasons with his correspondent, gives good advice, consoles, and asks for mutual prayer—on needing to be reminded that there is a point beyond which return becomes impossible; on the ordinary remedies for overcoming fears; and on the need to seek psychiatric help if the fears become extreme, if one despairs.*[9]

---

[6] Matthew 25:31–63.
[7] Philippians 2:12.
[8] Philippians 2:13.
[9] *Letters III*, 1340–1341.

11 MAY 1962

I also once ceased to believe and told others there is no God. In fact you and I both lost our faith and then returned to it. But surely we did not return on our own steam? Surely we were re-called by God? For no man can come, nor come back, to God unless God send for him. The grace He has thus shown us for a second time is the proof that He has forgiven us. He has not cast us aside even though we, for a time, cast Him aside.

Don't forget that Bunyan, as he himself tells us, thought that he had at one time committed the unforgivable sin.[10] Yet he lived to write the *Pilgrim's Progress* and to be a great Christian champion.

It has always puzzled me very much that Our Lord should have told us there is an unforgivable sin and yet not told us what it is. If it is a particular act which could be done at a particular time, the warning does not seem to be any use—like being told that there is a poisonous vegetable but not told which it is. But it may mean persistence in ordinary sin, a final refusal to repent or even to *try* to reform. If so, the warning would then be useful, a reminder that there is a point beyond which return becomes impossible. His purpose would be to fix the danger in our minds, but certainly *not* to set us looking through all our particular sins and trying to guess if some one of them was It.

As far as you (and I) are concerned I have no doubt that the fear you mention is simply a temptation of the devil, an effort to keep us away from God by despair. It is often the devil working through some defect in our health, and in extreme cases it needs a medical as well as a spiritual cure. So don't listen to these fears and doubts* any more than you would to any obviously impure or uncharitable thoughts.

With hearty good wishes.

*Of course, like other evil temptations, they will not be si-lenced at once. You will think you have got rid of them and then they will come back again—and again. But, with all our tempta-tions of all sorts, we must just endure this. Keep on, do your duty,

---

[10] Mark 3:28–29; Matthew 12:31–32.

say your prayers, make your communions, and take no notice of the tempter. He goes away in the end. Remember I John iii, 20 'If (= though) our heart condemn us, God is greater than our heart.' Let us sometimes pray for one another.

TO MRS. JOHN R. ROLSTON, *who had written Lewis to thank him for* A Grief Observed.[11]

14 MAY 1962

Thank you for writing. We are only two in the huge number of mourners, but it is cheering when two of us thus meet. Let us remember all the others in our prayers. With all good wishes.

TO MR. GREEN: *Another care-filled letter about coping with the fear of having committed the unforgivable sin.*[12]

16 MAY 1962

I was not only baptised in infancy, but, what seems to me for worst, I was already an apostate when I hypocritically allowed myself to be confirmed and made my first communion—in a state of total unbelief.

You'll find Bunyan's story (about how he thought he had committed the unforgivable sin) in *Grace Abounding to the Chief of Sinners*. I find also that our chaplain—a very good young man—once thought that he had done the same thing. He, by the way, took the view that those who had *really* done it would be the very last people to be bothered about it (in this life), for they would be hardened, which you—and, I dare to add, I—obviously are not.

There is a lovely passage in Pascal where he represents Our Lord as saying to the timorous soul, 'Be comforted. Unless you had found me, you would not be seeking me.' God bless us both.

---

[11] *Letters III,* 1343.
[12] *Letters III,* 1344.

TO EDWARD LOFSTROM: *A letter of great encouragement for someone who had been struggling with excessive self-awareness.*[13]

10 JUNE 1962

You are of course perfectly right in defining your problem (which is also mine and everyone's) as 'excessive selfness'. But perhaps you don't fully realise how far you have got by so defining it. All have this disease; fortunate are the minority who know they have it. To know that one is dreaming is to be already nearly awake, even if, for the present, one can't wake up fully. And you have actually got further than that. You have got beyond the illusion (very common) that to *recognise* a chasm is the same thing as building a bridge over it.

Your danger now is that of being hypnotised by the mere sight of the charm, of constantly *looking at* this excessive selfness. The important thing now is to go steadily on acting, so far as you can—and you certainly can to some extent, however small—as if it wasn't there. You can, and I expect you daily do—behave with some degree of unselfishness. You can and do make some attempt at prayer. The continual voice which tells you that your best actions are secretly filled with subtle self-regards, and your best prayers still wholly egocentric—must for the most part be simply disregarded—as one disregards the impulse to keep on looking under the bandage to see whether the cut is healing. If you are always fidgeting with the bandage, it never will.

A text you should keep much is mind is I John iii, 20: 'If our heart condemns us God is greater than our heart.' I sometimes pray 'Lord give me *no more* and *no less* self-knowledge than I can at this moment make a good use of.' Remember He is the artist and you are only the picture. You can't see it. So quietly submit to be painted—i.e., keep on fulfilling all the obvious duties of your station (you really know quite well enough what they are!), asking forgiveness for each failure and then leaving it alone. You are in the right way. *Walk*—don't keep on looking at it.

---

[13] *Letters III,* 1349–1350.

TO MR. GREEN: *A rare letter of retraction of advice.*[14]

11 JUNE 1962

You are kind enough to say that I helped you. This emboldens me to make a very serious request of you, almost an entreaty. Cancel your order for *Grace Abounding,* or, if it is too late, *don't* read it. I implore you not to. It is a strange request, you will say, since I first directed your attention to the book. But the whole point of that was to convince you that a man can come through all that nightmare about the unforgivable sin and live to be a great Christian.

But for you, who have just got out of it, to go back and steep yourself in another man's sinister nightmare, might do dreadful harm. When a man has just got over malaria one doesn't advise him to go back to a malarial district. I now blame myself—God forgive me—for having mentioned the book at all. A line from you promising not to read it —not for 10 years or so—would be a very great relief to me.

TO MR. GREEN: *On the reasons why Lewis withdrew his recommendation of the book by Bunyan—Bunyan's method of interpreting the Bible is very misleading, and reading such a book will lead to further introspection when introspection is to be avoided for the time being.*[15]

21 JUNE 1962

Dismiss from your mind all idea that Bunyan's *Grace Abounding to the Chief of Sinners* contains any *facts* from which I wish to shield you. Bunyan's crisis, as anyone can see to-day, was far more pathological than spiritual. The way he got into the trouble and the way he got out of it were both irrational. The one need not alarm, and the other can hardly help, any sane person. What I feared for you was the mere *infection* of steeping yourself in a very vivid account of all the emotions felt by a man in a condition from which you have so lately emerged yourself.

This *is* something to be learned from the book, and I will now tell it you. It is this: that the habit of taking isolated texts from the

[14] *Letters III,* 1350–1351.
[15] *Letters III,* 1352–1353.

Bible and treating the effect which they have on one in a particular mood at a particular moment as direct messages from God, is
very misleading. It fills some people (who are in one state) with
morbid terror, and fills others (who are in a different state) with
presumption. This, I say, *can* be learned from Bunyan but I don't
think that is what *you* would get from him at present. No very
introspective book—no books in which a man is wholly preoc-
cupied with his own spiritual state—would be very safe reading
for you just now. Convalescents need a careful diet! You need
something that will direct your attention away from yourself to
God and your neighbours.

I suggest G. K. Chesterton's *The Everlasting Man* and George
MacDonald's *Sir Gibbie* (if you can manage the Scotch dialect).

Be regular in prayer and the Sacraments: do all the good to
those you live among: and trust to God. May He bless us both.

TO MARY WILLIS SHELBURNE: *On the spiritual profit to be made from
imposed mortifications during convalescence.*[16]

3 JULY 1962

Yes, we do seem to be having a certain amount of experience
in common! Perhaps if we had done more voluntary fasting before God would not now have put us on these darn diets! Well,
the theologians say that an imposed mortification can have all the
merit of a voluntary one if it is taken in the right spirit.

We are also both ruled by cats. Joy's Siamese—my 'step-cat' as
I call her—is the most terribly conversational animal I ever knew.
She talks all the time and wants doors and windows to be opened
for her 1000 times an hour.

Yes, and one gets bored with the medicines too—besides always wondering 'Did I remember to take them after breakfast?'
and then wondering whether the risk of missing a dose or the risk
of an over dose is the worst! All my sympathy. In haste.

---

[16] *Letters III*, 1355–1356.

TO MARY WILLIS SHELBURNE: *On the different ways women and men respond to being ill.*[17]

31 JULY 1962

Yes, it *is* strange that anyone should dislike cats. But cats themselves are the worst offenders in this respect. They very seldom seem to like one another.

I have a notion that, apart from actual pain, men and women are quite diversely affected by illness. To a woman one of the great evils about it is that she can't do things. To a man (or anyway a man like me) the great consolation is the reflection 'Well, anyway, no one can now demand that I should *do* anything.' I have often had the fancy that one stage in Purgatory might be a great big kitchen in which things are always going wrong—milk boiling over, crockery getting smashed, toast burning, animals stealing. The women have to learn to sit still and mind their own business: the men have to learn to jump up and do something about it. When both sexes have mastered this exercise, they go on to the next.

In your present *ménage* you seem to be getting a foretaste of this! If I were you I wouldn't 'do all you can'. It probably only bothers the other lady and, as you say, makes you ill.

I think I continue to improve physically. As I get better I feel the loss of Joy more. I suppose the capacity for happiness must reawake before one becomes fully aware of its absence.

Yes, one gets sick of pills. But thank God we don't live in the age of horrible medicines such as our grandparents had to swallow.

TO MARY WILLIS SHELBURNE: *On regrets and humiliations over past blunders and the unintended consequences of past actions.*[18]

3 SEPTEMBER 1962

Our situations are curiously reversed: you live in fear that an operation may be necessary, and I in hope that one may become

---

[17] *Letters III,* 1361–1362.
[18] *Letters III,* 1366.

possible. (At least it ought to be *hope,* but sometimes the flesh is weak!) Nausea is horrible, isn't it? Worse than all but really severe pains: at least it dominates the mind and the emotions more.

I am surprised that you should doubt your forgiveness for sins from which you have doubtless long since received absolution. Especially as what apparently troubles you is not malice but the unforeseen results (or things only possibly the result) of behaviour whose intention was innocent. No doubt, as I know only too well, the knowledge that one's acts have, contrary to one's intention, led to all sorts of dreadful consequences, is a heavy burden. But it is a burden of regret and humiliation, isn't it?, rather than of guilt. Perhaps we all dislike humiliation so much that we tend to disguise it from ourselves by treating blunders as sins?

Of course you always have my prayers.

My idea of the Purgatorial kitchen didn't mean that anyone had lately been 'getting in my hair'. It is simply my lifelong experience—that men are more likely to hand over to others what they ought to do themselves, and women more likely to do themselves what others wish they would leave alone. Hence both sexes must be told 'Mind your own business,' but in two different senses!

TO KEITH MANSHIP: *On the slow process of being more in Christ; and on doing one's duty, especially the duty to enjoy.*[19]

13 SEPTEMBER 1962

You state the problem very clearly, and the fact that you can do so really shows that you are very much on the right road. Many don't even get so far.

The whole problem of our life was neatly expressed by John the Baptist when he said (John, chap 3, v. 30) 'He must increase, but I must decrease.' This you have realised. But you are expecting it to happen suddenly: and also expecting that you should be clearly aware when it does. But neither of these is usual. We are doing well enough if the slow process of being more in Christ and less in ourselves has made a decent beginning in a long life (it will be completed only in the next world). Nor can we *observe* it happening. All our reports on ourselves are unbelievable, even in

---

[19] *Letters III,* 1368–1369.

worldly matters (no one really hears his own voice as others do, or sees his own face). Much more in spiritual matters. God sees us, and we don't see ourselves. And by trying too hard to do so, we only get the fidgets and become either too complacent or too much the other way.

Your question what to *do* is already answered. Go on (as you apparently are going on) doing all your duties. And, in all lawful ways, go on *enjoying* all that can be enjoyed—your friends, your music, your books. Remember we are told to 'rejoice'.[20] Sometimes when you are wondering what God wants *you* to do, He really wants to *give* you something.

As to your spiritual state, try my plan. I pray 'Lord, show me just so much (neither more nor less) about myself as I need for doing thy will *now*.'

TO MARY WILLIS SHELBURNE: *On what Lewis learned from the behavior of cats and dogs.*[21]

2 OCTOBER 1962

I am glad to hear you have rehabilitated a displaced cat. I can't understand the people who say cats are not affectionate. Our Siamese (my 'step-cat') is almost suffocatingly so. True, our ginger Tom (a great Don Juan and a mighty hunter before the Lord)[22] will take no notice of *me*, but he will of others. He thinks I'm not quite socially up to his standards, and makes this very clear. No creature can give such a crushing 'snub' as a cat! He sometimes looks at the dog—a big Boxer puppy, very anxious to be friendly—in a way that makes it want to sink into the floor.

TO MARY WILLIS SHELBURNE: *On Lewis's own rule for assisting panhandlers; and on the suffering and eternal destiny of animals.*[23]

---

[20] Philippians 4:4.
[21] *Letters III*, 1374–1375.
[22] Genesis 10:9.
[23] *Letters III*, 1376–1377.

26 OCTOBER 1962

I do most thoroughly agree with your father's principles about alms. It will not bother me in the hour of death to reflect that I have been 'had for a sucker' by any number of impostors: but it would be a torment to know that one had refused even *one* person in need. After all, the parable of the sheep and goats[24] makes our duty perfectly plain, doesn't it? Another thing that annoys me is when people say 'Why did you give that man money? He'll probably go and drink it.' My reply is 'But if I'd kept [it] *I* should probably have drunk it.' . . .

I am sorry to hear of the little dog's death. The animal creation is a strange mystery. We can make some attempt to understand human suffering: but the sufferings of animals from the beginning of the world till now (inflicted not only by us but by one another)—what is one to think? And again, how strange that God brings us into such intimate relations with creatures of whose real purpose and destiny we remain forever ignorant. We know to some degree what angels and men are *for*. But what is a flea for, or a wild dog?

TO MARY WILLIS SHELBURNE: *On how much harder it is to live alone than with others, but how hard it is to avoid the sins of the tongue (which include our look, manner, and intonation).*[25]

8 NOVEMBER 1962

Yes, I can well understand how you long for 'a place of your own'. I nominally have one and am nominally master of the house, but things seldom go as I would have chosen. The truth is that the only alternatives are either solitude (with all its miseries and dangers, both moral and physical) or else all the rubs and frustrations of a joint life. The second, even at its worst, seems to me far the better.

I hope one is rewarded for all the stunning replies one thinks of and does not utter! But alas, even when we don't *say* them, more than we suspect comes out in our look, our manner, and our

---

[24] Matthew 25:31–46.
[25] *Letters III,* 1379.

voice. An elaborately patient silence can be very provoking! We are *all* fallen creatures and *all* very hard to live with. It is not only Episcopalians who behave as if they had never read St. James.[26]

I do hope the operation will turn out to be unnecessary.

TO MARY VAN DEUSEN: *On the difficulties of moving and on the lessons moving teaches us—"We must 'sit light' not only to life itself but to all its phases. The useless word is 'Encore!'"*[27]

21 NOVEMBER 1962

I think I share, to excess, your feeling about a move. By nature I demand from the arrangements of this world just that permanence which God has expressly refused to give them. It is not merely the nuisance and expense of any big change in one's way of life that I dread. It is also the psychological uprooting and the feeling—to me, as to you, intensely unwelcome—of having ended a chapter. One more portion of oneself slipping away into the past! I would like everything to be immemorial—to have the same old horizons, the same garden, the same smells and sounds, always there, changeless. The old wine is to me always better. That is, I desire the 'abiding city'[28] where I well know it is not and ought not to be found. I suppose all these changes should prepare us for the far greater change which has drawn nearer ever since I began this letter. We must 'sit light' not only to life itself but to all its phases. The useless word is 'Encore!'

TO MARY WILLIS SHELBURNE: *On the resurrection of the body and of all creation; and on the goodness of the bodies we now have.*[29]

26 NOVEMBER 1962

My stuff about animals came long ago in *The Problem of Pain*. I ventured the supposal—it could be nothing more—that as we are raised *in* Christ, so at least some animals are raised *in* us. Who knows, indeed, but that a great deal even of the inanimate cre-

---

[26] James 3:1–12.
[27] *Letters III*, 1382–1383.
[28] Hebrews 13:14.
[29] *Letters III*, 1383–1384.

ation is raised *in* the redeemed souls who have, during this life, taken its beauty into themselves? That may be the way in which the 'new heaven and the new earth'[30] are formed. Of course we can only guess and wonder.

But these particular guesses arise in me, I trust, from taking seriously the resurrection of the body: a doctrine which now-a-days is very soft pedalled by nearly all the faithful—to our great impoverishment. Not that you and I have now much reason to rejoice in having bodies! Like old automobiles, aren't they? where all sorts of apparently different things keep going wrong, but what they add up to is the plain fact that the machine is wearing out. Well, it was not meant to last forever. Still, I have a kindly feeling for the old rattle-trap. Through it God showed me that whole side of His beauty which is embodied in colour, sound, smell and size. No doubt it has often led me astray: but not half so often, I suspect, as my soul has led *it* astray. For the spiritual evils which we share with the devils (pride, spite) are far worse than what we share with the beasts: and sensuality really arises more from the imagination than from the appetites: which, if left merely to their own animal strength, and not elaborated by our imagination, would be fairly easily managed. But this is turning into a sermon!

TO MARY WILLIS SHELBURNE: *On the illusion of independence.*[31]

10 DECEMBER 1962

Thanks for your letter and the amusing enclosure. . . . About ancient lineage (I haven't any myself). My feeling is that all such things can legitimately be enjoyed provided one takes them lightly enough. Like tinsel crowns worn for private theatricals! And the prig who considers himself *above* enjoying his tinsel crown is perhaps as far astray as the paranoiac who mistakes it for gold. This goes for things like beauty, talent, fame, *et cetera* as well as for blood (Of course a great deal of so-called 'democratic' feeling against the claims of blood is really based on a desire to make the claims of money all important: and of all claims to distinction money is, I suppose, the basest).

---

[30] Revelation 21:1.
[31] *Letters III,* 1390–1391.

There is much that is cheering, along with much that isn't, in your letter. One must get over any false shame about accepting necessary help. One never *has* been 'independent'. Always, in some mode or other, one has lived on others, economically, intellectually, spiritually. Who, after all, is *less* independent than someone with 'a private income'- every penny of which has been earned by the skill and labour of others? Poverty merely *reveals* the helpless dependence which has all the time been our real condition. We are members of one another whether we choose to recognise the fact or not.

I get on fairly well. My chief trouble is a difficulty in sleeping at night and keeping awake by day. Perhaps I am turning into a nocturnal animal. Bat? Wolf? Owl? Let's hope it will be owl, the bird of wisdom (and I always *was* attracted by mice!).

1963

TO MRS. LEON EMMERT, *who had written Lewis from the Congo: On a mature sense of one's parents; and on sexual morality.*[1]

2 JANUARY 1963

Thank you for your kind and most interesting letter. Yes—how one's view of one's parents begins to change when one has discovered the beam in one's own eye![2] I have had that experience too. And when one has grasped the right view of marriage, how all the current gabble about 'sexual morality' is reduced!—as if it did not consist almost entirely in applying to sexual behaviour the same principles of good faith and unselfishness which have to be applied to all behaviour.

A good many of my books might not interest you. Write for the list to . . . MacDonald is nearly all out of print.

You are all facing a terrible situation out there; may God support and protect you.

TO MARY WILLIS SHELBURNE: *On the need to take care of oneself and not of things.*[3]

8 JANUARY 1963

I don't mind betting that the things which 'had to be done' in your room didn't really *have* to be done at all. Very few things really do. After one bad night with my heart—not so bad as yours, for it was only suffocation, not pain—my doctor strictly rationed me on stairs, and I have obeyed him. Of course it is hideously *inconvenient*: but that can be put up with and must. What worse than inconvenience would have resulted if you had left those 'things' undone? Do take more care of yourself and less of 'things'!

Still snow-bound.

---

[1] *Letters III*, 1402.
[2] Matthew 7:3.
[3] *Letters III*, 1404.

TO MARY WILLIS SHELBURNE: *On the strange and terrifying things that happen to us and are really for our benefit.*[4]

8 FEBRUARY 1963

I'm not surprised at Son Suez's [a cat] reaction. She couldn't possibly know that this inexplicable arrest, exile, and imprisonment had a kind intention. It suggests the comforting thought that the strange and terrifying things which happen to *us* are really for our benefit. That's an old platitude of course: but seeing it the other way round, in relation to the cat, somehow brings it to life.

Still snow!

TO MARY WILLIS SHELBURNE: *On Lewis's nonchalance and even humor in the face of death.*[5]

19 MARCH 1963

I'm sorry they threaten you with a painful disease. 'Dangerous' matters much less, doesn't it? What have you and I got to do but make our exit? When they told me I was in danger several months ago, I don't remember feeling distressed.

I am talking, of course, about *dying,* not about *being killed.* If shells started falling about this house I should feel quite differently. An external, visible, and (still worse) audible threat at once wakes the instinct of self-preservation into fierce activity. I don't think natural death has any similar terrors.

I am thrilled to hear that Son Suez has a sweater! Is this part of the *demarché* [formal presentation] (it's in all our papers) which a body of American women are making to the President to get animals properly clothed 'in the interests of decency'? Can it be true? If so, not only what insanity, but also (as in all super-refinements) what fundamental foul-mindedness! But also, what fun! The elephant looks as if he wore trousers already, but terribly baggy ones. What he needs is *braces* [suspenders]. The Rhino seems to wear a suit much too big for him: can it be 'taken in'? What sort of collars will giraffes wear? Will seals and otters have ordinary

---

[4] *Letters III,* 1410–1411.
[5] *Letters III,* 1415–1416.

clothes or bathing suits? The hedgehog will wear his shirts out terribly quickly, I should think....

Yes, private communions (I shared many during Joy's last days) are extraordinarily moving. I am in danger of preferring them to those in Church.

TO MRS. DUNN, *who seems to have asked about Jesus' destruction of the fig tree in Matthew 21:19: On the purpose of death in the natural world.*[6]

3 APRIL 1963

Yes, a very puzzling passage. I think it *is* a moral allegory enforced by an actual miracle. It would be shocking if a man, or even a beast, were destroyed just to point a moral. But a vegetable? After all, every tree that dies (and they all die) anywhere in the world does so by God's will. 'Not a sparrow falls to the ground *et cetera*'.[7] Mustn't we face the fact that He wills deaths as well as lives? He has made the natural world to depend partly on death—'unless a seed die'.[8] At least, that is how I look at it.

TO FATHER PETER MILWARD, SJ: *On the evil of Christian disunity; and on prayer and cooperation in works of charity as the means of reunion.*[9]

6 MAY 1963

Dear Padre,

You ask me in effect why I am not a Roman Catholic. If it comes to that, why am I not—and why are you *not*—a Presbyterian, a Quaker, a Mohammedan, a Hindu, or a Confucianist? After how prolonged and sympathetic study and on what grounds have we rejected these religions? I think those who press a man to desert the religion in which he has been bred and in which he believes he has found the means of Grace ought to produce positive reasons for the change—not demand from him reasons *against* all other religions. It would have to be *all,* wouldn't it?

---

[6] *Letters III,* 1420–1421.
[7] Matthew 10:29.
[8] John 12:24.
[9] *Letters III,* 1425–1426.

Our Lord prayed that we all might be one 'as He and His Father are one'.[10] But He and His Father are not one in virtue of both accepting a (third) monarchical sovereign.

That unity of rule, or even of *credenda* [things to be believed], does not necessarily produce unity of charity is apparent from the history of every Church, every religious order, and every parish.

Schism is a very great evil. But if reunion is ever to come, it will in my opinion come from increasing charity. And this, under pressure from the increasing strength and hostility of unbelief, is perhaps beginning: we no longer, thank God, speak of one another as we did over 100 years ago. A single act of even such limited co-operation as is now possible does more towards ultimate reunion than any amount of discussion.

The historical causes of the 'Reformation' that actually occurred were (1.) The cruelties and commercialism of the Papacy (2.) The lust and greed of Henry VIII. (3.) The exploitation of both by politicians. (4.) The fatal insouciance of the mere rabble on both sides. The spiritual drive behind the Reformation that ought to have occurred was a deep re-experience of the Pauline experience.

Memo: a great many of my closest friends are your co-religionists, some of them priests. If I am to embark on a disputation—which could not be a short one, I would much sooner do it with them than by correspondence.

We can do much more to heal the schism by our prayers than by a controversy. It is a daily subject of mine.

TO MARY WILLIS SHELBURNE: *On how to rehearse for death and how to diminish fear.*[11]

17 JUNE 1963

Pain is terrible, but surely you need not have fear as well? Can you not see death as the friend and deliverer? It means stripping off that body which is tormenting you: like taking off a hair-shirt or getting out of a dungeon. What is there to be afraid of? You have long attempted (and none of us does more) a Christian

---

[10] John 17:21.
[11] *Letters III*, 1430–1431.

life. Your sins are confessed and absolved. Has this world been so kind to you that you should leave it with regret? There are better things ahead than any we leave behind.

Remember, though we struggle against things because we are afraid of them, it is often the other way round—we get afraid *because* we struggle. Are you struggling, resisting? Don't you think Our Lord says to you 'Peace, child, peace. Relax. Let go. Underneath are the everlasting arms. Let go, I will catch you. Do you trust me so little?'

Of course, this may not be the end. Then make it a good rehearsal.

Yours (and like you a tired traveller near the journey's end)
Jack

TO MARY WILLIS SHELBURNE: *On why God might delay death so that the dying might finish the spiritual work they were meant to do; and on the spiritual work the dead might do for us.*[12]

25 JUNE 1963

Tho' horrified at your sufferings, I am overjoyed at the blessed change in your attitude to death. This is a bigger stride forward than perhaps you yourself yet know. For you *were* rather badly wrong on that subject. Only a few months ago when I said that we old people hadn't much more to do than to make a good exit, you were almost angry with me for what you called such a 'bitter' remark. Thank God, you now see it wasn't bitter: only plain common sense.

Yes: I do wonder why the doctors inflict such torture to delay what cannot in any case be very long delayed. Or why God does! Unless there is still something for you to do. As far as weakness allows I hope, now that you know you are forgiven, you will spend most of your remaining strength in *forgiving*. Lay all the old resentments down at the wounded feet of Christ. I have had dozens of blood transfusions in the last two years and know only too well the horrid—and *long*—moments during which they are poking about to find the vein. And then you think they've really got in at last and it turns out that they haven't. (Is there an allegory

---

[12] *Letters III,* 1431–1432.

here? The approaches of Grace often hurt because the spiritual vein in us hides itself from the celestial surgeon?) But oh, I do pity you for waking up and finding yourself still on the wrong side of the door! How awful it must have been for poor Lazarus who had actually died, got it all over, and then was brought back—to go through it all, I suppose, a few years later. I think he, not St. Stephen, ought really to be celebrated as the first martyr.

You say too much of the very little I have been able to do for you. Perhaps you will very soon be able to repay me a thousand-fold. For if this *is* Good-bye, I am sure you will not forget me when you are in a better place. You'll put in a good word for me now and then, won't you?

It will be fun when we at last meet.

TO MARY WILLIS SHELBURNE: *On how to be very ill; and on Christian hope.*[13]

28 JUNE 1963

It was anaemia that endangered my life the winter before last, but of course trifling compared with yours. I think the best way to cope with the mental debility and total inertia is to submit to it entirely. Don't *try* to concentrate. Pretend you are a dormouse or even a turnip.

But of course I know the acceptance of inertia is much easier for men than for women. We are the lazy sex. Think of yourself just as a seed patiently waiting in the earth: waiting to come up a flower in the Gardener's good time, up into the *real* world, the real waking. I suppose that our whole present life, looked back on from there, will seem only a drowsy half-waking. We are here in the land of dreams. But cock-crow is coming. It is nearer now than when I began this letter.

TO JOCELYN GIBB, *who had asked Lewis how he wanted* Letters to Malcolm, Chiefly on Prayer, *described on the book jacket: On Lewis's sense of his vocation as writer.*[14]

---

[13] *Letters III,* 1434.
[14] *Letters III,* 1434–1435.

28 JUNE 1963

I've thought and thought about the blurb but find I just can't write it—apparently I can hardly write the words either! I'd like you to make the point that the reader is merely being allowed to listen to two very ordinary laymen discussing the practical and speculative problems of prayer as these appear to them: i.e., the author does *not* claim to be teaching.

Would it be good to say 'Some passages are controversial but this is almost an accident. The wayfaring Christian cannot quite ignore recent Anglican theology when it has been built as a barricade across the high road'?

I wouldn't stress your point about my not having given tongue very recently. It can't *feel* like that to the public. They must get the impression that I bring out a book once a fortnight. And your denial, however true in fact, will, like the sculptor's fig-leaf, only draw attention to what it would fair conceal.

I enclose a new passage for the last letter. This will make that letter unusually long but that legitimate in a finale. Anyway, I like the new bit.

TO MARY WILLIS SHELBURNE, *whose difficulties with her daughter and son-in-law continued: On the experience of forgiving; and on the tedium of dying.*[15]

6 JULY 1963

All one can say about Lorraine is that if she is really so brainwashed as you think, she is then no more morally responsible than a lunatic. I fully admit that as regards her husband you have been set as difficult a job in the forgiving line as can well be imagined.

Do you know, only a few weeks ago I realised suddenly that I at last *had* forgiven the cruel schoolmaster who so darkened my childhood. I'd been trying to do it for years: and like you, each time I thought I'd done it, I found, after a week or so it all had to be attempted over again. But this time I feel sure it is the real thing. And (like learning to swim or to ride a bicycle) the moment

---

[15] *Letters III*, 1438–1439.

it does happen it seems so easy and you wonder why on earth you didn't do it years ago. So the parable of the unjust judge[16] comes true, and what has been vainly asked for years can suddenly be granted. I also get a quite new feeling about 'If you forgive you will be forgiven.'[17] I don't believe it is, as it sounds, a bargain. The forgiving and the being forgiven are really the very same thing. But one is safe as long as one keeps on trying.

How terribly long these days and hours are for you. Even I, who am in a bed of roses now compared with you, feel it a bit. I live in almost total solitude, never properly asleep by night (all loathsome dreams) and constantly falling asleep by day. I sometimes feel as if my mind were decaying. Yet, in another mood, how *short* our whole past life begins to seem!

It is a pouring wet summer here, and cold. I can hardly remember when we last saw the sun.

Well, we shall get out of it all sooner or later, for

> even the weariest river
> Winds somewhere safe to sea.

Let us pray much for one another.

TO MARY WILLIS SHELBURNE: *On treating one's doctors with understanding (and Lewis's humor at who will die first!).*[18]

9 JULY 1963

I can well understand with what mixed feelings you received what is obviously, in the ordinary medical sense, very 'good' news. Aren't you a trifle fierce about the doctor? It can't be much fun attempting to explain the details to 100 bio-chemical patients who have no knowledge of bio-chemistry and who, one knows, won't really understand, however hard one tries. I was always only too glad to let mine off with the merest skeleton account of my own state—I found it such a boring subject. Also, aren't your doctors (like ours) hideously overworked? I know my specialist,

---

[16] Luke 18:1–8.
[17] Matthew 6:14–15.
[18] *Letters III,* 1439.

when I was in hospital, had a working day which had begun at 8.30 a.m. and was still going on at 9.45 p.m. Doesn't leave much elbow room.

Our hearts, by the way, must be different. When yours is worst you have to lie flat. When mine was worst I had to *sit* up—night and day for months.

By the way, as you come out I may possibly go in. Swollen ankles—the Red Light for me—have returned. I see the doctor about this to-morrow. My fear is that he will forbid me to go to Ireland on Monday as I had arranged, and put me back in hospital.

Our friends might really get up a sweepstake as to whose train really will go first! Blessings.

TO RUTH BROADY: *Lewis's last letter to a child about Narnia.*[19]

26 OCTOBER 1963

Many thanks for your kind letter, and it was very good of you to write and tell me that you like my books; and what a very good letter you write for your age!

If you continue to love Jesus, nothing much can go wrong with you, and I hope you may always do so. I'm so thankful that you realized the 'hidden story' in the Narnian books. It is odd, children nearly *always* do, grown ups hardly ever.

I'm afraid the Narnian series has come to an end, and am sorry to tell you that you can expect no more.

God bless you.

TO MR. YOUNG: *Lewis's last letter of direction—on the virgin birth; on the glorified body of the risen Christ; on atonement theories; and on the wrath of God.*[20]

31 OCTOBER 1963

1. I believe in the Virgin Birth in the fullest and most literal sense: that is, I deny that copulation with a man was the cause of the Virgin's pregnancy.

---

[19] *Letters III,* 1474.
[20] *Letters III,* 1476–1477.

2. It is not easy to define what we mean by an 'essentially human body'. The records show that Our Lord's Risen Body could pass through closed doors, which human bodies can't: but also that it could eat. We shall know what a glorified body is when we have one ourselves: till then, I think we must acquiesce in mystery.

3. When Scripture says that Christ died 'for' us,[21] I think the word is usually υπερ (on behalf of), not αντι (instead of). I think the ideas of sacrifice, ransom, championship (over death), substitution *et cetera* are all images to *suggest* the reality (not otherwise comprehensible to us) of the atonement. To fix on any *one* of them as if it contained and limited the truth like a scientific definition would in my opinion be a mistake.

4. All associations of human passions to God are analogical. The wrath of God: 'something in God of which the best image in the created world is righteous indignation'. I think it quite a mistake to try to soften the idea of anger by substituting something like disapproval or regret. Even with men real anger is far more likely than cold disapproval to lead to full reconciliation. Hot love, hot wrath. . . .

Your questions are not in the least offensive.

Yours sincerely

C. S. Lewis

---

[21] Romans 5:8.

INDEX

BIBLICAL INDEX